Picture Freedom

Picture Freedom

*Remaking Black Visuality in the
Early Nineteenth Century*

Jasmine Nichole Cobb

NEW YORK UNIVERSITY PRESS

New York and London

NEW YORK UNIVERSITY PRESS
New York and London
www.nyupress.org

ISBN: 978-1-4798-1722-1 (hardback)
ISBN: 978-1-4798-2977-4 (paper)

For Library of Congress Cataloging-in-Publication data,
please contact the Library of Congress.

References to Internet websites (URLs) were accurate at the time of
writing. Neither the author nor New York University Press is responsible
for URLs that may have expired or changed since the manuscript was
prepared.

New York University Press books are printed on acid-free paper, and
their binding materials are chosen for strength and durability. We
strive to use environmentally responsible suppliers and materials to the
greatest extent possible in publishing our books.

Manufactured in the United States of America
10 9 8 7 6 5 4 3 2 1

Also available as an ebook

THE
AMERICAN
LITERATURES
INITIATIVE

A book in the American Literatures Initiative (ALI), a collaborative
publishing project of NYU Press, Fordham University Press, Rutgers
University Press, Temple University Press, and the University of Virginia
Press. The Initiative is supported by The Andrew W. Mellon Foundation.
For more information, please visit www.americanliteratures.org.

For the ladies, especially Lottie Cobb and Helen Webster

Contents

Color images appear as an insert following page 110

Acknowledgments

This book is complete because of an extensive network of family, friends, colleagues, and students who supported me throughout the process. I first owe endless gratitude to the Black women of this study who left an archive for me to consider and lived their freedom in ways that continue to defy documentation. In tracing their lives, I first visited holdings at the Library Company of Philadelphia, with support from their Andrew Mellon fellowship program. I am forever indebted to Phillip Lapsansky for his vast knowledge and good nature, and also to Erika Piola, Cornelia King, Charlene Knight, Krystal Appiah, and Nicole Joniec, who make the Library Company a place to which I will always return.

New York University Press is another significant institution that shaped this project. I appreciate the commitment of Eric Zinner and Alicia Nadkarni, editors for the America in the Long 19th Century series, the American Literatures Initiative, and, most especially, my editors, Badia Ahad and Cecelia Cancellaro.

My intellectual community is vast and charitable. John L. Jackson Jr., my advisor, has offered unwavering support for my ideas, and me, even from the very beginning; I continue to rely on his guidance and friendship. Kali N. Gross, Kathleen Hall Jamieson, and Paul Messaris read the earliest iterations of these ideas, along with Oscar Gandy Jr., offering critical insights. Beverly Henry, Nadine Gabbadon, and Robin Stevens, along with Khadijah White and Aymar Christian, helped me thrive at the University of Pennsylvania, making the Annenberg School for Communication a place in which I could study. Dan Berger, Gershun Avalez, and Tshepo Chéry variously continue to amaze me, inspire me, and keep me honest. Then and now, Riley Snorton remains a generous reader, great counsel and a good friend. Shawnika Hull, added much robustness to my life in Philadelphia and remains a close confidant.

I am also thankful to the Africana Research Center at Pennsylvania State University for fellowship and an expanded community. I am grateful to Lovalerie King, Cary Fraser, Tracy Beckett, Kirt Wilson, Dawn Noren, Alyssa Garcia, and especially Ariane Cruz. I count them among a network of mentors and dear friends, to include Robin Means Coleman, Maghan Keita, Crystal Lucky, Carol Anthony, Teresa Nance, Ed Goff, Charles Cherry, Kevin Miles, Bryan Crable, Marcia Dawkins, Deborah A. Thomas, Martha Jones, Daphne Brooks and Erica Armstrong Dunbar.

Northwestern University has offered the support of generous colleagues, including Angela Ray, who read a full draft, along with E. Patrick Johnson and Jan Radway, the ever-luminous Richard Iton, Jasmine Johnson, Huey Copeland, Joshua Chambers-Letson, Miriam Petty, Michelle Wright, D. Soyini Madison, Dilip Gaonkar, Bob Hariman, and Pablo Boczkowski. I appreciate the helpful administration, as well as the Northwestern University Research Grants Committee, which provided partial funding for this publication. Also, a special thank-you to the students in my graduate seminars for contributing to spaces of experimentation and contemplation. Conversations with Rhaisa Williams, Dwayne Mann, Cecilio Cooper, and Chelsea Ferguson have been particularly helpful, alongside the exceptional assistance of Caitlin Bruce, Amina Asim, and most especially, Juliette Lim.

Most of all, I thank my family, including a host of aunts, uncles, cousins, siblings, parents, and grandparents, who encouraged me throughout this process. Lottie Cobb, Daryl Cobb, and Helen Webster have always been divine, even while on earth. Clinton Webster has been a blessing in my life; I would not have made it here without his love and devotion. I am most grateful to my mother, Caryl Harris, who has always fostered my curiosity, even when inconvenient. She has supported me in everything I have ever attempted, escorting me on every wild endeavor and filling my room with books. Danielle, Darrell, Dana, Nyall, and especially Monique cheered me on the entire way, along with my aunts Jean Webster and Marilyn Johnson, who nurtured me. I am also immensely grateful for friendships that travel, like family, surviving space and time: Lynette Lee, Keyanna Pompey, Shanice Jackson, and Precious Daniels. Finally, I am thankful for my chosen family, which sustains me everyday. Loie faithfully attended work daily, under my desk, until this book was complete. Kenyon Whittington teaches me something new every day and supports me in ways far bigger than I can dream. I could not have finished this book without you; thanks for ceaseless love and dedication. Thank you all for the support.

Introduction: Parlor Fantasies, Parlor Nightmares

Freedom put color in the cheeks of Black people in the nineteenth century. African descendants who sat for daguerreotypes around 1855 made sure to document self-possession with proper attire and a little rouge for the flesh, such as members of the Dickerson family in antebellum Philadelphia.[1] Though this marker of vitality appeared in many daguerreotypes, Black people sitting for early photographic portraits marked themselves against the deprivation and sallowness demanded by slavery with such details. Black women, such as the unidentified sitter in figure I.1, showed up at the studio highly decorated for the occasion of portraiture, dressed in fine garments of thick satin with lace embellishments that were punctuated with modest hoop earrings. While the unidentified Black men in the Dickerson family portraits needed to be proper only from the bust up, much of a lady's body appeared in the image, so her dress needed to drape perfectly. Every aspect of the self demanded perfect execution for picture taking in the mid-nineteenth century. Self-proclaimed ladies and gentlemen of African descent likely braved stares on their way to the studio as they prepared to create a new visual archive of Blackness before the abolition of slavery. Privileged Black people convened to represent freedom.

The unknown people pictured in the Dickerson daguerreotypes commissioned these images several years before the Civil War. Free people who wanted portraits worked with an artist, in this case, likely Robert Douglass Jr., a Black artist and daguerreotypist who snapped pictures at an art studio near Philadelphia's Twelfth and Arch Streets.[2] The daguerreotype—predecessor to the modern photograph—was then in vogue, and these customers could afford this expensive process, many having patronized Douglass since the 1840s. His earliest customers paid approximately five dollars for each image and its morocco case. Together with the artist, Black patrons made decisions about how to pose, whether or not to add

Figure I.1. Portrait of an unidentified woman from the Dickerson Daguerreotype Collection, ca. 1850. (Courtesy of The Library Company of Philadelphia)

color to their cheeks, and what casing to use to preserve the image.[3] These women staged smartness with clothing and jewelry, and, with the books they included within the frame of the photograph, they staged intelligence and literacy. Common studio props such as tables, chairs, and vases appear in these images to ground the subjects in furnished, home-like settings. Framed in small leather cases that open like books on metal hinges, these prized possessions document the look of free communities in the mid-nineteenth century. The cases protect miniature archives of Black self-making and early pictures of freedom in the decades moving toward the end of U.S. slavery.

Black people appearing in early daguerreotypes used this new media form to picture freedom, to image and imagine people of African descent as self-possessed and divorced from slavery. Such illustrations countered a long history of contemptuous representations of Black people by portraying "black pride and identity" in daguerreotypes.[4] These people were not just creating distance between freedom and slavery's mediation of Blackness, as distributed in auction advertisements, for example. They were reimagining and reconstructing Black visuality removed from the cultural logics of slavery. Daguerreotypes offered a sense of "truth" in representation, with images that seemed unencumbered by human interpretation like hand-drawn illustrations. Daguerreotypes employed technological intervention for the capture of nature; and many free Black people enjoyed them as tools of "critical black memory," countering a fifty-year history of Black subjugation via visual representation with their own images.[5] The occasion to sit for a Black photographer meant the opportunity to archive a changing Black visuality and the new visibilities exhibited among free people of African descent. These materials evidenced the gaze of the free Black photographer shot through the lens of the camera, the gaze of the free Black person seated as subject looking through the other side, and, finally, the gaze of any visitor who viewed these daguerreotypes on display in the home. Blacks pictured in these early photographs used portraiture to seize control over representation of the free Black body. With the artist, these patrons created a palpable record of freedom and Black visibility that bolstered the contemporaneous displays of autonomy staged within Black communities. These images documented the existence of free "Americans" of African descent, even as the issue of Black freedom and national belonging remained in question. Pictures of freedom in Black homes of the antebellum North simultaneously wielded "spectacle and possession," documenting the way in which people of African descent appeared within various conceptions of the domestic; they display ownership of the self as distinct from slavery.[6] These daguerreotypes circulated in a preemancipation context where viewers consumed a bevy of other renditions of Black freedom—items that were variously hostile, humorous, obscure, affirmative, and persistent.

Mainstream media pictured Black freedom quite differently for White Americans who were uncertain about or downright unhappy with the idea of Black freedom as well as with the dissolution of slavery. A robust genre of "racial Americana" emerged at the turn of the nineteenth century, weaving an "American" folk culture tapestry of U.S. nationalism and fetishizing racism that appeared on theater stages, as well as in cartoons, print ephemera, and sheet music.[7] The racial caricaturist Edward Williams Clay illustrated Black freedom with a popular lithographic series, titled "Life in Philadelphia," that depicted free Blacks engaged in ridiculous forms of civic and domestic life. Clay's vision of Black freedom emphasized elaborate dress and improper speech to portray free people as foolhardy and self-important. His illustrations positioned people of African descent as ill-prepared to experience liberty or autonomy. Examples such as figure I.2, which depicts a Black man, overdressed in top hat and waistcoat, making a house call to "Miss Dinah," used speech, gesture, and physical space to turn Black freedom into a humorous notion. Although the unseen Dinah imagines herself as too important to answer the door, Dinah's servant reveals that her mistress is "bery petickly engaged in washing de dishes." In lieu of a visit, the gentleman caller leaves a card at the door for the woman of this basement "parlor." While polite rules of conduct required a lady of the house to receive all her guests unless she was ill, Miss Dinah denied her visitor because she remained engaged in the lowly domestic work of dishwashing. The joke of the image is that arrogant free Black people like Dinah, her servant, and her visitor remained in feeble social and *domestic* positions. Clay used the pitiable cellar to symbolize the truth about self-important people of African descent; even in freedom, Black people remained too connected to slavery and low socioeconomic standing to move out of the basement and into the above-ground space of the house, or the parlor of the home. Clay created many images like this scene, often overwhelming the page with commentary on the rules of proper decorum and inverted social conventions to portray Black freedom as ridiculous or implausible. Responding to a small, but growing number of free Black people gaining economic stability and building independent communities in the urban North, Clay used pictures to rethink the consequences of freedom.

This book explains how seemingly divergent cultural productions were engaged in the same project of domesticating Black freedom during the slaving era—rendering *free* African descendants as part of the U.S. landscape and translating their belonging for dominant culture. It takes up modes of *picturing* Black freedom before the Civil War and before the daguerreotype to trace its emergence in the transatlantic imaginary.[8] By

Figure I.2. Edward Williams Clay, *"Is Miss Dinah at Home?,"*
1828, "Life in Philadelphia" series. (Courtesy of The Library
Company of Philadelphia)

"picturing," I refer to a whole set of embodied processes involved in the act
of creating a picture, as well as to a means of theorization.[9] I argue that the
visual practices of both free Whites and free Blacks attempted to represent Black freedom as belonging within the purview of the home space—
variously defined as the house, the nation, and the Atlantic world—called
together by trade among slaving empires, and diverse schemas employed
within to dissolve slavery.[10] I show how *picturing freedom* before the
advent of photographic technologies reorganized Black visuality, repositioning Black people within the conceptual space of the Atlantic world,
summarily making inroads into the eventual abolition of slavery. Visual
culture represents a site wherein free Black people organized new ways of
existing within the domiciles of slaving nations. It was also a vehicle for
Whites to experiment with notions of Black freedom. Picturing freedom

enabled different, but interrelated, modes of situating Black people within the empire as a home space. Such a cultural practice was necessary for disentangling Blackness from slavery within the shared space of the nation. Competing conceptualizations of Black freedom were essential to how Black and White viewers reimagined national belonging and racial identity between lithograph and daguerreotype, between the years of gradual emancipation laws emerging in 1780 and the Fugitive Slave Law of 1850.

Women and Black Visuality

Black women, and Black feminist visual practices, are central to *Picture Freedom* for what each reveals about the relationship between visuality and domestic belonging near the end of the transatlantic slave trade. Black women were essential to the maintenance of slave societies in the Atlantic world because they replenished a stolen labor force through giving birth. Laws about the matrilineal nature of slavery determined the slave status of children based upon the status of their mothers.[11] In slavery, Black female bodies served as sites for sexual violence as well as labor production, beginning as early as the initial disembarkation of the transatlantic voyage. Many African women suffered rape onboard slave ships before arriving in the "Americas," where their lives were "characterized, above all, by incessant work."[12] Accordingly, early visual portrayals of Black women's bodies represent them as unique emblems of exploitation. Image captures of slavery, such as Louis Agassiz's infamous nude daguerreotypes, reflect how evidence of nursing and whipping written on Black women's bodies were fascinating to White spectators.[13] Yet, in these images of unfree people, Black women who "calmly reveal their breasts" also offer "detached, unemotional, and workmanlike" attitudes toward the camera.[14] Mythologies of Black women's bodies were essential to slavery, but when constructed for the purposes of representation, unfree Black women managed to organize means of distancing an inner self from the material body that appeared before the lens. The "emancipatory" parsing of the body from the flesh that "enabled the slaves and their descendants" to organize a "countermemory" to dominant organizations of the body, making slavery part, but not the sum, of Black women's experiences, describes this important distinction.[15] Conceptualizations of Black female bodies were entirely relevant to discourses of visibility, even as the histories of Black women's flesh are dissimilar across designations of free and unfree.

Free Black women provide the most robust examples of the cultural work required to imagine freedom during slavery. Despite their relative privilege, freedom for African descendants, in the context of slavery, was a "fragile" determination, according to Erica Armstrong Dunbar, even for elite or upper-class Blacks.[16] Free Black people, and especially women, also suffered from the peculiar racial decorum that proliferated during slavery, even as the law did not consign them to masters on paper. While Black men contended with the fact that freedom required "the non-traditional political activities and education of their wives, sisters, and daughters," free and elite Black women remained entangled in discourses of Black visibility and demands for their public activism to buttress a larger Black community.[17] For these reasons, my determination of Black freedom is not limited to political and civic frameworks of citizenship, although ensuing ideals of self-possession and property are relevant to this study. I am interested in what it meant to make freedom visually manifest in the context of slavery. How did people of African descent make freedom visually evident? Accordingly, my discussion focuses on Black women, and Black people, whom I variously, even if controversially, consider *free* for the *purpose of illustration*. I read the image of freedom through items pertaining to fugitives and manumitted persons as well as Black people who were "born" free to mothers who were not enslaved. Black freedom as a problem of imagination was not limited to the juridical notions of "free," as realized in numerous accounts of Black people who behaved as free, despite having "owners." Orlando Patterson offers the idea of a "tripartite" freedom—personal, sovereign, and civic—to discuss a continuum of individual and social autonomy.[18] *Picture Freedom* considers Black freedom in popular imaginaries, which in many instances superseded or ignored the lawful determinations of liberty, but reveal freedom as something demonstrable and as a posture toward visual discourses. Not to be discounted in the context of slavery, the cultural underpinnings of Black freedom were indeed political, even if they were different from juridical conceptions of autonomy. The unlikely examples I discuss demonstrate that "freedom is active and creative."[19] The trajectory of this argument does not conflate enslavement with freedom or assign complicity to the unfree; instead, by including diverse examples of "free," my aim is to consider the array of concepts relevant to imagining Black freedom in its earliest relevance to the Atlantic.

Picture Freedom considers efforts to imagine both Black men and Black women as free in the context of slavery, but as a study in Black feminist visual theory, the analysis simultaneously considers "the black female body and the gaze" rather than treating each as a distinct entity.[20] I emphasize the ways in which Black women's bodies were particularly important to imagining freedom and to accepting free people of African descent into the folds of empires. In *Picture Freedom*, free Black women's bodies are not simply passive victims of dominant scopic regimes but are also disruptive vessels that Black women manipulated to evidence a female gaze. My approach to early-nineteenth-century visual culture employs feminist theories of spectatorship and explores Black women's early contributions to shaping Black visuality. *Picture Freedom* considers Black women as visual theorists whose contributions to the historical evolution of visual praxis in U.S. Black culture are easily overshadowed by those of the Black men who produced nationally circulated print media in the nineteenth century. Black women help accentuate the way in which slavery also required people of African descent to develop multivalent self-concepts, to manage both inward understandings of Black raciality and outward displays of regard for public concepts of racial caste.

Although I often turn to images to think through freedom in the visual culture of slavery, my focus in this study is on the issue of Black visuality. Visibility is central to this concern, as the way one is seen in the eyes of others is relevant to larger conceptualizations of what the visual means. However, Black visuality as taken up in recent scholarship does the important work of turning scholarly attention away from questions of authenticity and propriety, to focus instead on the ways in which the issue of race within the field of vision is far more complex than surface-level appearances. Visuality, "a problem of the conceptual scheme of modernity and representation," is best understood through the act of picturing as a tactile reference to diminished visual encounters.[21] Explorations of Black visuality broaden the context for understanding Black life, drawing on a wider array of visual evidence to think through questions of culture. Likewise, an examination of Black visuality also moves beyond individuated concerns about vision or spectatorship. Hal Foster's canonic text couples vision and visuality but specifies the latter "as a social fact" that "involved the body and the psyche."[22] The sociality of the visual draws in issues of vision but traffics in so much more than the fickle thing of sight. Black visuality is a complex notion because the articulation of race compounds the significance of the visual.

In *Picture Freedom*, I consider Black visuality through various sense making mechanisms associated with the eye, and rather than as a specific thing or a single instance, I theorize Black visuality within a complicated interplay between subjectivity, social context, and cultural representations as circumscribed by the trauma of slavery. With my approach, I mean to deconstruct the still–a priori organization of Blackness as Other or as a thing first seen before becoming a subject who looks at others—a residual effect of slavery's visual logics. Black visuality is a complicated quest to reveal, to make visible, the themes of subjectivity that lie at the other end of the visual encounter. It is about the ways in which the racialized object, in fact, has eyes, casts a gaze, and consciously construes a way of being visible. At the same time, Black visuality is also about the ways in which people of African descent lived within the shroud of invisibility and reveled in it as a nascent element of a Black experience. Often denoted in situations of its absence or a "mostly invisible black visuality," this notion is about the unseen elements of the visual encounter.[23] Slavery's emphasis on the visible markers of Black raciality, such as hair texture and skin color, failed to attend to the unseen aspects of visual culture. Just as the perpetual surveillance of the Black body in slavery and the forced spectacle of the coffle are foundational to theorizations of Black visuality in the early republic, so, too, are the subversive measures and invisible methods of undermining these visual logics.

The visual theorist Nicole Fleetwood describes Blackness as a "troubling vision" where the visible Black body poses an enduring nuisance to the very scopic regimes that rendered it problematic and locates this foundation in "captivity and capitalism."[24] *Picture Freedom* builds on this work to explicate the extent to which slavery zeroed in on the Black body as a site of production, and as a way of life, proliferated through a racialized visual order with which early demonstrations of freedom needed to contend. When persons of African descent acted outside of this order, via the flicker of a glance or a disingenuous presentation of self, they revealed slavery's visual logics of race as fallible. Thus, we might think of the troubling nature of Blackness in the field of vision as masterfully contrived, initiated in the ways in which the fugitive free decisively troubled slavery's ocularity as a means of resistance. The genius of fugitivity (which I discuss in chapter 1) was that it revealed to Whites that Black visuality was not simply Black visibility—that the social fact of Blackness in the visual field entailed surprising complications. Black visuality—the entire sum of the visual as experienced by people of African descent—helped to undermine slavery's visual codes. Psychic and subjective, Black visuality as shaped by the experience of slavery pertains to the Black figure's awareness of how she was perceived, and the sense of possession she felt toward her own body that allowed her to master and manipulate outward constructions of her visibility.

Picture Freedom is related to, but distinct from, an art history of free Black people during slavery because it focuses on popular culture, specifically. Popular cultures offer an opportunity to think about the everyday experience of living among images of Black freedom, and not just questions of negative or positive publicity.[25] Print media supported the minstrel performances that invited Whites to imitate "perceived Blackness."[26] Through Jim Crow plays, Blackface performances in traveling circuses, and racial ephemera in the home, Blackness came to instantiate what would become U.S. popular culture. The materials of everyday life that variously "pictured" Black freedom in its earliest conceptualizations offered a coping mechanism for transatlantic audiences trying to interpret the significance of free Black populations and mass resistance to slavery. Through depicting Blackness as foreign to itself, as hypervisible but lacking critical awareness or visual capacity, images discouraging emancipation settled into the cultural fabric of the nation and offered routes through which White viewers could accept abolition much later in the century. Significant volumes such as the *Image of the Black in Western Art* are, at least in part, revisionist efforts to illuminate the history of Black representations as far more lengthy and complex than the Middle Passage.[27] Such treatments rally against the idea of slavery as an inception for explorations of Black life, especially because slavery ignited a host of unflattering portrayals of Black people. However, slavery remains an important, even if controversial site for considering revolutions relevant to Black visuality because of its indelible mark on the way in which people of African descent resisted its limited conceptualizations of racial difference. African-descended peoples existed within slavery's complicated visual culture and were consistent forces in its maintenance and deconstruction. Early ruminations on freedom during slavery offer up another moment in which to explore Leigh Raiford's charge that Black visuality "is inextricable from African American movement efforts to change the conditions of black people's lives."[28] Slavery's visual organization of Black raciality represented an exigency for the performance of freedom, and thus it remains essential to historical cultural analyses of how Black people re-presented themselves apart from bondage.

My exploration of Black visuality draws upon mediated and unmediated modes for reconceptualizing Blackness as free when such a notion was most disruptive. Practices of picturing freedom among people of African descent were more complex than a single mediated moment, but instead existed as day-to-day methods of survival, submission, and resistance to the prevailing codes of looking. In this study, I parse Black visuality through the silent, but dialogic, visual interactions across difference that rendered Blackness as *representable*. *Picture Freedom* explores Blackness as both visual and visible along with the complex web of cultural practices. The emergent and cohesive Atlantic world taking shape outside the home was one of instability and unsustainability, hastening demands for an unchanging parlor anchored by symbols of empire.

The Transatlantic Parlor

The issue of Black freedom in the context of slavery is an inherently transatlantic concern.[29] British slavery helped compel U.S. slavery, and whether by profitability or morality as a motive, British abolition inspired U.S. activists to suppress the slave trade.[30] Moreover, Black people who asserted their freedom in the wake of imperial wars, and apart from organized antislavery efforts, simultaneously declared their own transatlanticism. For example, a number of Black Loyalists, who supported the British Crown against the United States in the Revolutionary War, fought for freedom through movement from Virginia, to Canada, and ultimately, Sierra Leone.[31] Enslaved Black people in bondage throughout the Americas were aware of the stakes associated with changing imperial relations, whether in the United States or in the European colonies.[32] The interdependent Atlantic world linked through bondage and colonialism meant that the corollary violent resistance to slavery by unfree Blacks was also internationally relevant. When people of African descent rebelled against slavery in Saint-Domingue in 1791—giving way to the emergence of independent Haiti in 1804—their uprising unnerved supporters of slavery and inspired Black people throughout the Atlantic world. The Haitian Revolution unsettled practices of enslavement not only under French rule, but throughout the Americas, as news of the insurrection inspired resistance in other locales.[33] Whereas the Atlantic world served as a setting for cycles of human chattel and imported goods, it was also host to contemplation about the meaning of freedom. The Atlantic world functioned as what Mary Louis Pratt calls the "contact zone," a space of clashing and combining "asymmetrical relations of power," to include both slavery and its abolition.[34] Laws such as the Act for the Abolition of the Slave Trade passed by British Parliament in 1807 attempted to maintain an interconnected Atlantic world through suppressing the transportation of Africans across the Atlantic Ocean.

Just like Britain and France, the U.S. scenario for slavery carried with it specific attributes that were relevant to the Atlantic world as a contact zone. First, unfree Blacks and White slavers lived together in the domestic confines of the nation, and thus White lawmakers could not geographically disaggregate the question of Black freedom, such as was the case for European metropoles and colonies. European visitors to colonial America gave "particular attention" to U.S. slavery, since there was no "European equivalent of the plantation slave system as it existed in the American South."[35] In this context, Black freedom in the United States posed immediate questions relating to home and nationality. Under what conditions do people of African descent *belong* within the United States? Second, and related to this, lawmakers decided the judicial abolition of slavery on a state-by-state basis in the United States, making the early republic "a microcosm of the multiple judicial structures of freedom in the Atlantic world as a whole."[36] Unfree Black people from throughout the Diaspora who sued for their liberty in U.S. courts, much like White slave owners who used the law to retain their claims to human property, found the confluence of Atlantic world slavery laws in the U.S. court system.

Accordingly, this book emphasizes the northeastern U.S. territories for how they were explicitly conversant with an imagined Atlantic world. People in these locales circulated much paper about their early antislavery efforts, and Philadelphia plays an important, but not defining, role in efforts to picture freedom.[37] To begin with, Philadelphia was of national significance to the early U.S. republic. It served as a temporary capital after the Revolutionary War, and by the turn of the nineteenth century, Philadelphia was "the second largest city in the English-speaking world with a population of about 75,000."[38] From 1794 until the 1828 election of President Andrew Jackson, Philadelphia served as home to nationally important institutions, including the President's House; Independence Hall, which served as the State House; as well as three important commercial banks.[39] Slavery commenced alongside these landmarks, but by the first decades of the nineteenth century, free Black people developed a noticeable presence in the city. Literate and wealthy by the period's standards, "middle-class" free people like Robert Douglass and his friends developed identifiable Black neighborhoods. Free people of African descent comprised the wealthiest 1 to 2 percent of all Philadelphians of the period.[40] Although Black Philadelphia was distinguished by its wealth and size, people here suffered just like free Black people in other northern cities like Boston, New York, and Providence, where organized violence at the hands of White rioters destroyed Black institutions.[41] However, Philadelphia was also home to the first ever U.S. lithograph—a highly innovative printing process that made color prints cheaply and quickly—so that this combination of finance and racial mixture resulted in great fodder for commercial artists.

Picture Freedom locates diverse conceptions of Black freedom in the parlor, and more specifically, the *transatlantic parlor*, as a place for dissimilar groups of people and cultural producers to convene around visions of Blackness separated from slavery. The parlor, as a historically specific architectural space, refers to an area within the home for receiving visitors and demonstrating the social status of the family. The parlor entailed its own "visual vocabulary," inviting entrants to "read for its symbolism" in the material cultures contained within.[42] The parlor is where families entertained guests, practiced piano, and enjoyed early print cultures—it was the best room of the home, and a place for representing home dwellers to outside visitors. Filled with luxurious upholstery and heavy decor, the middle-class parlor demanded formality even in posture, constricting the body to stiff, prescribed comportment through rigid furnishings and delicate bric-a-brac.[43] In the United States, the parlor thrived from the colonial and early national periods, becoming most popular in the nineteenth century with the rise of urban versus rural culture.[44] Later, the parlor took on a specifically British connotation and was called the "Victorian parlor" in association with Victorian arts and culture attributed to the reign of Queen Victoria beginning in 1830. This designation captures the way in which many Victorian parlors emphasized fantasy and contradiction in response to oppressive social conditions denoted with this era.[45] Home dwellers frequently filled parlors with items competing for attention, weighing the room with covered surfaces draped with lace cloths, books, vases, decorative china, and ornaments. By filling parlors with consumer items that indicated their cost and value, inhabitants of the parlor used consumption to bring a sense of order to a time characterized by doubt and transition.[46]

Literature and popular cultures of the mid-nineteenth century illustrated the ideal parlor as a space for White women, specifically. *Godey's Lady's Book*, the preeminent U.S. women's magazine, printed images of

City Interiors.—Parlor. For Description, see Household Furnishing Department.

Figure I.3. "City Interiors—Parlor. For Description, see Household Furnishing Department," *Godey's Lady's Book,* May 1884.

parlors alongside advertisements for furnishings and reading materials that should appear in the setting (see figure I.3).[47] This color plate reveals a bedecked parlor along with a story detailing the decorative choices made in the room. Velvet furniture, curio cabinets, and mirrors characterize the parlor as a place for respite and display. The author further explained the parlor as "the *face* of a house," demanding "a richer style of furnishings, and a more fastidious taste" to mark its distinction within the home.[48] An accompanying floor plan indicates that in a two-story home, a parlor should be the largest room in the house. In the cultural imaginary, this room sheltered a delicate woman from the outside world with brocade curtains and draping. In design, the Victorian parlor was intended to convey beauty, respectability, and an astute lady of the house who was well versed in the demands of the woman's sphere; it was a middle-class dwelling for the White "lady" who did not leave the house, but spent her day reading, sewing, playing music, and entertaining company. The parlor displayed her penchant for decoration, which was akin to her personal appearance. Victorian parlors included an overabundance of "decorative objects" that displayed the period's obsessions with social status through the collection of things, the myth of privacy, and the rigid differentiation of the internal domestic space along gendered lines.[49] Other terms for the parlor such as the "drawing room," shortened from the "withdrawing room," indicate the spatial impulses of concealment and the protection of White women. The drawing room as a "private place removed from more public reception areas" symbolized both social status and gender separation within the structure of the home.[50] Existing as two things at once, "the domestic and the gala," the parlor represented a stage for White women's class presentations, portraying "ownership, possession, and permanence" through the parlor and its entailments.[51]

Only members of the community, friends of the family, or organizational associates entered one's parlor for a visit or entertainment. The parlor's constitution in multiple positions of privacy and publicity rendered it as a "parochial realm," as a space that was both open to nonfamily members but closed off to people outside of the family's social network. Bringing together friends as well as neighbors, "parochial realms" only welcomed visitors already acquainted with, or tangentially familiar with, the home dwellers.[52] In its politics of inclusion, the philosophical underpinning of the parlor provided a barrier to individuals outside its classed derivations. Parlors were public in that they welcomed people from outside of one's family into the space to witness the staged performances of middle-class and gender decorum. At the same time, parlors were private in that they closed off individuals who were not already within, or in close proximity, to one's social circles. Parlors staged public displays for private audiences.

It is in these details that a free Black woman's appearance in an early-nineteenth-century parlor would have been a curious event, whether as an animate body or a representative image. The idea of the parlor provided a setting for the dominant culture's "true" woman, a White woman too fragile for "the harsh social realities of expansive industrial capitalism" who could escape to the protection of a delicate domestic space.[53] Parlors were not just for women, but also for "ladies" with privileges. While that excluded many White women in the early nineteenth century, the parlor fundamentally contradicted the lives of Black women in the context of slavery. In the eyes of the early republic, Black women were too closely associated with slavery to be considered fragile or worthy of protection, even if born free. "Ladies were not merely women; they represented a class," and Black women were theoretically barred from the parlor because "no Black woman, regardless of income, education, refinement, or character" could be a lady.[54] Aside from the symbolic notions of womanhood, slavery intervened on the material as well, and blatantly disregarded the "opposition between the family at home and the exterior workplace."[55] Nineteenth-century slavery in the North situated Black women's work within White homes, but even in freedom, many women continued harsh labor for low wages away from their own domiciles, away from their children. Dominant paradigms of private-sphere women, housed away from the paid labor market, were inapplicable to Black women, even after emancipation. Slavery ran counter to the parlor's architectural idea of domesticity, thus excluding Black women. Whereas "U.S. gender ideology" emphasized the separation of men and women via public and private spaces of work, slavery left Black families bereft of these private/public sphere distinctions.[56] No matter her civil status, occupation, or wealth, a woman of African descent did not belong within the conceptual space of the parlor or its indispensable notions of domesticity.

Nonetheless, in the United States, a small number of free Black people maintained parlors, against the prerequisites of middle-class belonging. Emma Lapsansky explains that the economic demand for Black women's labor distinguished their "middle-class" identities from White women who were meant "to be dependent [and] self-effacing."[57] While well-off White women readily married influential White men, Black women who married important Black leaders remained restricted within the limited degree of power enjoyed by their husbands. Many free women of color who enjoyed fine parlor items like pianos and clocks simultaneously represented a diverse range of financial stability, from those who housed boarders for extra income to those who hired their own domestic live-in servants.[58] These Black women were especially noticeable and especially problematic in a context uncomfortable with free Blackness within middle-class spaces.

In *Picture Freedom*, I mobilize the parlor as a metaphor for thinking through projects of domesticity and domestication that took place through the visual cultures of this interior space. Specifically, I offer the notion of the transatlantic parlor to discuss pictures of freedom as tools of sense making that helped reorient parlor dwellers to changing conceptions of the nation and the Atlantic world, each as representative of home. Parlors served as settings for what Simon Gikandi describes as the "culture of taste," supporting the "conceptual gap [that] separated the leisure of drinking coffee or tea from the brutality of slavery."[59] By referring to the transatlantic parlor I mean to call attention to the idyllic global home that traversed the Atlantic, simultaneously providing solace to constituents of empires, and terror to those subjected to domination. The transatlantic parlor represents a site of leisure and sense making, a place of reprieve and rehearsal, where both Whites and Blacks turned to deal with transformations happening around them. The transatlantic parlor serves as a metaphor and an analytic that underscores the spatial commitments of display that were significant for understanding Black freedom in the slave era. The transatlantic parlor is a place of multiple domesticities: the Atlantic world as a unified home of slaving empires and a place for domesticating presumably uncivilized Africans through enslavement.

I offer the transatlantic parlor as "one single, complex unit of analysis," much like the ships that Paul Gilroy uses to discuss slavery and its reverberations in a transnational and intercultural perspective.[60] Similar to the "living means" by which Gilroy imagines the enjoining of disparate points across the Atlantic Ocean, I use the transatlantic parlor to emphasize the issues of display and spatial belonging that influenced interpretations of emancipation.[61] While the figurative slave ship traveled the sea to create a sense of transient nationalism for people of African descent, the parlor represents the space where Whites and Blacks retired to reconcile that aftermath. Rather than the mobility symbolized in the slave ship, the parlor provided a rigid setting for disciplining Black freedom into belonging through visual practices. A transatlantic parlor made more luxurious because of the sailing ships that Gilroy describes, rife with more opulence and decoration through capitalistic exploitation, also represents a place where Whites and Blacks collectively experimented with the free Black body and visions of national inclusion. I reimagine the stagnant (but not static) parlor, overrun with the items picturing Others, to discuss the transformational notions about Black belonging. Picturing freedom functioned as a method to assuage anxieties about Blackness and its place within the transatlantic. The parlor—a very dark, heavy, and overly ornamental domestic space, often overrun with tokens of exoticism—was itself tied to slavery in that the refined home dwelling was meant to counter everything happening outside of the space. The parlor protected its inhabitants from the chaos of the exterior world, including colonial expansion, and thus becomes particularly important as a space for thinking about how viewers staged early notions of Black freedom as at home within the empire.

The parlor as metaphor calls upon the messiness of "manifest domesticity," as Amy Kaplan describes it, "the imperial project of civilizing" as it happens through the idea of the home and determinations of the foreign.[62]

The metaphor of the parlor makes it possible to think about how the centrality of Whiteness, gender norms, and middle-class status heavily relied upon the palpability of Otherness, rendered through physical objects and pictures. Moreover, the domesticating work that took shape in the parlor acted on Whites and Blacks alike, helping viewers to intensify visualizations of belonging as was necessary to the formation of a nation and the contemplation of emancipation. The parlor as a private-public space remained open to international influence via the incorporation of material cultures, but it also signifies attempts to close off the home to foreign interests through the enactment of geographic borders. Across these various needs, parlor occupants anxiously considered issues of belonging, both international and domestic, as they were destabilized by the question of Black freedom. Parlor dwellers variously read prints, handled material cultures, and turned to the visual to contemplate a new positionality for people of African descent within a multifaceted home. These items helped people figure Blackness as permanently situated *throughout* the Atlantic world, outside the experience of slavery. Whereas the parlor simultaneously addressed issues of colonial relationships and transatlantic belonging, it presents an opportunity to think about how parlor activities helped the developing United States fit into the larger transatlantic as a cohesive space.

The potential for emancipation to make room for Black people within the parlor, visible as guests and owners rather than invisible facilitators, threatened to disrupt still-fragile notions of Whiteness and nationhood structured within the very idea of the space. Whereas the structural domain of the parlor meant to exclude the living Black body, invitations for printed Blacks to appear in this space offer up an interesting counterpoint. The proliferation of critical and complimentary images of free people of African descent amid the earliest legislative enactments of abolition queries issues of production, circulation, and function. How did the printed, free, Black body belong within the parlor when the animate Black body did not? Did the print culture existence of Black freedom within the parlor of the home make way for Black bodies to physically exist there in the larger cultural imaginary? To picture freedom in the context of slavery was to imagine empire without slavery, inasmuch as it was about reconceptualizing people of African descent. Free Black communities posed a number of questions in their very existence, causing Whites to query issues of permanence and national identity. What should slaving empires do about free Black people? Where do free Black people belong? Most important, how did viewers of the Atlantic world incorporate and exclude free Blackness, simultaneously?

The Archive of Freedom

Slavery and its corresponding philosophies of the visual have marred the antebellum archive of Black visuality. A specifically nineteenth-century desire for "coherence, accuracy, and completion" in representations of race meant limited variation among illustrations of Black freedom before the photograph.[63] The preemancipation archive of Black freedom is rampant with reluctance to depict the Black body as interested in or prepared for the act of picturing. Stephen Best points out the "emptiness" in the "visual archive of slavery," where there are no visual equivalents to the slave narrative in early U.S. history; whereas "slaves [were] not the subject of the visual imagination," but instead "its object," Best points to a foreclosed visual imagination among unfree Blacks that does not *appear* in the archives.[64] Such an observation might seem hard to fathom given the ubiquity of Black representations in archives of the early United States, beginning in the late eighteenth century. However, recent scholarship further reveals the complexity scholars face in parsing Blackness in the visual culture of the nineteenth century. The archive demonstrates Black visuality as a utility, often a source of revelation; the visual occurs as a productive site where African Americans demonstrated fitness for citizenship or divulged the ruthlessness of slavery.[65] Questions about visual imagination, especially outside the confines of propaganda, become difficult to trace. People who lived, loved, worked, played, and resisted a multitude of atrocities every day are noticeably absent in pictorial representations before the middle of the nineteenth century. Before the daguerreotype, images of the runaway, the eugenicists' sketches of scientific racism, and the pervasive caricatured renditions of Africanness collectively constitute early conceptualizations of Black freedom.

The preemancipation archive of Black freedom also features critical portrayals of free Black communities, items that do the double work of representing people of African descent who actually existed, but also reveal contemptuous White attitudes toward Black emancipation. My triangulation of artifacts, even those in conflict with one another, offers a contextualization of the meanings in circulation as free people took to the streets of northern cities. Caricatures (which I discuss in chapter 3) are part of my larger attempt to make the very fleeting moment of sight palpable for the sake of critique. Since seeing is a disappearing practice, difficult to pin down and examine some centuries after the fact, I trace a complex web of transient interactions through both the cheap prints produced to comment on emancipation and in the "high culture" iterations of freedom in other formats. The cadre of characters discussed in *Picture Freedom* signify often conflicting approaches to Black visuality, symbolizing the complicated ways in which viewers across race grappled with the projected end of slavery. While Whites who were hostile to abolition used print to disparage the idea of Black freedom and national identity, free Black people and cultural producers carefully transformed their relationships to the visual.

Many of the Black people I explore in this study were quite dogmatic culture producers, insistent about racial propriety and representation. Consequently, their preoccupations with the "respectable" shaped an archive with few images of free Black bodies produced by people of African descent. They documented Black freedom in ways intended to avoid "negative stigmas and caricatures," treating Black publicity in the slave era in ways that suggest a "deliberate concession to mainstream societal values."[66] Indeed, before the emergence of daguerreotype and the expansion of Black portraiture, people of African descent infrequently reproduced the Black body on the page. Prominent activists such as Frederick Douglass advocated for "the transformation of dominant conventions" around representations of Black people, but Black elites largely avoided picturing freedom in the quotidian formats of popular culture.[67] While their parlors included a plethora of books and newspapers, their records primarily focused on the textual at the expense of a more picturesque archive. Similarly, free Black abolitionists who were active in the antislavery movement did not appear in its bastion of material culture and imagistic propaganda; much of abolitionist propaganda promoted the end of slavery with depictions of the unfree.[68] Far less obvious than caricature's abrasiveness, Black archiving of the visual emerges in the invisible. It is what does not appear on the page—including explicit racialization—that gives us insight into what Black visuality meant to those fortunate enough to be free, but who also remained unsafe and marginal in the early republic.

I have construed an archive that draws on a variety of items to discern the landscape of Black visuality and visualizations of Black freedom in the early nineteenth century. I piece together racial caricatures, lithographs, abolitionist newspaper writings, runaway notices, sentimental literatures, joke books, and scenic wallpaper to create a more robust depiction of Black freedom in the transatlantic imaginary. *Picture Freedom* seeks to bring the emergent appearance of Black freedom into sharper relief by excavating the ways in which Black people presented themselves as free within a visual culture built upon a perverse concept of Black visuality. It asks and answers questions about how formerly enslaved people of African descent reformulated notions of vision and visuality to present themselves as free to a hostile public. At the same time, this text considers how White viewers evolved practices of looking to cope with the chaos set in motion by the emergence of Black freedom. Through a critical cultural analysis of pictures, performances, looking practices, and plays on spectacularity, I explore the ways in which Whites and Blacks engaged Black freedom in preparation for abolition.

Overview

The people and pictures in this book reveal various postures toward the idea of Black freedom. They present early cultural experiments with vision and visibility, as well as new engagements with Black raciality. Rather than a chronological order, the organization of *Picture Freedom* mimics the movement of antebellum visual cultures as the emergence of emancipation restructured racial ways of seeing. The chapter order foregrounds the visual culture of slavery as the context for the earliest pictures of freedom, and proceeds to describe how viewers in Black homes and White homes variously used print to address the visual problems associated with Black freedom. I discuss evolving considerations of domesticity with a reflection on the parlor across chapters. *Picture Freedom* considers life on the street, race in the home, and Blackness within the northern United States and in the transforming Atlantic.

Chapter 1, "A Peculiarly 'Ocular' Institution," theorizes the visual underpinnings of slavery in order to contextualize the cultural crisis represented by free Black people at the end of the eighteenth century. I take up the various ways in which slavery established a visual logic of race in order to underscore the emergence of Black freedom as a spectacular occurrence. I offer the language of the "peculiarly 'ocular' institution" to describe the visual practices of slavery as foundational and unwavering; it is from this established way of seeing race and visuality that questions about seeing Black freedom became complicated. I theorize the institutionalization of slavery's visual culture through unique methods of social interaction and the circulation of "slaving media"—items such as the runaway notice that captured Blackness on the page or supported the system of slavery.

The remaining chapters examine various methods for picturing freedom in the late eighteenth and early nineteenth centuries, against a backdrop of slavery's visual logics. Chapter 2, "Optics of Respectability: Women, Vision, and the Black Private Sphere" explores emergent visual practices developed by elite free Black women within the confines of Black parlors. This chapter critiques free Black women's friendship albums, a popular form of sentimental print culture usually produced for middle-class White women, to explore how notable Black abolitionist women cultivated critical looking practices and subversively engaged perceptions of free Black womanhood.[69] I use the friendship album as a basis for imagining the parlor and the production of privacy (such as interiority) in the lives of Black women who cultivated new self-perceptions in these spaces to coincide with experiences of freedom. Different from historical analyses of the friendship album, this chapter considers theories of feminist spectatorship to treat the album as a media artifact and to think about private practices of visual culture among free women in the slave era. I read the use and circulation of the friendship album to theorize the development of a Black female gaze connected to the production of innocuous floral paintings and sentimental prints. Exploring the visual practices of Black parlors offers a chance to think through how free people of African descent transformed Black visuality amid changes happening around them. In the "intimate publics" of Black parlors, free women used sentimental literatures to connect with one another and to legitimate their claims to middle-class belonging.[70] The homes of free Black people provided semipublic locations for contemplating Black visibility and emancipation. Friendship albums represents moments of "encoding" and "decoding," where free Black women acculturated one another into dominant hegemonic definitions of seeing themselves, and into critical reflexivity, based in "situated logics," about the norms of visual culture.[71]

Chapter 3, "'Look! A Negress': Public Women, Private Horrors, and the White Ontology of the Gaze," argues that White viewers retreated to their parlors and used caricature to retool White dominion over the visual in response to street encounters with free Blacks. I analyze the development of Clay's "Life in Philadelphia" lithograph series, which mocked free Black Philadelphians for their public displays of freedom in order to discuss

White perceptions of the social changes compelled by gradual emancipation laws.[72] This chapter constructs free people and women in particular as individuals who performed dissident "looks," rather than as figures ontologically dislodged by the gaze.[73] I reconsider existential phenomenology's idea of the "look" (as theorized by Jean-Paul Sartre and Frantz Fanon), to argue that such linear constructions of the gaze also describe dominant (White) experiences of vision, disrupted by confrontations with difference.[74]

Chapters 4 and 5 diverge from discussions of domesticity in the localized arena of the home space in chapters 2 and 3, to instead think through the nation and the Atlantic world as sites of domestication. Here, I transition from a discussion of private interiors to one of public spaces, beginning with the urban North. Chapter 4, "Racial Iconography: Freedom and Black Citizenship in the Antebellum North," considers domestic portrayals of freedom circulating in the Black press and in White media venues. It explores the manner in which free Black people published their own periodicals and worked as activists in northern cities to publicize civic participation.[75] I argue that this collection of representations excluded free Black people from definitions of U.S. national belonging, and that neither venue cultivated a picture of Black citizenship. This chapter analyzes pro- and antislavery media together, as items that compounded the notion of racial hypervisibility, and explores early depictions of Black freedom throughout U.S. print culture. It describes the treatment of Black freedom in the Black press and explains how the powerful combination of words and images in caricatures became the unchecked representation of Blackness in the larger cultural imaginary. Chapter 4 moves toward thinking about the relationship between Black freedom and U.S. national identity.

I conclude *Picture Freedom* by discussing the transatlantic utility of Black freedom in internationally circulating representations. Chapter 5, "Racing the Transatlantic Parlor: Blackness at Home and Abroad," draws upon the transatlantic parlor as a metaphor of inter/national belonging and a place for situating Black domesticity. I argue that viewers domesticated Black freedom—made it fit within the purview of the home—through depictions that simultaneously included and excluded people of African descent within visions of empire. I analyze the evolving form and content of print portrayals of free Blacks shared across U.S., British, and French parlors, with a detailed analysis of the caricatured origins of "Vues d'Amerique du Nord." Produced in 1834, this scenic French wallpaper used an image from Clay's original caricature to portray Black freedom in North America. My analysis offers a detailed reading of the transatlantic visual culture focused upon problematizing Black emancipation as a method for broaching Black belonging.

Picturing Freedom

Picture Freedom considers the emergent visual culture shaped by competing representations of free Blacks, realized in the relationship between items like the daguerreotype and the caricature I discussed in the beginning of this introduction. Both types of objects are constitutive elements of an inter/national narrative about Blackness as a thing apprehended by the eye and seen/scene to a host of other visual interactions unspecific to modern technologies. Black women were not just figures that other artists thought to include in their cultural works; they also invented their own accounts of Black visuality in the changing context of transatlantic slavery. Sarah Mapps Douglass, artist, abolitionist, and sister to the aforementioned daguerreotypist Robert Douglass, created a number of illustrations like this Black butterfly (figure I.4) and shared them with an exclusive group of friends.[76] On its own, this resting creature, painted in a scene of leaves and flowers, may seem unremarkable. However, read in the context of hostile illustrations of Black women, such as figure I.5, *Back to Back*, Douglass's seemingly innocuous offering demarks an important point of contrast from this "cutting" vision of Black freedom.[77] The illustrated Black butterfly set in nature, reads quite differently from this ornately dressed woman, who only serves as an accompaniment to an equally extravagant male partner. The delicacy of butterfly wings is distinct from the abrasive shoulders of the woman in caricature, the former marking a fragility to free Black womanhood that is entirely absent from the hostile approach to picturing freedom, and generally unrecognized in a context focused upon kidnapping and enslaving Black women.

Black women's modes of picturing freedom were essential to the parlor as a place for preparation—a private place to perfect new Black visibilities. African descendants, and Black women in particular, cultivated national identities through developing different postures toward the visual. Free Black people produced multifocal visions of Black visuality that oscillated between resisting and submitting to the logics of slavery. In the presence of hostile images like *Back to Back*, the racial animus of slavery never quite disappeared, and in fact, only materialized in internationally

Figure I.4. Sarah Mapps Douglass, *"A token of love from me, to thee,"* ca. 1833, Amy Matilda Cassey Album. (Courtesy of The Library Company of Philadelphia)

popular forms of cultural production. Ironically, graphic humor made for coping with the actual sight of "uppity" free Blacks— plastered in shop windows that sold prints and present in homes that entertained company— also made Blacks more visible in public culture. Through the fashionable consumption of ostentatious Black bodies in pictures, free Black people became more popular through images that re-presented them for amusement. Thanks to efforts to picture freedom, Blackness became ubiquitous and a permanent staple in the U.S. popular imaginary.

Figure I.5. Edward Williams Clay, *Back to Back*, 1829. (Courtesy of The Library Company of Philadelphia)

This book offers a new way to think about Black visuality and emancipation by proposing Black freedom as a visual problem that Whites and Blacks variously managed with practices of picturing. Different from antislavery rhetoric and political documents, visual cultures captivated with the prospect of Black freedom used strange and unexpected practices to resituate Blackness within the transatlantic imaginary. Transatlantic slavery produced a visual order to everyday life by organizing unfree Blacks into cadres of invisible helpmates that lived and worked in destitution but in close proximity to Whites. Images that groped through Black freedom amid de jure and de facto slavery circulated the Atlantic Ocean while living Black people who made themselves visible in contradistinction to slavery worked hard to create distance from a legacy of bondage and exploitation. These artifacts archive the manner in which Black freedom presented a crisis to national and international codes of looking at race and nationhood. They intimate a desire for sense making about freedom and illustrate the ways that ordinary people and image producers alike attempted to make "free" status meaningful for others through depiction. Welcomed into the parlor on sheets of paper, relegated to fleeting pieces of popular ephemera, free Black people provided a platform for experimenting with ideas of home. Although Black women were entirely uninvited as animate visitors in certain parlors, excluded from the concept of "guests" that might sit on a White woman's sofa, White homes strangely welcomed free Black men and women as silent objects with no gaze of their own, in ridiculing depictions.

1

"A Peculiarly 'Ocular' Institution"

An amorphous Atlantic took shape around the enslavement of African peoples. Black bondage fortified a perimeter around the Atlantic world and constituted a burgeoning U.S. identity, as both New England and the U.S. South "flourished under slavery."[1] The execution and the abolition of slavery in the United States functioned to constitute the early republic as part of the Atlantic. As the Atlantic world expanded, playing host to a sprawling dispersal, "changes across [its] time, space, and jurisdiction" appear at the intimate level of a single household up through the remote relations of metropole and colony.[2] Visual culture provided measures for the assessment of fitness or belonging, as both pictures and practices represent sites of confrontation among unfree African descendants and Whites who held them in captivity.

Fugitive Freedom in the Atlantic

Elizabeth "Mumbet" Freeman sat for her portrait (figure 1.1) as a free woman in 1811.[3] This amateur painting by Susan Anne Livingston Ridley Sedgwick pictures Freeman well dressed in Federalist-period clothing. In addition to her blue dress, Freeman dons a white fichu to cover her cleavage and a white bonnet to cover her head. Her clothing choices depict Freeman as a respectable free woman in possession of her own body, while the adornment of her gold necklace adds a flourish of conspicuousness to the image (figure 1.2). Freeman's portrait reflected her "regal love of the solid, & the splendid wear" of fine "chintzes and silks."[4] Although her body sits askew from the artist, Freeman's side-eye stare meets the viewer of her portrait. This image, in a gilded frame, pictures a woman who achieved emancipation by confrontation and by a clear sense of entitlement to the founding values that defined the colonial United States in the context of an evolving Atlantic world. Freeman's decision to sit for a portrait represents

Figure 1.1. Elizabeth "Mumbet" Freeman, 1811. (Courtesy of the Massachusetts Historical Society)

a conscious invocation of the visual on her part, a moment in which she applied her sense of self-possession to the terms of looking and being seen that, in part, defined chattel slavery.

Freeman's other very poignant disrespect to slavery's structure of the visual is central to the story of her formal pursuit of freedom. Catherine Maria Sedgwick drafted a lengthy account of Freeman's life as a free and paid servant to the Sedgwick family, which the English literary magazine *Bentley's Miscellany* published in 1853.[5] According to Sedgwick, "action was the law" of Freeman's "nature," and thus, for her, "servitude was intolerable."[6] Sedgwick's account of Freeman's life begins with an account of Freeman's servitude under her abusive former violent mistress, Ms. Ashley. One day, when "making the patrole of her kitchen" [*sic*], "Madame Ashley" observed that Freeman's sister Lizzy, "a sickly timid creature," had reserved scraps of dough from a "wheaten cake" she had baked for the Ashley family in order to make her own. Madame Ashley, enraged, labeled Lizzy a "thief" before she "siezed [*sic*] a large iron shovel red hot from cleaning the oven, & raised it over the terrified girl." However, before the shovel could land on Lizzy, Freeman "interposed" her body, taking the

Figure 1.2. A bracelet of gold beads made from Freeman's necklace. (Courtesy of the Massachusetts Historical Society)

blow instead. Ashley cut Freeman to the bone with the hot shovel, leaving her with "a frightful scar" for the rest of her life. However, in a recurring act of resistance, Freeman regularly brandished the scar to visitors of the Ashley home. When Freeman reflected on the incident, she explained that although she had "a bad arm all winter," she made sure that "Madam had the worst of it." Freeman refused to cover the scar, and when visitors asked Freeman what happened, she replied, "ask Misses." Freeman displayed her wounded body to undermine Ashley's womanhood, purposefully using her insurrectionary exhibition to pose the question, "Which was the slave, & which the real mistress?" Freeman's question queried domesticity as a White woman's gender norm as well as a privilege determined by the space of the home. The sympathy Freeman intentionally invoked from visitors when exposing her scar potentially dislodged Ashley's designation as "mistress" of the house, even if briefly. Freeman used the scar to assert her own domesticity and to punish Mistress Ashley. Where the home served as the arena for White women to display domesticity, Freeman's presentation took up that space as a site of refutation and reassertion. She ignored slavery's customary practice of denying Black pain and White culpability, she undermined predeterminations of domesticity through the way in which she maneuvered within the Ashley home, offering her body as evidence of her owner's malfeasance.

Freeman confronted the racial visual order of slavery, both through the portrait and through the ability to conjure sympathy via the display of her wound. Freeman refuted the daily practice of Black women's subjugation within the intimate confines of the home and at the hands of White women through recourse to the visual. Social interaction in the context of slavery required that unfree Black women like Lizzy and Freeman live and work as invisible helpmates who made life easier for White women like Ashley. Free-man challenged these conventions by drawing attention to White crimes and Black women's corporeal needs. In this context, Freeman's acts func-tioned as cultural transgressions. Freeman's offering of a free Black woman for portrait and her confrontation with Mistress Ashley represent measures that destabilized slavery's architecture of visual domination. In the intimate proximity of the master's home, Freeman used her body in defense of her sister, Lizzie. She then revealed her body to shame Mistress Ashley in front of others, and finally, she covered her body but focused her eyes for the sake of creating a picture. In all of these instances, Freeman defied a visual ter-rain steeped in the suppression of Black women's self-possession and unac-customed to Black women's self-appointed pictures.

My aim in this book is to discuss the ways in which picturing freedom intervened in slavery's institutionalized visual culture and to reveal exhi-bitions of freedom as disruptive to this visual landscape. Although the *picturing* element of this scenario involves some actual illustrations, like Freeman's portrait, we can also think of the flickering glance that might have accompanied the display of her wound as another tool that Freeman used to force Ashley to picture freedom. Each of these appeals to the visual divulges the way in which Black people's demonstrations of freedom in the context of slavery were problematic. In this chapter, I describe the way in which the organization and maintenance of chattel slavery intertwined the racial and the visual. I argue that this intricate formulation made the appearance of freedom a difficult thing to discern in its earliest occur-rences. Drawing on the language of the "peculiar institution," I describe slavery as a "peculiarly *ocular* institution" that utilized an unstable visual logic of race to enslave persons of African descent and to protect Whites from the threat of the gaze. The term "peculiar institution," coined by South Carolina senator John Calhoun in the nineteenth century, describes slavery as oddly intransient given its conceptual necessity to White pros-perity.[7] Referring to slavery as "the peculiar institution" helped to dimin-ish the unpleasant realities of slavery and allowed its advocates to argue for the perpetuation of bondage while removing the human connotation associated with the term. Offering a theory of the "peculiarly 'ocular' insti-tution," I mean to underscore slavery's visual culture as an impediment to recognizing freedom. Moreover, I offer this notion to contextualize Black visuality as shaped by and resistant to slavery's visual culture. This theory of the peculiarly ocular nature of slavery frames the reception of freedom and the new tactics of spectatorship that I describe throughout this book.

The mediation of slavery was also central to the institutionalization of this peculiar visual culture as early print media helped to circulate a set of racio-visual codes to readers and viewers throughout the Atlantic world. Much of the print material involved in the transatlantic transport of Africans for enslavement, from auction advertisements to runaway notices, emphasized physical traits, sometimes with the help of illustrations, and targeted White viewers. I offer an analysis of these items below to explain how media conjured a racio-visual logic in support of slavery. Thinking through visual culture as a "generative" site for the deployment of slaving ideologies, I describe the runaway and the *mediation* of the runaway as distinct, but interrelated, examples of slavery's visual assumptions.[8] Whereas media supporting slavery helped proliferate the visual construction of race, the runaway forcibly destabilized these presumptions.

Media in support of slavery points to the runaway as a distinctive problem, but I collect these reclamations of freedom under the rubric of *fugitivity*. While slavery alone was enough to initiate a perpetual state of "not belonging" for people of African descent, the fugitive conditions of homelessness and obscurity also correspond to *exhibitions* of freedom in the context of slavery. Whites often curiously regarded demonstrations of freedom among Black people in the context of slavery, receiving such displays as out of place. Even someone like Freeman might have been somewhat of a mystery to Whites, both in her ability to manipulate the visual terms of slavery in the Ashley house as well as in her demonstration of freedom through portraiture. Yet, the confounding nature of Black freedom in the context of slavery did not result from the "fugitive vision" of exceptional Black people who transformed from unfree to free cultural producers, but from the way in which slavery intertwined race and visuality.[9] I argue that displays of Black freedom took up the questions of legibility and home that defined fugitivity and haunted the transatlantic. The idea and the image of the Black fugitive symbolized insurgence against both a specific master who properly "owned" the runaway, and against the state, which depended upon Black people's compliance with slavery as the rule of law. Blacks who ran away were fugitives from justice but also fugitives from an evolving conception of the Atlantic world as home. While slavery constructed people of African descent as legible and comprehensible, freedom and fugitive freedom took up illegibility as permanent conditions that countered the parlor's reliance on slavery.

Even the juridical demand for freedom took up the issue of fugitivity in the face of the transatlantic slave trade. Freeman's reclamation of liberty explicitly proposed questions about home and belonging in a transatlantic landscape. Freeman managed both local and large-scale notions of domesticity in the process of resisting slavery. She was one of the first people of African descent to sue for liberation in the United States, filing one of the earliest "freedom suits" in the state of Massachusetts in 1781.[10] In Sedgwick's narrative of Freeman's life, she reports on Freeman's experience of hearing a public reading of the Declaration of Independence in Sheffield, Massachusetts, from which Freeman discerned that U.S. Americans' right to liberty from England translated to her right to freedom from Whites and from slavery. On hearing "that paper read yesterday that says 'all men are born equal—&, that every man has a right to freedom,'" Freeman asked, "'wont the law give me my freedom?'"[11] Freeman's idea that the Declaration of Independence applied to her is indicative of her notion of a transatlantic belonging as a precedent to U.S. national identity. Her pursuit of emancipation was not yet about her right to U.S. citizenship, but about her right to the freedom to which people in the colonial United States were entitled in the Atlantic world.

My interest is about how the fugitive element of exhibitions of freedom in the context of slavery called attention to the ways in which people of African descent confronted the visual conditions of slavery by acting outside its institutional presets of interracial interactions. Spectacular exhibitions of freedom problematized and abraded the visual culture of slavery. Fugitive free Blacks reveal that the enslaved might outwardly appear resigned even while calculating escape. Fugitive free people of African descent masterfully understood assumptions about race, vision, and visuality, and then used this knowledge to steal themselves and upend the foundational assumptions of slavery's visual culture. The ascertainment of freedom by way of fugitivity suggested a calculated incongruence between the outward appearance of the Black body and the internal perceptions of the unfree person. Freeman's commitment to her sister may have made running away a less likely choice for her—a notion consistent with the fact that most runaways were men.[12] Nonetheless, her method of achieving liberty still conjured questions of domestic belonging and an opaque display of freedom meant to torment her abuser. My description of slavery's peculiar visual culture is meant to situate early exhibitions of freedom within a fraught and domineering context for reception. This chapter explains the visual culture of slavery as one undergirded by an unreliable praxis that depended on "visible" signifiers of race to conflate seeing and subjectivity, to racialize the eye/I. Whereas the practices of transatlantic slavery institutionalized a visual construction of race and racial ways of seeing, late-eighteenth-century assertions of Black freedom offered interruption.

A Peculiar Ocularity

Slavery functioned as a peculiarly "ocular" institution. Its daily execution thrived in a racio-visual economy that determined ways of seeing and ways of being seen according to racial difference. In trying to imagine the visual culture of slavery, one might most immediately consider the routine monitoring of bondspersons' behavior on plantations since this was central to slavery's policing tactics. C. Riley Snorton asserts that "plantation governance schemes" and the role of the overseer, in particular, were chief among slavery's practices of visual domination.[13] Additionally, the whole process of chattel slavery relied heavily upon visual culture wherein the idea of the eye was a matter of racialization. Indeed, to possess both the eye and an "I" was a matter of raciality in the context of slavery. The divisions of social power into White or Black also parsed the faculty of sight into discrete racial categories. More specifically, slavery organized an omniscient White eye/I to police and manage Black bodies, constructing sight as a racially distinct experience, and as the sovereign domain of Whiteness. Summarily, slavery parsed visibility along racial lines as well, distinguishing and racializing people of African descent from Whites through the presumption of an innate visibility. Whereas practices of enslavement relied on the eye within social encounters, the visual culture of slavery constructed race and racialized the act of seeing.

But slavery's peculiar ocularity was more than the mere visual habits that made slavery possible. By slavery's peculiar ocularity, I mean the very specific visual idiosyncrasies and contradictions utilized within the visual logics of slavery that were at once contrary and commonplace in early U.S. life. These visual logics of racial decorum were irrational, unreliable, and often collided with one another, even as they were crucial to enslavement philosophies. For example, while Whites exercised visual authority over Blacks, there were also numerous instances of Black overseers or "drivers"; these Black overseers could be as cruel or more benign than their White counterparts, but their race meant that their authority was limited by law. Black slave drivers existed somewhere between official White overseers and enslaved Blacks in this peculiar visual culture.[14] To think of slavery as a peculiarly ocular institution is to think of how systemic bondage fetishized a connection between vision and race in ways that were simultaneously nonsensical and naturalized. Slavery entailed a tautological, and thus self-sustaining, visual rationale. The peculiar visual practices of slavery happened in the day-to-day processes of enslavement that inconsistently used the eye to determine signifiers of race, and thereby determine social, economic, political, and visual possibilities. Slavery organized a strange approach to race that emphasized sight and intertwined raciality with visuality. The hegemony of slavery's peculiar ocularity relied on visibility to enslave, and relied on invisibility to carry out slavery with feigned innocence. Slavery coded Black raciality as visible, and thus associated the denial of freedom with racial perceptibility. Not only did the sight of persons of African descent first suggest they should be enslaved, but, more importantly, the habitation of an observable racial identity coincided with enslavement, over time. This kind of racio-visual logic persisted, making it necessary for free Black people to furnish paperwork to prove their freedom to random Whites in northern U.S. states, and for all persons of African descent to live under the suppressive scrutiny of various "codes" to legislate proper behavior.[15]

Saidiya Hartman's canonic text offers up the term "scenes of subjection" as language useful for thinking through the overdetermination of Blackness in the field of vision, or hypervisibility, where forced displays of jubilee and the sight of the coffle were essential to characterizations of Blackness as inherently spectacular.[16] The theater of slavery—the scenes of violence and order—existed for disciplining race, with noted accentuation on pain and the "spectacle of power."[17] The visible Black body appeared on display for the sake of White pleasure and Black terror. In the moment that Black bodies met the subjugation of slavery, they simultaneously encountered the visual ordering of race. In written details about skin color, hair texture, and overall physicality, slavery theorized Black raciality as an observable phenomenon as early as the moment of purchase. Unfree Africans were often "graded" in the slave market, delineated as "Second Rate or Ordinary Men," sometimes "Extra Girls or No. 1 Girls," as "slave speculators" tried to rate the value of human cargo against other goods like cotton or sugar.[18] Not only did these tactics assign fiscal value to Black bodies, but descriptions were part of an overall practice of closely examining unfree people. Scenes of subjection happened through both intimate and distant forms of social contact. The peculiarly ocular institution transformed the display of individual unfree people into a large-scale cultural practice of constant observation, prefiguring Black bodies and people of African descent as demanding surveillance. This approach to the visual imagined the Black body as intrinsically visible, as decipherable. The construction of vision and visibility in the context of slavery also organized Black raciality around an inherent need for management or oversight from Whites.

Ironically, although slavery's visual matrix positioned Blackness as a visible phenomenon, this unreliable visual culture also projected unfree people of African descent as deftly capable of a sly invisibility. Mainstream belief in the idea of Black visibility happened in concert with a perpetual suspicion about unfree Blacks trying to escape. Although the coffle situated the Black body as an entity on view for the White eye/I, the ever-present possibility of escape also positioned unfree Black people as likely to avoid observation. This coupling imagined people of African descent as simultaneously easily observable and also requiring special techniques of visual policing. Black bodies were both hypervisible and yet capable of a certain invisibility. For example, in mid-eighteenth-century New York City, Whites in local government enforced laws requiring enslaved persons to be indoors after sundown or to carry candle lights (as well as explanatory passes) after dark; lawmakers made it illegal for an unfree Black (body) to be unlit after dark.[19] The idea that technological intervention helped illuminate the Black body advanced the idea that without help, Black people could easily avoid White surveillance in the colonial United States. These social practices imagined that Black skin was able to evade visibility, or the White gaze, despite the way in which Black corporeality was thought of as uniquely palpable. Mandating Black illumination constructed Black skin as textured in such a way as to avoid visual faculties. Accordingly, slavery required surveillance and public vigilance against a deceptive Black visibility. Such beliefs fanaticized the Black body's inherent ability to evade observation and its ability to deceive even the most astute White observer.

This condition of hypervisibility depended upon the suppression of a Black gaze. Although slavery constructed the Black body as deceptive, the matrix also construed unfree Black people as devoid of the ability to properly see, prefiguring them as visible objects that lacked the ability to consciously manipulate notions of visuality. The matrix of slavery's peculiar visual culture meant to suppress the Black eye/I. In the daily practice of slavery, many Whites failed to recognize that enslaved Black people engaged in processes of observation, or that they monitored Whites' behaviors. Likewise, the system of slavery failed to entertain the existence of an inner Black subject, with a sense of will, who realized her own mistreatment or violation.[20] These social beliefs appear in records of unfree Black house servants who listened in on White people's conversations.[21] In this rubric, slavery's atrocities happened to individuals who were supposedly unable to critically observe acts of sexual assault and kidnapping. When Whites did not presume that Black people were unable to cast a critical eye on the system of slavery, they demanded that unfree people look away. For example, if a bonded man or woman delivered the wrong kind of "look" toward a free White, such an offense was deemed disrespectful to the individual and to slavery's power relations—a punishable crime in the state of Virginia.[22] Whites socially mandated that people of African descent avoid issuing looks in service of the maintenance of slavery.

Accordingly, slavery's peculiarly unreliable visual culture entailed a number of inconsistencies that helped maintain constant distinctions of race. African descendants could not avoid visibility, but the law required that they make themselves visible to White sight. Similarly, unfree Blacks inherently lacked any kind of critical perception, but the law forbade them from looking at Whites. The peculiar nature of visual culture in the context of slavery mimicked the strange nature of ocularity in the eighteenth and nineteenth centuries. In the presence of transatlantic slavery, "a deep belief in knowing by seeing" emerged as "key" to race relations.[23] Cartesian dualism lent visual credence to its power structures, producing an unrelenting faith in the "disembodied eye" in popular culture as well as within intellectual discourses. Whereas within this "ontology of sight," as described by Martin Jay, "the one who casts the look is always a subject and the one who is its target is always turned into an object," ocularity within the context of the Enlightenment easily attached itself to philosophies of race and enslavement.[24] The subjective "I" found its underpinning in the Cartesian "eye," and thus the racialization of subjectivity also enlisted the visual. To put it differently, early ruminations on the eye/I always already trafficked in conceptions of race. Enlightenment theories of the visual were imbedded within the proliferation of slavery. The eye as dissociated from corporeality accommodated a larger context that severed Whiteness from the body. Similarly, emphasis on the utility value of the Black body or Blackness as pure embodiment rendered persons of African descent as devoid of ocular faculties. The construction of ocularity in the period of Enlightenment established the ability to see, or the state of being visual, as connected to raciality. Bodies prefigured as visible, and thus racialized, necessarily remained distant from any practices of looking. Slavery united the racial and the visual through everyday practices. These philosophical ruminations on the eye, perspective, and corporeality (as associated with Descartes) are not severed from the practices of slavery that they helped to facilitate. These racial distinctions within the visual neatly connected to the Cartesian notion of subjectivity, problematically parsing the individual into mind *or* body, eye or embodiment.

Although a number of laws and social practices emphasized the significance of the Black body and unfree Black people to the system of slavery, notions of the White eye were also fundamental to the inconsistent nature of this peculiar institution. Acts such as locating Africans for kidnapping and identifying individuals who were "strong" enough to withstand the Middle Passage constructed slavers as gifted in assessing bodies for subjugation. Particularly when it came to purchasing chattel, slavery demanded an expert White eye/I to examine the bodies of potential purchases. Yet, while it took a certain innate visual skill to choose people of African descent who were good investments, slavery's marketplace actively existed as a place of illusions where Whites oiled unfree people to make them appear strong, fed Blacks enough to make them look healthy, and prodded them to seem joyous. Walter Johnson explains that "being a 'good judge of slaves'" was an important attribute for southern White men, making "the inspection and evaluation of black slaves" a central part of social hierarchy and one's "public identity."[25] The "White man's" ability to "see" enslaved people was a notable skill, even as Johnson notes that Whites in charge of trading took care to physically alter Black bodies for sale, shaving beards, dying hair, feeding them fatty diets, and forcing them to dance.[26] In the transactions of slavery, the Black body represented the terrain on which Whites attempted to trick other Whites, or to demonstrate their own expertise. The White eye/I could simultaneously exist as expert at the slave market, and as one who suffered deception there as well.

The investiture of Whiteness with exceptional visual abilities is one of slavery's most peculiar offerings. The cultivation of Whiteness through the faculties of the eye represents a key element of slavery's visual domination. Although "slavery operated behind a certain invisibility, as far as its European beneficiaries were concerned," where European colonists could avoid visual encounters with enslaved peoples and colonized territories geographically removed from the empire, slavery also helped to render Whiteness invisible by diminishing the specificity of the White body.[27] The establishment of "White" as a racial group happened through a number of processes in the U.S. context, and slavery's visual culture was one of them. Matthew Frye Jacobson describes the "making" of "Caucasians," where the cultivation of White raciality "is not merely [about] how races are comprehended, but how they are seen." Jacobson exposes the intertwining of citizenship with Whiteness in the nation's founding documents, simultaneous to questions of immigration, naturalization, and the abolition of slavery.[28] Connecting Whites and citizenship made ascending to Whiteness a politically salient project for immigrants. Over time, White bodies became unmarked by race as the "possessive investment in whiteness," from the colonial period onward, happened through the articulation of non-Whiteness, through emphasis on the specificity of Native, African, Asian, and Mexican American bodies.[29] The importance of distinction helped to obscure White raciality by rendering Whiteness as an achievement, by making "White" a thing of racial ascendance for European ethnic immigrants trying to assimilate. To be recognized as White was to be recognized in relation to both Black and White servitude. Of the vast number of unskilled Europeans who immigrated to the colonial United States, one-half to two-thirds of them sold themselves into indentured service for five to seven years, facing hardships similar to slavery on a day-to-day basis, notwithstanding the "length of bondage and the involuntary and hereditary nature of slavery" as a unique and unfortunate distinction for African descendants.[30] White servants in the colonial United States often identified as English, Scots, Irish, and German immigrants, and they also ran away from servitude because of brutal punishment. The appearance of "white" skin helped many indentured servants escape, although, at times, Celtic accents or tattered clothing gave them away, leading to their recapture.[31] Nonetheless, these instances reveal how tracking down Whites to reinstitute their servitude required attending to multiple characteristics besides the appearance of the body. So while some would-be Whites could not instantly lay claim to slavery's organization of White invisibility, the ability to call on the privileges of Whiteness in social interaction and, more importantly, the ability to be seen as other than a "slave" brought some degree of leverage for European immigrants that people of African descent were not afforded. A White "convict servant maid, named SARAH WILSON" ran away from her master and changed her name to "lady Susanna Carolina Matilda," which she offered to make "the public believe that she was his Majesty's sister." Along with the name change, Sarah/Susanna made her clothes "with a Crown and a B" to support her story.[32] Sarah/Susanna could move into another kind of visibility in the context of the colonial United States, transitioning from the object of surveillance to presenting herself as fit for observing others.

The remarkable White runaway Benjamin Franklin provides another useful example of how some indentured servants could utilize the visual apparatus of slavery to their advantage. Franklin's body was rife for surveillance when he suffered a brutal apprenticeship under his brother James Franklin of Boston. Like other White indentured servants, Franklin lived under conditions that inherently involved scrutiny and management by some other more powerful person. However, Franklin quickly took to self-invention and began to act as free during his brother's incarceration for printing seditious comments in his own newspaper. Franklin's White privilege enabled him to establish relationships with other Whites and flee to Philadelphia under the auspices of "being" a free man.[33] The idea of Franklin's White body created opportunities for other kinds of visibilities, apart from servitude, allowing him to run away and pass into a class of seemingly self-made free White men. Franklin navigated the early republic as a nondescript, free White, and not simply a European ethnic, because of the ways in which the public received Whiteness in a slave society. Not only could he refuse the positions of surveillance that came along with servitude, but he could also presume visibility at his pleasure. When Franklin decided to publish essays and put his name on the masthead in his brother's *New England Courier* newspaper, he assumed a right to be seen as a free White man, even as he remained unfree on paper.[34] Franklin's servitude and his freedom demonstrate how, although not every European descendant automatically achieved the full privileges allotted to Whiteness on a spectrum of race, they also were not visually barred from national inclusion solely and permanently on the basis of skin color. Franklin moved from indentured to free because he could rely on a viewing public to treat him as free, despite what his brother might say. White servitude illustrates ownership as a factor in the achievement of invisibility, although it is not the entire story. White servants could not claim invisibility in the same ways that White owners could, but many indentured servants aspired toward this visual role, and slavery's raciovisual order provided various routes to this position. As David Waldstreicher writes, "Whites must be seen to be white," and yet "whiteness as power is maintained by being unseen."[35] Slavery organized White invisibility around the cultivation of Whiteness as unhinged from the physical body. Whiteness existed in privileges exclusive of or closed off to people of African descent. Through slavery, Whiteness became the racial identity that seemed, strangely, least racialized and yet best able to morph into other racial performances at will.[36] The emergence of Blackface minstrelsy exacerbated the constructed irrelevance of White corporeality within slavery's visual culture. David Roediger explains that minstrel performers were self-consciously White, using Blackface to illustrate that fact for audiences, and issuing playbills that emphasized the contrasts between the "reality" of the White performer and the transformation into a performance of Black raciality.[37] Visually, the peculiar institution helped to diminish the significance of White corporeality. Slavery's peculiar ocularity advantageously denied the way in which the White body remained just as present in the act of slavery as the Black body. Whites used Black bodies in the most utilitarian sense, to plow, to build, to labor, to nurse, to pleasure, and although White bodies remained ever-present in these encounters, the position of visual authority helped to diminish White corporeality. Whiteness earned invisibility within the social processes of slavery by occupying multiple roles of surveillance within the procedures of enslavement. Unfettered by the physical body, the White I/eye could be everywhere, and always. Here, Whites were always on the lookout, and never to be looked at.

Mediating the Runaway

Media in support of slavery typically figured Whites as particularly gifted in the realm of sight. Print items hailed White viewers, objectified Black bodies, and nurtured Whiteness as a viewing position. A diverse array of print ephemera, such as auction advertisements, runaway advertisements, and pickup notices, traveled to readers throughout the northern and southern U.S. states. White viewership became essential to the institutionalization of slavery's visual culture, as print media undergirded the slave economy. Slaving media, then, normalized Whiteness as a disembodied viewing position by excluding slavers, auctioneers, purchasers, owners, and catchers from the page. Instead, these items announced the arrival of new chattel for sale or called on the White viewing public to assist in the reclamation of enslaved property—all summarily emphasizing the specificity of the Black body and deemphasizing the White body. A still-burgeoning U.S. media industry became central to the buying and selling of chattel persons with advertisements that invited free White viewers, specifically, to visit auction sites and view scantily clad Black bodies for display and for purchase.

Print media offered a strong foundation for the reification of a peculiar visual culture. Various advertisements in support of slavery appeared in colonial newspapers and cheap broadsides during the first one hundred years of U.S. news printing, after the 1690 issue of the *Publick Occurrences Both Foreign and Domestick*, and before the expanded circulation of the penny press.[38] While real-time racialized practices of looking governed interracial encounters within domestic personal spaces such as the farm and the home, print cultures mediated Black bodies and Black freedom as unnatural and unlawful in the domestic space of the nation. These items buttressed a visual culture of domination by disseminating visual codes of race to larger and more varied audiences. While a limited number of free Whites might have been present to see a designated number of enslaved Africans sold at auction, the auction advertisement perpetuated this culture of looking at Black bodies by sharing information about the sale across a large geographical area to more viewers than might have been convened to witness the marketplace. With its wide and regular occurrence—printers could issue their papers on a daily basis by the late eighteenth century—the print media connected to slavery made the institution's governing racial precepts more permanent and prevalent in the public imaginary.

Media portrayals representing unfree Blacks calcified slavery's peculiar ocularity by further enlisting White viewers into skewed visual dynamics. Although these materials targeted property-owning Whites, the cultivation of Whiteness as a viewing position cut across designations of free, indentured servants and property owners. At the level of interpellation, slaving media "hailed" White viewers, asking them to understand that print materials were speaking to them, directly.[39] Print media called upon Whites to imagine themselves as the intended audience for the mediation of slavery and to participate in slavery's culture of surveillance. Slavers readily enlisted print to help control the "slave population" by cultivating "a network of interested onlookers" to protect Whites from property loss.[40] Slavery advertisements functioned as perceptual documents, as materials that taught Whites *how* to see Blackness, but also encouraged Whites to believe that Blackness was a thing to see, and that White subjectivity functioned as a domain for looking. Slavery's media further promoted the development of a White eye/I by focusing attention on Black bodies and away from White bodies, especially away from Whites who were actively involved in the processes of enslaving others. Print media insinuated a White audience—a band of readers for whom literacy was not outlawed.

It further invested Whiteness with the power to look, and encouraged Whites to remain on the lookout for people of African descent.

The runaway notice was the most prevalent and most powerful example of media used to develop White viewership. Runaway advertisements in regional newspapers circulated across state boundaries to inform the public, both literate and illiterate, that an owner or an overseer needed (and would pay for) assistance in retrieving fugitive property. Runaway notices are important to the visual archive because they were among the earliest pictures of Black freedom; they portrayed people of African descent more negatively than all of slavery's media materials did. These items pictured Black freedom as stolen, situated among other kinds of theft; frequently, they marked runaways as unstable individuals who represented a danger to law-abiding persons. Runaway notices detail Blacks doing more than just absconding; Blacks are also depicted as stealing clothes, passing as White, and using "passes" given to run errands in order to escape. The accompanying illustrations are standard images of "free" men and women, Blacks depicted without chains and shown in motion, often with one foot off the ground. Images of an enslaved figure seemingly on the run, in possession of stolen goods, the body itself a stolen good, shown with an enlarged monetary amount on the page, called out to Whites to watch for Black fugitives and to remain attentive to free Black people, in general. Runaway materials imagined fugitive Black people as elusive figures who treacherously evaded visual attention by deploying various tricks to manipulate their bodies and to deceive White owners. Runaway notices *picture freedom* (unlike the abolitionist material I discuss later) as the sly cultivation of tropes that tricked the eye. They reveal fugitive Blacks as "confidence men" and women who seized clothing, literacy skills, manual labor skills, and local spatial knowledge to escape enslavement and to erode public confidence in the institution of slavery.[41] Media meant to assist in the capture or retrieval of Black bodies imagined them as uniquely visible, open to the scope of the White gaze or duplicitous in their attempts to "pass" for free. Ironically, these publications also revealed how runaways capitalized on slavery's peculiar visual culture, showing that while slavery demanded a deferred gaze from unfree persons as a signal of deference, fugitive free Blacks actively manipulated these demands on Black spectorial practice.[42] Such a discrepancy only intensified anxieties of observation.

Picturing freedom in slavery's media meant imagining Black freedom as wholly problematic. Runaway notices indicate that the first and farthest-reaching illustrations of freedom were derogatory. Quite simply, in their existence and their format, runaway notices imagined Black freedom as misbegotten and volatile. Postings with bold letters that described "RUNAWAY," both as a person and an action, illustrated with a Black figure in motion, helped to assert freedom as a stolen entity, further diminishing the sense that slavery purloined life and labor from Black bodies. Additional details included in runaway advertisements also organized Black freedom as dangerous. Many runaway ads described multiple kinds of theft: the fugitive body, clothing taken for disguise, as well as pilfered horses and weapons. Runaway advertisements were intended to help the public identify very specific individuals who escaped custody. Printed notices about fugitive free Blacks attempted to give precise details about "the demeanor, dress, speech, character, abilities, background, and possible destination of runaway slaves" to describe them more robustly than any other depiction of unfree persons during this period.[43] Through word and image, these materials "recreated the slave's body as a living and moving text" that encouraged viewers to *read* the Black body, to find the scars, brandings and wounds described in the announcements on the physical person.[44] Runaway notices attended to the specificity of the individual fugitive rather than to the collective bounty. Runaway advertisements helped to parse unfree Blacks into legible groups or "personality types" such as "'surly,' 'sour,' 'impudent,' and 'bold'" in one category; "'shy,' 'complaisant,' and of 'meek countenance'" in another; and "'cunning,' 'artful,' 'sensible,' 'ingenious,' and 'smooth tongued'" in a third.[45] These descriptors represented the needs of White owners attempting to make sense of Black runaways, after the fact. They pictured free Blacks as crafty and visually fraudulent, disrespectful and wild, for running away from slavery.

The specificity of the individual runaway notice was somewhat undercut by pairing them with images of Black bodies taken from larger sheets of newspaper cuts or prototypes. The salience of advertising to the early U.S. print industry emphasized the role of pictures in relaying messages to consumers. These advertisements similarly imaged the figure of a mobile Black body bound for escape, despite other kinds of textual distinctions. Images were an important aspect of the mediation of slavery because depictions of Black bodies may have made runaway notices and auction advertisements understandable to an illiterate populace. Most Whites throughout the colonial United States remained illiterate well into the nineteenth century, although literacy rates for White adults in the northeastern states were generally higher than in the southern and western territories due to their unique economic, geographic, and historical conditions.[46] Literacy rates were difficult to determine, even once U.S. census takers began accounting for the "literate" and "illiterate" class for the 1840 survey. Moreover, a literate individual might have been able to read or write, but not necessarily both, since many people learned to read first, and then received separate instruction in writing. The ability to sign one's name was often a marker of literacy in the colonial United States, but this determinant only revealed itself in a class of people privileged to sign property documents, such as wills and deeds.[47] Pictures cut across all of these designations, appealing to various kinds of readers. Both literate and illiterate Whites could discern the meaning of the stereotyped figure of a runaway. Numerous advertisements for runaways often appeared on a single page of a newspaper, like the sheet from the *South Carolina Gazette* shown as figure 1.3. Both ads are headlined "RUNAWAY," but the top notice for "a tall, slim, black negro wench, named JENNY" may not have been as accessible as the lengthier ad below for "Saul," "Charlotte," and "Fortune," a man "notoriously known for his Villainy." This notice illustrated three different people with the stock illustration of a presumably "African" person—in motion, clad in nativist garb, carrying a stick.[48] Not only does the image distinguish one ad from the other, but it also helps the longer ad stand out on a page among other kinds of images.

Black women were in precarious positions once framed within the confines of the runaway notice. First, as mothers, Black women runaways needed to choose between leaving their children behind or taking them on the run. A number of Black women ran away from slavery while pregnant. Although "it was not easy to feed, clothe, care for, and protect children" in these scenarios, a number of women did, as indicated by notices that list an infant "at the breast" of a runaway.[49] Still, other women who were not nursing children might find their bodies described in advertisements in ways that invited sexual objectification. A "mulatto woman, named Silvie" ran away with a fifteen year-old boy, "Joseph," but the ad directs readers to look for a "flat belly, and a mark on both sides of her breast" when trying to identify this woman.[50] Such a description gave further license to any would-be captor to examine Silvie's body—or that of any Black woman presumed to be Silvie—should they find her.

This objectification might have informed Harriet Jacobs's method of getaway. In Jacobs's retelling of her escape from the Norcom plantation to her grandmother's house, she navigates the flight by passing for a free Black sailor. Jacobs describes "Linda Brent," the pseudonymous Jacobs, donning "a suit of sailor's clothes—jacket, trousers, and tarpaulin hat."

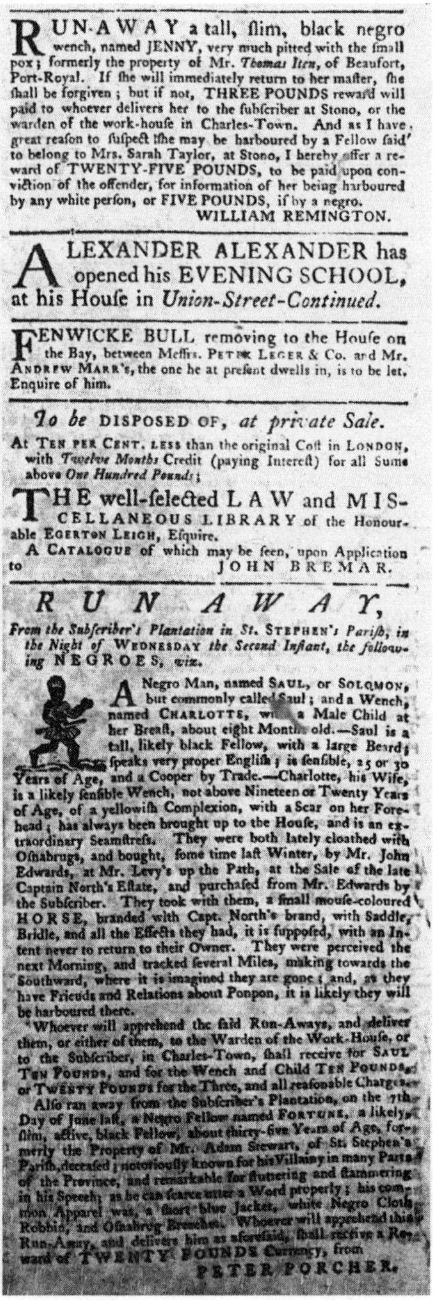

RUN-AWAY a tall, slim, black negro wench, named JENNY, very much pitted with the small pox; formerly the property of Mr. *Thomas Iten*, of Beaufort, Port-Royal. If she will immediately return to her master, she shall be forgiven; but if not, THREE POUNDS reward will paid to whoever delivers her to the subscriber at Stono, or the warden of the work-house in Charles-Town. And as I have great reason to suspect she may be harboured by a Fellow said to belong to Mrs. Sarah Taylor, at Stono, I hereby offer a reward of TWENTY-FIVE POUNDS, to be paid upon conviction of the offender, for information of her being harboured by any white person, or FIVE POUNDS, if by a negro.
WILLIAM REMINGTON.

ALEXANDER ALEXANDER has opened his EVENING SCHOOL, at his House in *Union-Street-Continued.*

FENWICKE BULL removing to the House on the Bay, between Messrs. PETER LEGER & Co. and Mr. ANDREW MARR's, the one he at present dwells in, is to be let. Enquire of him.

To be DISPOSED OF, *at private Sale.*

At TEN PER CENT. LESS than the original Cost in LONDON, with *Twelve Months* Credit (paying Interest) for all Sums above *One Hundred Pounds*;

THE well-selected LAW and MISCELLANEOUS LIBRARY of the Honourable EGERTON LEIGH, Esquire.
A CATALOGUE of which may be seen, upon Application to JOHN BREMAR.

RUNAWAY,

From the Subscriber's Plantation in St. STEPHEN's *Parish, in the Night of* WEDNESDAY *the Second Instant, the following* NEGROES, *viz.*

A Negro Man, named SAUL, or SOLOMON, but commonly called Saul; and a Wench, named CHARLOTTE, with a Male Child at her Breast, about eight Months old.—Saul is a tall, likely black Fellow, with a large Beard; speaks very proper English; is sensible, 25 or 30 Years of Age, and a Cooper by Trade.—Charlotte, his Wife, is a likely sensible Wench, not above Nineteen or Twenty Years of Age, of a yellowish Complexion, with a Scar on her Forehead; has always been brought up to the House, and is an extraordinary Seamstress. They were both lately cloathed with Osnabrugs, and bought, some time last Winter, by Mr. John Edwards, at Mr. Levy's up the Path, at the Sale of the late Captain North's Estate, and purchased from Mr. Edwards by the Subscriber. They took with them, a small mouse-coloured HORSE, branded with Capt. North's brand, with Saddle, Bridle, and all the Effects they had, it is supposed, with an Intent never to return to their Owner. They were perceived the next Morning, and tracked several Miles, making towards the Southward, where it is imagined they are gone; and, as they have Friends and Relations about Ponpon, it is likely they will be harboured there.

Whoever will apprehend the said Run-Aways, and deliver them, or either of them, to the Warden of the Work-House, or to the Subscriber, in Charles-Town, shall receive for SAUL TEN POUNDS, and for the Wench and Child TEN POUNDS, or TWENTY POUNDS for the Three, and all reasonable Charges.

Also ran away from the Subscriber's Plantation, on the 7th Day of June last, a Negro Fellow named FORTUNE, a likely, slim, active, black Fellow, about thirty-five Years of Age, formerly the Property of Mr. Adam Stewart, of St. Stephen's Parish, deceased; notoriously known for his Villainy in many Parts of the Province, and remarkable for stuttering and stammering in his Speech, as he can scarce utter a Word properly; his common Apparel was, a short blue Jacket, white Negro Cloth Robbin, and Osnabrug Breeches. Whoever will apprehend this Run-Away, and delivers him as aforesaid, shall receive a Reward of TWENTY POUNDS Currency, from
PETER PORCHER.

Figure 1.3. "RUNAWAY, From the Subscriber's Plantation in St. Stephen's Parish," *South Carolina Gazette,* September 26, 1771.

She punctuated this ensemble with a masculine "rickety gate" and by "blackening" her face with "charcoal."[51] Jacobs's decision to present herself as a free Black sailor rendered her "invisible on the street" in a way that she might not have experienced if she merely stole typical dress clothes and ran away.[52] Jacobs intended this theatrical appearance to place her among numerous Black sailors for whom no one in particular may have been looking. Free and enslaved Black seafarers sailed through every north Atlantic seaport from as early as 1740.[53] Moreover, if Jacobs anticipated her owner issuing a runaway notice for her capture, this presentation bore little resemblance to the description of her in the advertisement. James Norcom's published description of Jacobs in an 1835 issue of the *American Beacon* typified runaway advertisements, presuming that Jacobs manipulated her race and costume in effort to escape. Describing Jacobs as a "light mulatto" with thick black hair "that curls naturally" but can "be easily combed straight," Norcom suggested that Jacobs might not be immediately recognizable as someone else's property. Offering extensive details, Norcom warned the public that Jacobs may be on the run, "tricked out in gay and fashionable finery," clothing that she likely made herself.[54] Norcom imagined Jacobs through slavery's peculiar visual culture and its corresponding media framework. Within this structure, Jacobs should be seeking Whiteness and dressing as a free woman, not accentuating her Blackness. Jacob's successful escape reveals her ability to evade the structuring vision of the runaway notice, as well as the surveillance of the Norcom plantation.

Conversely, media advertising Black people for sale were far more imaginative than items issued for their recapture. Purchase materials encouraged Whites to visit the auction to choose from an array of able-bodied Black people. In general, media advertising the sale of enslaved persons encouraged more enthusiastic perceptions of Black people. Many of these items eschewed the vilifying language of Black racial identity that appeared on other kinds of advertisements and instead offered favorable reviews about able Black bodies for sale. One advertisement for a "private sale" emphasized the availability of "valuable slaves, mostly this country born" listing nameless persons variously described as "a driver and very good cooper," a "fisherman boat negro and field slave," and "a wench who is a good cook, washer and ironer, and dairy and poultry woman."[55] While the actual auction positioned unfree persons as inanimate objects, media promoting the sale of enslaved persons constructed bondspersons as able-bodied service persons. Slave auction advertisements convened audiences to participate in the spectacle of the sale and helped to whet buyers' appetites. Many of these notices lumped people and objects together such as one ad for "A NEGRO WENCH" listed as a "cook and washerwoman" for sale alongside "a clock, a billiard-table, a chariot," random other home furnishings, "a parcel of lumber, bricks" and "plantation tools."[56] A number of auction advertisements mentioned the sale of people alongside the sale of hogs, cows, and mules—many listing an entire plantation for sale, one replete with "Three Slaves, about Thirty Hogs, and a Stock of Cattle" to go with several hundred acres of land.[57] Most auction advertisements diminished any sense of individuality for enslaved men and women, instead remaking once-free Africans into a large, collective Black mass of washed and oiled bodies available for purchase. And while these descriptions did not recognize the humanity of individual men, women, and children, advertisements did more than promise buyers that the cargo was healthy and capable, paradoxically flattering unfree people as skilled workers.

The images on these materials were distinct as well. A full column of one southern newspaper moved through the various images of Black bodies in the context of slavery, denoting each position with a different image (figure 1.4). The three separate ads for auction emphasized the "CARGO" of "NEGROES" for sale, "choice and healthy," as indicated by the chiseled muscles. These images positioned the human cargo as ready to work; Blacks are shown wearing loincloths, facing the viewer of the paper, open chested, holding work implements, and waiting for direction. These images contrast sharply with the two figures assigned to the runaway notices. Although the "cargo" is described as docking from Sierra Leone, Barbados, and the Gold Coast, it is the runaways who are imprinted as "foreign," depicted in nativist garb, holding tools that now signal weaponry, and with one foot off the ground to indicate their movement.[58] Arguably, enslaved people of the colonial period were often from identifiable locations outside the United States. However, the contrast in these images depicts the conscious use of indicators of "Africanness" and foreignness to distinguish between people who are committed to working as unfree and people who have broken this agreement by running away. Blackness read as Africanness becomes more relevant, and visible, for Black people who act outside the dictates of slavery's visual and social contracts.

Pickup notices similarly described the physical attributes of captured Blacks to readers. Jailers used public notices to capture fugitives and to notify owners of the whereabouts of their escaped property. Again, these items connected the idea of the residual "Africanness" of some runaways

TWENTY POUNDS REWARD,

For each of the following RUN-AWAYS, viz.

JAMES, a likely, young Mulatto man, the property of Mr. Moncrief, of St. Augustine, and arrived here lately with Captain Bishop; he formerly belonged to Colonel Byrd of Virginia, was brought to Carolina when he was a boy by Mr. Levi, and now pretends that he is free. CATO, a stout negro man, well known in Charles-Town, late Major Butler's, and now belonging to Dr. Spence; they are artful and sensible, and will endeavour to ship themselves as seamen. All masters of vessels are therefore hereby cautioned not to carry them off the province. TWENTY POUNDS reward will be given for each of them; and any person who harbours them, will be prosecuted with the utmost rigour of the law.

ALEXANDER ROSE.

Charles-Town, June 26. 1772.

TO BE SOLD,

On MONDAY the 6th of JULY, on the usual TERMS,

A CARGO OF
TWO HUNDRED and EIGHTEEN
WINDWARD COAST
NEGROES,
IN GOOD HEALTH,

JUST arrived in the Ship AFRICA, Captain WILLIAM WALLACE, directly from SIERRA LEONE.

JOHN LEWIS GERVAIS.

Charles-Town, June 29, 1772.

TO BE SOLD,

On WEDNESDAY the 8th Day of JULY,

A CARGO OF
TWO HUNDRED AND TEN
PRIME, HEALTHY, YOUNG
NEGROES,

Of the COROMANTEE and FANTEE Countries, Not one old, or ordinary among them,

BEING the FIRST CHOICE of a CARGO of 500, which came in a very short Passage to BARBADOS, and just arrived from thence in the Brigantine FRIENDSHIP, RICHARD WOOSTER, Master, by

ALEXANDER ROSE.

Charles-Town, June 30, 1772.

TO BE SOLD,

On THURSDAY the 9th Day of JULY,

A CARGO OF
THREE HUNDRED and FIFTY
CHOICE and HEALTHY
NEGROES,

ARRIVED Yesterday in the Ship Friendship, Captain James Cuming, directly from the GOLD COAST, by

MILES BREWTON.

RUN-AWAY from the subscriber, a negro boy named JAMEY, about eighteen years of age, remarkably artful, well known in and about Charles-Town; he may in all probability change his name, and make for the back country: Had on when he went away, a white negro cloth jacket and trowsers, much the worse for wear; he has several acquaintances at the plantation of Mr. Daniel Cannon, up-the-path, where he may in all probability be harboured. Whoever will give information of his being harboured by a white person, shall receive a reward of TWENTY POUNDS currency, and TEN POUNDS if by a negro, on conviction; and whoever will deliver him to the warden of the work-house, or to me in Charles-Town, shall receive a handsome reward, besides reasonable charges. All masters of vessels, particularly masters of schooners, are hereby cautioned not to carry him off the province, as they may depend upon being prosecuted with the utmost rigour that the law will allow of.

WILLIAM ROBERTS.

Brought to the WORK-HOUSE.

June 26, 1772. A new negro, of the Kisley country, says his name is JACK, he is about 30 or 35 years of age, 5 feet 8 inches high, has his country marks on his arms, and his ears bored, has on two white negro cloth jackets, brought with him two blankets. Taken up at Strawberry River, in the Marsh opposite to Mr. Nesbit's new house.

Figure 1.4. "TO BE SOLD," *South Carolina Gazette*, June 30, 1772.

to the act of fleeing, showing Africanness as a characteristic that accelerated fugitivity and made a captive status harder to maintain. One warden issued a lengthy list of detainees, including two Black women, Clarinds and Lyda, with "country marks" all over their bodies. The warden also reported that these women could report their own names, even though they "cannot" recall the names of their masters.[59] The warden does not indicate that Clarinds and Lyda might have purposefully withheld the name of their master. Instead, he focuses readers' attention toward their bodies and their "country marks."[60] This ad, like others, maneuvered within White certainty about Blackness as self-effacing and failed to consider Black people as calculating. Runaways destabilized certainty about how much Blacks ever genuinely submitted to slavery's ocularity and called into question every facet of social interaction that occurred before the crime of theft, including the apparent submission to surveillance and the ideology of an undeniably visible Black body.

Black Visuality and Performance

Runaways exhibited freedom, which theft helped to obscure. Whereas "performing Blackness" in the context of slavery meant the "'naturalization' of blackness" as constituted in "pained contentment," the expression of Black freedom in the form of fugitivity served as interruption.[61] Hartman expertly lays out the way in which the compulsory performances of Blackness under enslavement were about slavery's use of force and emphasis on the flesh to index a "truth" about Blackness. She goes on to explain that "stealing away" revealed the very sense of agency of which Black bodies were thought to be devoid, such that the runaway "transgressed the law of property" and conceptions of racial essence.[62] The act of running away destabilized slavery's philosophy of an innate and unconscious Black body by revealing the unfree person as calculating and capable of other kinds of presentations. "Performing Blackness" in refutation of slavery was different from the performative experience of subjection and spectacle because it accentuated the limits of domination.

I point this out in order to address the specific array of visual transgressions that distinguished behaving free from behaving unfree, and how those attributes were beyond the pale of the law. Runaways utilized an "intimate understanding of the dominant society's perception of freedom," sometimes acquired through watching the free people for whom they worked, to steal themselves and portray themselves as free.[63] By using dress, language, and knowledge of White perceptions of Blackness, fugitive free people cultivated carefully honed methods of exhibiting autonomy. In the processes of freeing themselves, the fugitive free made productive use of slavery's ill-conceived visual matrix by playing to the dictates of the peculiar institution and upending those assumptions at choice moments for escape. While it was illegal for an unfree person to liberate herself from slavery, and sometimes that theft invoked other companion thefts, running away involved a general disobedience about slavery's visual instructions that haunted the act of escape, even when no other "crime" was committed.

Black people who purportedly feigned freedom also exemplified a regard for the visual aspects of free performance.[64] White owners often used the phrase "Pretends to be free" in both northern and southern runaway advertisements, as such designations indicated a special kind of absconder. Runaways who "acted" free were doing more than transgressing the law of property; they were also conducting themselves as free through their interactions with Whites and how they maneuvered in public. These people could be especially devious because they stopped succumbing to slavery's visual imperatives the moment they left the site of their enslavement. When "A Negroe Wench, named Phebe" ran off from Marcus Hook, in Chester County, Pennsylvania, she did not let the numerous scars on her face and body from her owner's punishments stop her; she covered them with a handkerchief, took the name "Sarah," and presumably joined "free Negroes" in Philadelphia or Germantown.[65] The markings reported in the notice do not just help would-be captors find Phebe/Sarah, but they also suggest that the signs of slavery on her body do not interrupt her performance. A number of runaways duplicated this routine, even mingling with Whites in the process. When Cato, "alias Toby," ran away from Middletown, New Jersey, he also ignored the slave markings signed on his body. Richard Stillwell, Cato/Toby's former owner, warned the public that "he is a sly artful fellow, and deceives the credulous," potentially mingling with Whites "pretending to tell fortunes, and pretends to be free." With these tools in his repertoire, Cato stayed gone for at least a year.[66] These stories reveal that the stolen clothes were not just for covering the body or masking a "slave status" in quick and fleeting interactions in public. Many fugitives enlisted props for a very elaborate performance of Blackness as free people, performances where they encountered Whites and continued the "act."

Black runaways relied on elusiveness, and not just the absence of slavery, as an important element of liberty. "The fugitive exposes the groundlessness" of the "distinction between person and property," even at the potential cost of "silence, invisibility, and placelessness."[67] The choice to be obscure is a central part of redacting concepts of performing Blackness organized through slavery. People who ran away often conducted themselves in a way that resisted being read, despite slavery's repetitive treatment of the Black body as legible. Daphne Brooks calls the "spectacular opacity" of Black performance onstage a thing of resistance, sometimes erupting and sometimes proffered at will, meant to disrupt demands for transparency from Black performers.[68] Offstage, the indiscernible nature of Black performance in the flight to freedom occurred among people who exercised this opacity at will, by both removing themselves from the surveillance of slavery, but also by managing the body and engaging the White gaze in ways that refused transparent readings. Whereas "enslavement" as well as "the resistance to enslavement" constituted the "performative essence of blackness" and "black performance," the indefinable nature of fugitivity also becomes a constitutive element of Blackness in the field of vision.[69] Black runaways materialize the fugitive aspects of performed Blackness, the habitation of opacity and obscurity that occurs across experiences of freedom in the slave era.

The experience of not belonging as part of the fugitive condition manifested even for those African descendants who were born free in the context of slavery. Fugitivity, both as a state of rootlessness and of illegality, haunted all free performances of Blackness. In his description of Blackness as "inextricably bound" to fugitivity, Fred Moten locates the "right to obscurity," the right to "keep a secret" in the project of emancipation.[70] Enlightenment's overreliance on the eye as a means of objective knowledge formation and White demands for people of African descent to appear transparent in their motives circumscribed the lives of Black people who were born free and the reception of Black raciality. Consequently, slavery forcibly organized a distinction between the supposedly "real" Black-self as outwardly perceived and the internal ruminations on the entailments of Blackness; the racio-visual logics of slavery demanded distinctions between authenticity and sincerity.[71] Slavery's presumptions about Black raciality enforced a compulsory insincerity, an unavoidable choice between seeing oneself according to the dictates of the peculiar matrix or denying it altogether. Free performances of Blackness navigated these objectifying conceptualizations of Black visuality.

Fugitive free people denied slavery's ocularity, ignoring the supposedly fixed nature of Black visibility, as well as the idea of White omniscience. Formerly enslaved Blacks re/acquired freedom by playing upon racio-visual logics, tailoring performances of Blackness to undermine a peculiar visual culture. In a context that fixated on the eye during interracial encounters, Black visuality took shape in the acts of submitting to and resisting the visual cultures of slavery. Fugitive free Black people who stole items, ruined property and killed animals before deserting their owners simultaneously seized and subverted the White gaze. These acts of destruction, when coupled with the act of stealing away, reveal fugitives who capitalized on the failures of surveillance *and* on the moments when Whites would realize their misfortune. Fugitivity contradicted notions of a blind Black (non)subject. When a free person performed Blackness, as a runaway, she asserted her visual capacity. Although slavery's visual culture reimagined the fugitive as either docile or duplicitous, stealing one's self and portraying oneself as free also emphasized the ability to see and manipulate racial visibilities. Enslaved Blacks who ran away played on assumptions about the undeniable fact of the Black body and, in the process, deployed gazes that resisted slavery's ocularity.

The other fugitive element of the free performance of Blackness had to do with the fleeting nature of belonging. Fugitivity, as a state of being and a matter of fleeing justice, was also about the way in which the runaway had no clear place to go, no clear place of belonging in the context of slavery. "Fugitivity is not only escape" but is also "being separate from settling."[72] Some runaways ran north or adjacent, to blend in with communities of freeborn Black people. However, the idea of fugitivity as applicable to all free people of African descent points to the impending sense of homelessness for Black people in a slaving society. If the act of reading the Black body defined the way in which African descendants lived day-to-day in slavery, than the illegibility of fugitivity only complicated the runaway's claims to a home. The fugitive's displaced existence is not just about removal from a previous home or a given master's domicile but also from the idea of "home" as a place to return to through the act of running away. "Fugitives," by name, only have a place from which to flee, but no particular place to arrive. Again, this aspect of fugitivity marked the runaway as well as the juridical free person, as the task of emancipation involved creating a home. Read against the transatlantic parlor as a home space, fugitivity created a contest of belonging. The runaway implicitly queried the dichotomies between unfree and free, legible and illegible, native and foreign. Fugitivity meant trying to claim a cohesive Atlantic world as home when persons of African descent could not properly claim the nation and the nation did not properly claim fugitives. How could the inherent homelessness of Black freedom fit within the domestic space of the Atlantic world, especially marked against the parlor's penchant for display?

Some runaways revealed a remarkably expansive sense of transatlantic belonging and awareness of the parlor's decorum. Seizing an opportunity in 1771, James Somerset fled his master's custody. Somerset started his life on the western cape of Africa (the specific location unknown), before slavers kidnapped and delivered Somerset to Virginia for sale into bondage. Charles Stewart purchased Somerset, who remained Stewart's property from the age of eight and until Somerset freed himself at the age of thirty-three.[73] In Boston, Somerset ran errands and delivered messages on Stewart's behalf, laboring in relatively close contact to his master. Unfree Black people in the North were not only farmers. Many unfree men like Somerset worked in closer proximity to Whites than did some unfree Black women, who often worked outdoors until moving indoors to labor as domestics closer to the nineteenth century.[74] Somerset and Stewart sailed from Boston to England in 1769, where Somerset continued to move about alone on Stewart's behalf, learning his way around town and making his own acquaintances with Blacks and Whites. This bit of autonomy did not constitute freedom in Somerset's mind, although Stewart furnished his chattel with fine garments of silk and sometimes money. Few records of Somerset's procedures are recorded, but read in the context of runaway performances of Blackness, we can assume that by the time Somerset absconded on October 1, he may have been somewhat literate, but most assuredly he was decently dressed, familiar with his surroundings, and able to rely on friends to assist in his escape. Although slave catchers recaptured Somerset on November 26, 1771, he still made an astute decision to escape in England. In the United States, Stewart enlisted the public to capture Black fugitives, taking out at least one advertisement for another man who ran away, promising a "Pistole reward" to "whoever will apprehend and bring him to me."[75] These same networks of White surveillance were a little less effective for Stewart in England, however. Before Stewart could send the recaptured Somerset to Jamaica to suffer the brutal enslavement of plantation bondage, White abolitionists filed suit, arguing that Stewart could not detain Somerset; Judge Lord Mansfield determined that English law did not make clear provisions for chattel slavery to exist *within* England proper and freed Somerset. Stewart misread as fidelity Somerset's daily life as an unfree person, his leaving "home" on errands and returning in the evening. Somerset's escape reveals Black visuality as embroiled in the balance between illegibility and homelessness that is the fugitive condition.

Read in the context of innumerable runaways, Somerset is one of an unknown number of brilliant bondspersons who freed themselves in an environment built entirely upon Black captivity. Somerset's escape was comparable to that of many other fugitives documented in runaway notices. A number of enslaved persons gained their master's trust, acquired fine garments, made acquaintances, appeared content in their servitude, and then fled at a calculated moment. Although many times the fugitive just randomly took off, a greater number of runaways stole themselves at very important times, "when their absence was inconvenient and disruptive."[76] Like many others, Somerset's assertion of fugitive freedom revealed a schism between a Black bondsperson's outward appearances and self-perceptions, between visibility and vision.

The unique significance of this escape, however, is that it called upon the space of the transatlantic world for *freedom*, rather than bondage. Somerset's decision to run away suggested the willful deployment of fugitivity, both its illegibility and its punitive homelessness. Somerset engaged the issue of transatlantic belonging through the fugitive's opacity. News of Somerset's escape joined a transatlantic circuit already reporting insurrection among enslaved Africans in Surinam, St. Vincent, and Jamaica.[77] Somerset's well-timed escape may have drawn on a transatlantic consciousness of running away or, quite simply, on the existence of a supportive web of friends located outside the colonial U.S. territories. Regardless, Somerset's bid for freedom reveals his mastery of the Atlantic world as a domestic interior wherein his fugitivity—his illegibility and his displacement—entailed productive possibilities when used to exploit the visual assumptions of slavery.

The *Somerset* case became significant for what it meant about the amorphous space of the transatlantic. Newspapers on both sides of the ocean bandied about the horrors of slavery, the reach of U.S. property rights, and the meaning of Mansfield's decision as one that unabashedly condemned slavery on British soil.[78] Many proponents and detractors of the *Somerset* verdict understood the case as meaningful for the British Empire, with people of African descent benefiting in a corollary manner. The English lawyer Francis Hargrave published his argument on the trial, explaining that "questions arising on this case do not merely concern the unfortunate person who is the subject of it" because "they are highly interesting to the whole community." Hargrave recognized "the right claimed by Mr. Steuart to the detention of the negro is founded on the condition of slavery," a condition of the men's relationship before their Atlantic voyage. However, Hargrave contended, "if that right is here recognized, domestick slavery, with it's [*sic*] horrid train of evils, may be lawfully imported into this country, at the discretion of every individual foreign and native."[79] Essentially, lawyers on behalf of Somerset and his White abolitionist supporters argued, in part, that allowing Stewart to reclaim Somerset was to risk England's position in the transatlantic interior. Somerset's freedom was not simply about his own autonomy or the inhumanity of slavery toward people of African descent, but also about the danger of slavery to spatial boundaries of the British Empire and the relevant national identities of the English. Of course, these same concerns were important elements in arguments against Somerset's manumission as well. One anonymous tract argued that abolishing slavery in one territory "would not put an end to it; and if it is annihilated in the British dominions only, it can answer no other purpose, but to ruin a great many unoffending families, and to encrease the sugar colonies of France, Spain, Portugal, Holland, &c. upon the downfall of ours." Arguing that British slavery was less harsh than was the Portuguese, this writer contended the British "slave trade is not of that magnitude that is suggested by its opposers."[80] The *Somerset* decision threatened the innocent—namely, British benefactors of slavery. A unified transatlantic parlor connected through slavery meant a shared regard for the meanings associated with emancipation, including its moral and economic consequences.

Sense making about *Somerset* reverberated the power relationships between empires. Many eighteenth-century interpretations of Somerset's freedom wrongfully imagined that Mansfield's decree abolished slavery, even as this ambivalent decision simply assured that a master could not forcibly remove a bondsperson from England and that the bonded individual could "secure a writ of habeas corpus to prevent that removal."[81] Nonetheless, misinterpretations of Somerset's trial superseded the issue of accuracy and configured both Mansfield's decision and the British Crown as more sympathetic to slavery as problematic. Thus, *Somerset* fueled England's still-paternalistic position toward its colonies and compelled U.S. antislavery thinkers to consider the transatlantic perception of early America.[82] Although in truth *Somerset* ended de jure, not de facto, slavery in England, suppressing the legal basis for slavery in England, it ultimately became the crux for many early U.S. courts that "erroneously relied upon *Somerset* to help abolish slavery in the north," based on the British example.[83] This misperception about British benevolence proliferated even as many Black Loyalists found themselves marginalized in England and living in poverty after the Revolutionary War.[84]

Fugitives reveal the tactical management of racial visibility, showing African descendants subverting the hypervisible constructions of Black raciality circulating in advertisements, and cultivating critical spectator practices. Somerset's escape suggested that enslaved Blacks did not just run away, but that they might even be shrewd in selecting critical moments in which to flee. Runaways like Somerset intimated a keen awareness of presumptions about complacency, shyness, and impudence in the performance of Blackness. Somerset's well-timed escape suggested that Whites might never know the interior lives and ulterior motives of their bondspersons; thus, free performances of Blackness forced Whites to contend with the inherent failures of slavery's visual logic. While slavery presumed, even required, that Black people evade the visual, fugitives used these same assumptions to their advantage.

Previewing Freedom

The act of picturing freedom mediated the relationship between the parlor's demands for display and freedom's fugitive obscurity. On and off the page, it intervened in the transatlantic penchant for exhibiting the Black body and the free person's need for illegibility. Picturing freedom invited visual examination of Black bodies and welcomed viewers to scrutinize Black autonomy. The opaqueness of spectacular demonstrations of freedom remained fleeting and illegible unless transcribed to paper. Thus, to picture freedom in print, to attach the quotidian performance of Black freedom to the permanence of the page, made these demonstrations fit for the parlor. Print culture functioned as an essential element for fitting the free Black body into the domestic space of the transatlantic parlor, managing the simultaneous requirements of demonstration and disguise. Pictures of freedom were both things for display in the home and incomplete records for interpretation.

African descendants who pictured freedom in slavery resisted dominant organizations of the visual. Fifty-three kidnapped Mende people of

Sierra Leone ousted the crew of the *Amistad*, a Spanish slave ship, in 1839 as it sailed from Havana to Puerto Principe, Cuba. Portuguese merchants working for a Cuban trading company held the Mende confined in warehouses, selling them off into slavery under the cover of night. The abduction of the Mende people from Sierra Leone to Cuba was already illegal by this time since an Anglo-Spanish treaty of 1817 had established that Africans imported to Cuba after May 1820 were legally free.[85] However, the Spanish government maintained a lax attitude toward the treaty, as well as to British and U.S. efforts to outlaw transatlantic trade of Africans, because slavery in Cuba was increasingly profitable after the Haitian revolution.[86] Portuguese merchants illegally enslaved the Mende and were poised to profit off the sale once in Cuba, but when slavers made a second effort to transport the Mende from one locale to another, the captives revolted. They killed all but two of the ship's crew, including the ship's captain, sparing only those who could help them sail back to Africa. Although the two navigators purposefully misdirected the ship for several weeks, it was only during a stop for provisions in Long Island that the U.S. Navy illegally seized the *Amistad* and the captives, transporting them to New London and then New Haven, Connecticut, for trial on charges of piracy, mutiny, and murder.[87] Through this long and winding journey through the Atlantic, the people onboard the *Amistad* faced the subjugating glares of slavery and the spatial demands for transparency.

The indeterminate status of the Mende onboard the *Amistad* raised a number of questions that only heightened anxieties about the legible Black body in the Atlantic world. Were these people free? Were they enslaved? If they were unfree, to whom did they belong given the illegality of the slave trade? U.S. abolitionists argued that since the transatlantic importation of Africans for enslavement had been outlawed, that the *Amistad* captives were free people who resisted kidnapping. Antislavery advocates, including the businessman Lewis Tappan, Reverend Joshua Leavitt, and Minister Simeon Jocelyn formed the Amistad Committee to raise support for the Mende and fund their legal defense.[88] They argued this position against proslavery advocates who proposed that Africans on the *Amistad* were Cuban slaves subject to punishment by the Spanish government for insurrection and that the United States should return the captives to Cuba.[89] A lengthy court battle that extended up to the U.S. Supreme Court concluded by 1841, with former president John Quincy Adams and others successfully arguing on behalf of the Africans, and by 1842, the Mende were free to return to Sierra Leone. Despite this advocacy, U.S.

law enforcers were already out of their jurisdiction when they jailed the Mende people. Once the court ruled that the "Africans were not slaves or fugitives but free men," the Mende participated in abolitionist speaking tours and made handcrafts to raise funds for their return voyage.[90] The U.S. abolitionists used the Mende's captivity for reform, imposing English and Christianity during the captives' imprisonment to further the publicity of the *Amistad*'s antislavery campaign. Once free, the Mende represented the prowess of U.S. antislavery organizing to the benefit of the abolitionist movement.[91]

Efforts to picture freedom through the Mende practically defined their time on U.S. soil. Visions of the *Amistad* rebellion were popular in nineteenth-century print culture, especially reproductions of "Cinque," or Singbe Pieh, leader of the *Amistad* revolt. Robert Purvis, the freeborn Black abolitionist of Philadelphia, commissioned the most famous portrait of the noble warrior, clad in a tunic, bearing a bamboo staff in a tropical landscape, gazing away into the distance. The image of Cinque in a triumphant pose, refusing the gaze of the observer, met a controversial reception. Although Purvis was a prominent abolitionist, he could not get this portrait displayed at the annual exhibit of the Artist Fund Society in Philadelphia. Even in the North, "people were not ready for the spectacle of a strong, young African man, armed and at liberty" and thus "the image of the empowered black man vanished from the propaganda of the abolitionists."[92] The image of Cinque pictured freedom in a manner that was unhelpful to U.S. abolitionism at the time, whether for the implicit power signified in the leader of the *Amistad* revolt or for the nobility of a free African that did not rightly induce White sympathy about slavery. This and other popular illustrations offered viewers the chance to own the likeness of Cinque and place Black freedom within the parlor by combining the story of U.S. abolitionism with heroic visions of Black manhood. Modes of picturing freedom through controlled exhibition—rather than the unwieldy demonstration of mutiny—situated freedom within the parlor's dictates of unobtrusive visibility but also slavery's practices of surveillance.[93]

Viewers interested in the Mende as spectacle could also visit them in the Connecticut prison as a cultural attraction. One northern newspaper writer reported on his visit to the jail, where the Mende enjoyed comforts like "opportunities for exercise in the open air," as well as "cotton shirts and trowsers." Observed from prison "apartments" and kept under the watch of U.S. Marshall N. Wilcox, this jail was safe enough for the "multitudes" of people who visit, with "the keeper charging each one a New York shilling."[94] U.S. jailers capitalized on the chance to see a fugitive free Black pirate, purporting to use these funds first as compensation to the warden, and second for "benefit of the prisoners."[95] The jail only materialized the visual domination, as the carnivalesque nature of the Mende's imprisonment corresponded to the increasingly normalized subjection of free Black people to a public gaze.[96] Moreover, if viewers wanted to read the Mende in the context of actual enslavement, instead, they could visit wax statues of the *Amistad* captives on display through a traveling museum exhibit. Simultaneous to the prison term, the artist Sydney Moulthrop took molds of the Mende faces, and some of their hair shavings to "cast and arrange the figures at the peak moment of rebellion."[97] The exhibition of twenty-nine life-size figures also appeared at the Peale Museum in New York, illustrating "fidelity to nature," where "every muscle, every lineament of countenance is portrayed with all the appearance of life."[98] This popular portrayal traveled from New England to the Mid-Atlantic region, receiving positive reviews from both general audiences as well as from antislavery sympathizers. News writers reported witnessing "likenesses of the Africans" when the county jail keeper, Mr. Pendleton, put up "a representation of the deck of the *Amistad*" along with "very correct likenesses of most of the survivors; all done in wax by Mr. Moulthrop."[99] Readers of the Black press also learned that they could "visit" the "Amistad captives; not the great originals" but "their counterfeits, done in wax."[100] Viewers interested in seeing people who were at once fugitives and free could visit the prison or the life-size museum display.

The simplest of pictures reveal the way in which Whites understood the *Amistad* captives as a chance to render fugitive freedom on legible terms. William H. Townsend, a young White resident of New Haven, Connecticut, likely made his twenty-two sketches of the *Amistad* captives by visiting them in prison as well.[101] The pencil drawings do not portray the Mende in heroic scenes or romanticized backdrops, such as the Cinque portraits. Instead, these portraits illustrate people of African descent in the ambiguous space of freedom as rendered uncertain in the context of the Atlantic world. They are not set in a background of an imagined landscape, or even the background of the jails in which they remained captive. Freedom, as pictured in these images of the ambiguously captive, has no definite location. Sar's image (figure 1.5) suggests his circumspection, perhaps about having his picture drawn, as his furrowed brow hovers over a side-eye glance, which directly confronts the viewer. Sar's posture,

Figure 1.5. Sar, by William H. Townsend. (Courtesy of Beinecke Rare Book and Manuscript Library, Yale University)

and others like his, raise questions about having one's portrait rendered in the context of captivity. Did these people have any presuppositions about the purpose of these images? They certainly conceptualized themselves as free, as indicated in their resistance to enslavement. Men like Saby (figure 1.6) seem to have posed for the picture, not just in facing the artist head-on, but also by smoking during the process, which Townsend captures with a plume of smoke emanating from Saby's pipe. Other images,

Figure 1.6. Saby, by William H. Townsend. (Courtesy of Beinecke Rare Book and Manuscript Library, Yale University)

such as the portrait of Marqu (figure 1.7), a child and the only girl represented in Townsend's collection, look off into the distance, perhaps uncomfortable with the experience of portraiture or of confronting the artist with her eyes. The liminal nature of Black freedom during slavery is revealed in these pictures, and like the other attempts to picture freedom in the museum exhibit or in visits to the prison, the fugitive Black body is arrested, again, for the sake of visual sense making.

Figure 1.7. Marqu, by William H. Townsend. (Courtesy of Beinecke Rare Book and Manuscript Library, Yale University)

Undoing the Matrix

Picturing freedom became a means to experiment with new conceptualizations of the Black body as free and within the borders of the United States. The issue of Black freedom revealed itself to have visual ramifications for the transatlantic, with complex scenarios like the *Amistad* demonstrating how parsing the Atlantic into discrete notions of home had become quite difficult by the nineteenth century. The visual culture of slavery transferred to early images of freedom, making popular culture a site for the retention of slavery's peculiar ocularity and the contemplation of black emancipation. Together, Blacks and Whites variously emphasized and deemphasized black corporeality, rendering the Black body hypervisible and invisible simultaneously, in an effort to relearn racial visuality with the coming of emancipation. Instances of fugitive freedom made it difficult to discern if runaways who were variously described as intelligent, conniving, deceptive and ruthless in print advertisements were ever being their "true" selves. Was the figure that seemed soft-spoken during her enslavement actually gentle? Was the rabble-rousing unfree servant really so cantankerous? Did these behaviors fit into a larger ruse in service of the acquisition of fugitive freedom? Black people who ran away used slavery's notions of looking to their advantages. The act of escape placed White omniscience into doubt and asserted Blackness as operating within an unknown framework of visuality. Picturing provided answers to some of these questions.

Slavery enforced an unrelenting structure of the visual on Black people and, concomitantly, on their exhibitions of freedom. The performance of freedom—whether born free, manumitted free, or free by escape—necessarily incorporated fugitive elements of illegibility and dispossession. Persons of African ancestry who took up feelings of self-possession and autonomy retained indiscernibility and illegibility as part of the experience. Freeborn Black women, in particular, were committed to obscurity, employing these tactics in ways that began to shape approaches to Black people's national identities.

Slavery inspired "racial paranoia"; it necessitated a perpetual reliance on, yet distrust of, connections between racial visibility and internal drives.[102] The visual culture of slavery was entirely unreliable in that it necessitated surveillance, even as its chosen techniques of observation failed on a regular basis. Slavery theorized connections between race, vision, and embodiment but undermined these notions by investing in concepts of the crafty Black figure as untrustworthy and always on the verge of escape. Blacks were ontologically structured as unable to see, but contradictorily, in the context of slavery, legislation prohibited them from looking. Whiteness functioned as a sliding signifier, theoretically unbounded by the physical body but also requisite in moments of hostile social contact with Black bodies. Whiteness seemed invisible when understood in the context of bad behaviors, such as the day-to-day practice of slavery, but Whiteness, visually figured as the state of racelessness, remained the only discernible marker of a burgeoning U.S. identity.[103] Slavery's visual logics of race set up a system, a culture, of race relations that viewers could not dismantle, legislatively. The law could not reform ideas about the body, about the creation of the subject, and about racio-visual faculties. In fact, the law constantly sought to reinvigorate legibility.

Varied responses to the suppression of slavery at the end of the eighteenth century resulted in sharply bifurcated ideas about racial visibility and Black visuality by the turn of the nineteenth century. The evolution of slavery's visual logic entailed no clear paths for White or Black viewers. The slow erosion of the peculiarly ocular institution necessitated that both Whites and Blacks cultivate new ways of seeing the self and seeing the nation as eventually constituted without the practice of enslavement. On the one hand, Whites needed to develop new ways to construct and protect national identity from free Blacks. Moreover, these efforts implicitly meant to protect complex notions of the public and the private from the changes of emancipation as well. Even the most gradual processes of abolition meant that eventually people of African descent would be permanently at home within the developing United States. Accordingly, and on the other hand, the evolution of slavery's visual culture presented enslaved and free Blacks with the occasion to rethink Black visuality. While White sympathizers emphasized education as a necessary counterpart to preparing African Americans for citizenship, free Black abolitionists took to their own curriculums for visualizing Blackness after slavery. Freeborn and emancipated Black people were responsible for representing freedom in ways that made them discernible and legible to Whites. What did the performance of "legitimate" and legislative freedom look like, compared to the subterfuge of the runaway? While Whites increased hostility toward people of African descent, especially in the face of heightened fugitivity and gradual emancipation, free Blacks gave greater attention to questions about Black visuality.

2

Optics of Respectability: Women, Vision, and the Black Private Sphere

Small, but significant, communities of free Blacks established their own parlors by the early nineteenth century. Writers mentioned parlors in editorials to Black newspapers in the 1820s, describing the space as a site for weddings, funerals, and religious worship services. Growing numbers of Black people in northern cities worked for wages, using some of their money for leisure activities as well as home furnishings. Many "merchants, farmers, mechanics, [and] day-laborers" maintained "parlors and drawing rooms" that were "full of what they call splendor," decked out with "finery" like "valuable pictures."[1] Although many regarded the parlor as a middle-class space, labor and class diversity within free Black communities meant various approaches to the home. Increasing numbers of free people had established their own parlors by the early 1830s, and such spaces gained wider popularity after the Civil War, when Black newspapers began to advertise the sale of organs and cabinets for placement in the home with greater frequency.[2] Black parlors in the urban North represent particular kinds of spaces, serving as context for the evolutions of free Black life amid the continuation of slavery and decades before abolition.

The Gift of Sight

When young Mary Anne Dickerson sent her friendship album to her teacher in July 1846, Dickerson likely expected the instructor to read the other entries and add one of her own to an empty page. Manufacturers produced these blank scrapbooks with decorative covers, also known as personal albums, for inscription and display.[3] Since African American friendship albums functioned somewhat pedagogically by generally promoting "neatness, taste, and cultivated expression," Dickerson may

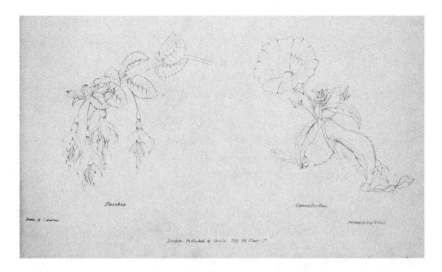

Figure 2.1. Template from *Lessons in Flower Painting: A Series of Easy and Progressive Studies*, 1836. (Courtesy of The Library Company of Philadelphia)

have looked forward to a gift from her teacher in the form of a poem, an essay, or a drawing.[4] In response, Dickerson received a watercolor painting likely copied from a tutorial flower-painting guide. A companion item to friendship albums in the nineteenth century, *Lessons in Flower Painting: A Series of Easy and Progressive Studies* featured a template for the same image pictured in Dickerson's album (figure 2.1). While antebellum print cultures ignored African American women consumers, many Black women engaged them anyway, inserting themselves into sentimental pastimes and the language of flowers as early as 1833.[5] Sarah Mapps Douglass, Dickerson's friend and teacher, copied the long branch of leaves and four bloomed fuchsias with well-defined parts, but also included lines of poetry to illustrate fuchsia for her pupil (figure 2.2). Douglass explained to Dickerson and whomever else might read the album that "All the spears of fuchsia droop their heads toward the / grounds in such a manner that their inner beauties can / only be discerned when they are somewhat above the eye / of the spectator." Since fuchsias typically face the ground, one needed to *see* them as higher and more exalted to understand their *inner* beauty—not their outer appearances. Douglass added, "for a meaner flower this might not / Attract attention but most of the fuchsias are / Eminently beautiful, both in form and color." While "meaner" flowers do not

Figure 2.2. Drawing accompanying the poem "Fuchsia," ca. 1841, Martina Dickerson Album. (Courtesy of The Library Company of Philadelphia)

garner as much attention when looking down, the form and color of fuchsias are so "eminently beautiful" that they cannot be ignored. She concluded that "the singular and peculiar / Beauty of the parts involved in the calyx," which "they would thus seem anxious to conceal," along with the "modest rendering of the head," helped fuchsias to "Beautifully and significantly" demonstrate modesty.[6] Although this poem and drawing may seem like an innocuous demonstration of aesthetic skill or a sentimental keepsake, in fact, "Fuchsia" also offered a profound meditation on Black womanhood as well as evolving concepts of free women's visibility and self perceptions in the slave era. With this curricular contribution, Douglass, as a token of friendship, offered thoughts on free Black women's bodies, the experience of freedom and new practices of spectatorship as a gift to Dickerson's keepsake.

Douglass paired a mass-produced floral stencil with copied lines of poetry, which she might have read in various other volumes of the period, including *Thoughts among Flowers* (1844) and *Magazine of the Rising Generation* (1846). Her inventive offering of "Fuchsia" spoke to issues of self-perception, decorum, and beauty that coincided with the emergence of free Black communities in the antebellum North. Black women activists were intensely aware of public perceptions of their femininity, especially since early abolitionism depended on Black women's credibility to advance the antislavery movement.[7] Free Black women accepted prominent positions of leadership in organizations like the Institute for Colored Youth (a segregated school), and supported annual antislavery conventions through fund-raisers.[8] Douglass addressed the simultaneous demand for visibility and invisibility by arguing that Black women viewers were uniquely capable of realizing the exquisiteness of Black women's beauty. In friendship albums, free Black women reframed public attacks on Black womanhood as jealous hate or envy. Framed in the space of the album, offered as a gift for her student, Douglass's contribution explained the spectacular visibility of free Black women in the slave era, and provided forms of affective and aesthetic support for other free women negotiating new visibilities. These nuances might have been uniquely legible to her specific community of friends. Such gifts provided education to a young pupil like Dickerson, and friendship to other adult women who read the album. Free Black women who submitted their own contributions worked together to articulate the complexities of a changing visuality and Black women's freedom. In the process, Douglass and her peers educated a younger generation on the early feminist construction of Black women's spectatorship and the management of free Black female bodies in the slave era.

This chapter explores the friendship album as a space wherein free Black women cultivated analytical visual practices to coincide with their experiences of freedom in the slave era. In the "affective scene of identification" and the inclusion of "consolation, confirmation, discipline, and discussion," Black women's friendship albums functioned as what Lauren Berlant has termed "intimate publics."[9] In these semiprivate spaces, free

Black women cultivated new ways of seeing themselves and seeing free Black womanhood against the backdrop of slavery's visual culture. Subtly critical but expressly subversive, African American women used friendship albums to position themselves as knowledgeable within White women's print cultures and to address the gender-specific exigencies of Black freedom. Central to this visual project, I argue that free Black women developed an "optics of respectability," an early feminist practice of spectatorship that free women organized and instructed through the circulation of African American friendship albums. I offer this theorization to think through the ways in which free women deftly engaged respectability as a visual discourse, and also to point to an early moment in U.S. culture from which scholars can recognize Black feminist practices of spectatorship. Free Black women who wrote in one another's friendship albums engaged a meaningful pastime with feminist consequences. Friendship album contributions contained discussions of womanhood, motherhood, marriage, and women's love relationships. In addition to the album serving as a venue for self-narration and self-representation, these items were also counterparts to a "black feminist agenda" of the early nineteenth century in that the inclusion of White abolitionists likely facilitated Black women's work in the antislavery movement, and enabled free women to comment on gender norms in antislavery periodicals.[10] A practice of feminist viewership, the optics of respectability served as the curriculum of the friendship album, making Black women's use of White women's print culture more complex than simple adoptions of dominant discourse.

Contributions such as "Fuchsia" disclose friendship albums as constitutive of larger practices of visual culture shared among free Black communities across the North, and especially among free women. "Fuchsia" theorized practices of looking among Black women who needed to see one another from various standpoints. Together, the image and the text of "Fuchsia" toggled between dominant and peripheral visions of womanhood, representing a view of Black women as beautiful figures with a unique way of seeing. Douglass's offering suggests a way in which free Black women understood the derogatory conceptions of Black femininity in circulation. She provided a way for Black women to see one another, and even to delight in being unseen or misrecognized. This contribution also offered the opportunity for women readers to theorize the construction and reconstruction of Black visual cultures as free women within the hostile context of slavery. Black women's personal albums were identical to White women's albums in their design, but distinct in their contributions.

At first glance, Black women's albums do not explicitly direct a reader's attention to their polysemic uses, but for Dickerson to *identify* with fuchsia's story, there needed to be a more complex set of meanings at work. She needed to *see* in a manner that dialogued with Douglass's own vision of misrecognized beauty, modesty, and intelligence. Both the writer and the reader needed to invest in a vision of Black womanhood that remained absent from sentimentalist literatures and companion popular cultures. Douglass's gift of fuchsia demanded a unique way of seeing born out of free Black women's shared experiences of hypervisibility and invisibility. "Fuchsia" addressed literate free women of means, and it relied on their shared experiences of alienation. These albums manifested the complexity of free women's relationships, revealing, as Farah Griffin explains, that African American women's friendships offered them ways "of seeing themselves through each other's eyes" and space for recuperating Black women from the hostile perceptions of White society.[11] Douglass's contribution suggests a method by which Black women readers critically engaged and reinterpreted hostile encounters.

"Fuchsia" also demonstrated for Black women readers how to be familiar with vernacular cultures and how to manipulate popular discourses to suit their own lives. Although painting and poetry were common White middle-class pastimes by the mid-nineteenth century, Douglass used these tools to address the personal concerns of free Black women who enacted new relationships to slavery's visual culture. In the language of sentimentalism, Douglass accentuated the importance of a downcast gaze and animated the life of a flower to avoid reproducing an image of the Black female body on the page. She denied the prevailing visual animus toward Black women through the personification of a flower. In an entry that reads like a Black women's guide to the management of hypervisibility, Douglass instructed her student to avert her eyes and represent her experiences through sentimental icons. "Fuchsia" offered a somewhat self-aggrandizing analysis of the experience of the gaze that capitalized on the semipublic and semiprivate nature of the personal album and the African American parlor. With a comment on beauty, Douglass addressed a shift in perspective that acknowledged the relationship between enslaved women's constructed hypersexuality and free women's awareness of the fetishization of black female bodies.[12] "Fuchsia" documented free Black women's recognition of one another as objects of sexual desire, and made a widely available image more personal and relevant to free women's experiences. Using mainstream media, Douglass offered her student a way to develop a critical Black visuality that corresponded to women's social obligations to one another and the larger free community during this period. The four known African American women's friendship albums circulated among an insular community of Black women and their abolitionist friends. Black women with the means and leisure for literacy and artistic hobbies lived throughout the Northeast Corridor, and their albums moved between Boston and Baltimore. Dickerson's parents might have gifted these decorative scrapbooks with beautifully embossed covers and printed pages during holiday seasons as sources of creativity and diversion for their daughters. However, a much larger community of Black women friends used friendship albums to develop lessons on self-perception and freedom in a still-hostile cultural climate. Sharing words and pictures with each other, elite Black women coconstructed a way of seeing to navigate the gendered and classed demands of comportment for respectable free women. Albums reveal the ways in which middle-class Black women integrated mainstream notions of femininity on a cursory level while also using their own unique experiences to revise dominant culture musings on womanhood.

A central part of this chapter focuses on the friendship album as a popular derivative of sentimentalism, as indicated in its generic inclusion of sympathetic prose and imagery to express morality and to evoke emotions in others. The friendship album was a place for insight, where Black women who were economically privileged by the period's standards, but constrained within a racist dominant culture, negotiated the evolution of Black life in the early nineteenth century. The flowers and poetry of the friendship album belong to the larger discourse of sentimentalism, which would have had legitimate value to free Black women trying to make sense of the constant flux of Black life in the North and the constant threat of slavery in the South.[13] Unlike White women's demonstrations of pity for the unfree, free Black women used sentimentalism to make sense of freedom within slavery's racially inflected visual culture. The sentimental metaphors appearing in African American friendship albums functioned to counter a host of negative conceptions of Black visibility that discredited Black women's liberty. African American women's friendship albums reveal these women participating in a mass consumer culture in the context of slavery as active agents, even though print culture markets did not target Black women as consumers and frequently took aim at them as objects of ridicule. The remainder of the chapter interrogates the ways in which Black women reconstructed domesticity within their parlor spaces by drawing on sentimental tropes and the display of the friend-ship album. These women utilized the ideological conceptions of wom-anhood and motherhood as tethered to the home or "woman's sphere," even as slavery troubled Black women's experiences of domesticity.[14] Although free women were not writing under the constraints of enslave-ment, (which necessitated, for example, Harriet Jacobs's presentation of her own experience as that of the pseudonymous Linda Brent), slavery undoubtedly shaped the lives and the gender consciousness of freeborn Black women. The parlor's penchant for display became a place where elite Black women could cultivate new approaches to the visual that coincided with the transformations of emancipation. In the maintenance of friend-ship albums, Black women successfully reappropriated mainstream print cultures and revamped prevailing notions of Black visuality, transforming the rigid parlor into a place of experimentation.

Optics of Respectability

Friendship albums, as glimpses into Black parlor culture of the early nineteenth century, encase meditations on freedom and visuality dur-ing the slave era. The elite group of literate and middle-class Blacks who maintained their own parlors in 1830s Philadelphia made critical use of the home and its media as personal spaces. While areas outside of Black homes featured stereotypical images of Black runaways and "Africans" for sale in local newspapers, many free Black women took up White women's print cultures in the privacy of their own homes. These women turned to their parlors and their friendship albums to fortify themselves against a visual culture of surveillance and slavery's discourses about visibil-ity. Parlors and the albums within them served as settings for cultivat-ing critical perspectives on the antebellum social context. Inside parlors and parlor literatures, African American women developed the "optics of respectability"—a spectator practice that evaluated proscriptions on free Black women's comportment and circulated as a critical perspective on free women's visibility.

Free African Americans mobilized the "politics of respectability" as a counterargument to negative conceptions of Black raciality in the nine-teenth century, treating respectability as an apparent or observable phe-nomenon determined through behavior. Free Black people gendered respectability by measuring women's virtue through marriage, chastity, and activism, and Black men's respectability in "thrift, temperance, cleanliness and sexual continence."[15] These ideals distinguished respectable women from the unsavory by judging their conduct for how it raised, or depressed, the social status of all African descendants. It policed Black women across class experiences, Evelyn Higginbotham explains, as it tightly controlled "sexual behavior, dress style, leisure activity, music, speech patterns, and religious worship patterns."[16] Vigilance over Black women's expressions of gender and sexuality supposedly offered ways to support Black men and Black families while at the same time undermining the derogatory narratives of Black womanhood in circulation in U.S. culture. However, in attempts to circumscribe individuals' behavior, respectability took "the emphasis away from structural forms of oppression," specifically racial, gender, and class prejudice, to instead problematize "low" culture practices.[17] In practice, the "politics of respectability" functioned as a bourgeois "schizophrenia" that vacillated between critiquing structural systems of oppression and criticizing particular values or lifestyles among free Blacks, especially of the lower socioeconomic class. Respectability fractured any idea of a cohesive Black womanhood by holding lower-class Black people accountable for mainstream conceptions of Black raciality. African Americans who worried "too much" about what White people thought, Frances White explains, only served to "authorize racist stereotypes."[18] Although all women of African descent experienced racial subjugation despite access to privileges of economic class or color, respectability obscured connections between Black women by creating a hierarchy of propriety.

Respectability, then, as a demonstrable ideal, also functioned as a visual discourse about comportment. It represented elite Blacks' hyperawareness about the public perception of the free community in the eyes of White society. Respectability politics connected racist assessments to Black peoples' actual behaviors. It attempted to hone Black visuality as antithetical to perceptions of promiscuity and lewd behavior, even though these narratives originated in the service of slavery. Conversant with slavery's visual culture, the politics of respectability promoted a diminished Black visibility, urging free people to suppress bodies and desires that seemed to reify racial logics. Purveyors of respectability policed Black public appearances even as they criticized the problem of White racial misperceptions. Many elite Blacks promoted ideologies of respectability in the pages of the Black press or used their leadership positions in churches to chastise other free African Americans toward respectability.[19] Respectability asked women of African descent to offer muted presentations such that they appeared barely there or unnoticeable as part of an attempt to assimilate into the U.S. mainstream—it asked Black women to suppress their supposedly undesirable, yet uniquely raced, differences.

Black women who fixated on respectability as a value also concerned themselves with *perceptions* of Blackness, both within and without African American communities; in turn, these women also cultivated respectability as visual culture, organizing "optics of respectability." A critical seeing practice, the optics of respectability speaks to how women of African descent simultaneously observed, deflected, and absorbed discourses about Black visibility. Optics, or "the scientific study of sight" as well as a "lens" or instrument of the eye, serves as a modifier, shifting the way in which we think of how respectability worked on practices of perception and observation.[20] Free women of African descent honed optics of respectability that variously managed the strictures of power working in the lives of Black women. While the politics of respectability were about viewing one another in light of the predominant constructions of true womanhood, I mean to call attention to the way in which free Black women developed this other way of seeing respectability, a way of seeing the dominant prescription for Black women's visibility. The optics of respectability provided Black women with critical distance from mainstream narratives of womanhood, a reflexive position from which they both participated in and analyzed discourses of domesticity from an alternative view.

The optics of respectability represents a form of Black feminist spectatorship in early mediated contexts. Scholars have variously argued for a third space of sight where women of color spectators realize the politics of the gaze through an out-of-body experience, or through viewing with a "third eye," as if from outside the encounter.[21] This other kind of awareness is displaced from a dialogic exchange of looks but instead places Black women in position to watch the experience of objectification. Black feminist spectatorship, as a rule, "transcends, critiques, and teaches" likeminded viewers about visual culture at the intersection of raced, classed, gendered, and sexed identities.[22] Feminist theorizations of Black women's viewing cultures recognize women as aware of their visual objectification but, at the same time, as unencumbered by it. These approaches construct Black women as viewers *first,* capable of realizing their objectification from within as well as from without encounters with hostile gazes. It is the experience of watching one's own body scoped through an antagonistic lens, even as it is happening—to be consciously present in the experience of racial spectacle. Black feminist theories of looking account for Black women's experiences of looking at others, their experiences of seeing how others view the Black female body, and finally, the experience of seeing one's own Black female body through the eyes of others. Not only does this way of seeing identify interracial encounters as telescopic or from the "outer" body, but this looking practice resists the uncivilizing narratives and linear histories of the racial gaze. Black feminist methods of seeing realize mechanisms of visual empowerment among women within an always already imbalanced power of racial gazing.

The optics of respectability served as a critical viewing practice to recuperate women of African descent from the peculiarly ocular institution. Whereas slavery's system of seeing denied the credibility of a Black looking practice even as it rigorously hailed Black viewers in scenes of violence, an optics of respectability compounded Black spectatorship as a layered experience. Through recognizing the social necessity for a respectability politics, even in all its flaws, free Blacks acknowledged visibility as a unique problem that they might manage with deliberate representational practices. Black women who engaged in optics of respectability met the demands for respectable appearances with a sense of purpose. The optics of respectability acknowledged demands on free women's decorum as a requirement of progress but also openly engaged studies of visibility as part of such a project. Black women mobilized critical visual practices well before the articulation of late-nineteenth-century theories of Black spectatorship, tethered to photographic technologies or marshaled by prominent Black men. For example, W. E. B. Du Bois theorized double consciousness to describe how African Americans operated with an intense awareness of skeptical public perceptions of Blackness. He connected respectability to the management of hypervisibility, where self-perception and recognition constitute the conflict of "two warring worlds" or "two souls."[23] In this conceptualization of the visual, respectability coincides with double consciousness to split the Black self into the subject viewed in the eyes of White society and the subject as she was known to herself and her (presumably homogeneous) Black community. In contrast, however, the third sight of respectability enabled Black women to cultivate dominant perspectives on Blackness and insights about demands placed on free Black womanhood, specifically. Free Black women of the preemancipation period operated within a critical visual framework without giving name to the practice whereby they managed visibility and reflected upon the charge to do so. These multifocal modes of perception were at work among Black women's communities simultaneous to the perpetuation of slavery and before the advent of daguerreotype.

The optics of respectability complicates scripted gifts like Mary Wood Forten's derived poem "Good Wives," contributed to the Amy Matilda Cassey album. Cassey, born free in 1809 to Sarah and Peter Williams Jr. of New York City, displayed respectability through her antislavery activism, as well as with her friendship album. Cassey maintained a scrapbook between 1833 and 1856, collecting notes from influential abolitionists like the businessman William Whipper and the activist Wendell Phillips. Yet, the optics of respectability as a viewing practice is revealed through the way in which Cassey's album provided a space for her Black women friends to demonstrate and discourse about respectability. Here, free women focused on portraying themselves as respectable women but simultaneously scrutinized notions of the respectable in what were inherently reflective maneuvers. To consider the optics of respectability is to consider how free Black women anticipated the display of their literary gifts in the parlor and under the watchful eyes of male contributors, even as they wrote these items directly for other women. "Good Wives" circulated to Black abolitionists of national prominence, who also contributed to Cassey's album. In paintings and poems that appear to be ordinary instances of women's writing, Black women friends used kind words and flower drawings to discuss ideas about womanhood without alarming a diverse audience of White and Black men readers. When Mary Wood wedded Robert Forten, she joined the Forten-Purvis family and a larger community of middle-class Black abolitionist women.[24] For her album contribution, Wood Forten prescribed that "Good wives to snails should be akin / Always their houses keep within." In an effort to be more discreet, they should "not to carry fashion's hacks / All they are worth upon their backs." Moreover, "Good wives like city clocks should chime / Be regular and keep in time / But not like city clocks aloud / Be heard by all the vulgar crowd." In their muted presence and silence, "Good wives like echoes still should do / Speak but when they are spoken to."[25] Wood Forten's poem accentuated the Victorian appreciation for privacy, punctuality, and control over one's person in a verse that dictated restraint as a necessary element of being a good wife. Although entries such as "Good Wives" resemble a commitment to dominant gender norms, such as true womanhood, this entry also used the language of admonishment to quip about mainstream constructions of women and marital relations. "Good Wives," as a popular and oft-cited poem, recognized the significance and "subjugation" of marriage, corresponding to how Black women "celebrated and critiqued" marriage in their pursuit of "Victorian Ladyship."[26] However, as an *exhibition* of "true womanhood," this widely circulated poem also traveled the semiprivate circuits of the friendship album. In this other frame, the poem portrays Black women rejoicing in traditional concepts of domesticity amid the surveillance of Black men readers like Forten's husband, perhaps her father-in-law, and even other Black women. Any of these individuals may have read friendship albums expecting to see signs of free women's commitment to respectability. "Good Wives" looks like a sincere sentimental musing on true womanhood, even as it analyzes such norms as well. When read through the optics of respectability, Wood Forten's contribution constructs the friendship album as a place to both uphold respectable visibility and to cocreate a multivalent understanding of respectability among Black women readers. The poem acknowledged expectations for free Black women to conform to mainstream ideas about womanhood, while also holding these ideas up for scrutiny and discussion. The optics of respectability—a way of seeing free women and dictates on their comportment—is about both *striving* for respectability, but also *displaying* respectability in a culture of surveillance. Wood Forten's inscription of "Good Wives" marked respectable womanhood as an important contribution to a free Black woman's friendship album. It also demonstrates the extent to which free Black women were mindful of revealing their commitments to domesticity. With "Good Wives," Wood Forten illustrates respectability as a goal and a routine, emphasizing it as a value and an obligation.

Albums circulated among a diverse audience of readers who encountered Black women's friendship albums and relied on free women to behave in ways that reflected positively on all Black people. Album contributors recognized the connection between acceptable gender comportment and the expectations of Black men as both life partners and community powerbrokers. While African Americans' partnerships contained some degree of equality in that most Black men and women labored outside of the home, some men expected Black women abolitionists to take decidedly subordinate roles when it came to institutional life.[27] The women's historian Deborah Gray White explains that hostility was "the price Black women paid for their feminism" as their public roles ignited distaste among Black men who regarded "female leadership with suspicion and resentment."[28] Creating balance in semipersonal arenas, such as the friendship album, provided free and activist Black women with central locations for accentuating feminine ideals acceptable among Black men, illustrating domesticity in ways that maintained fair standing among Black men powerbrokers.

Album contributors understood Black friendship albums as gendered, leading many Black men to negotiate the visual culture of the album by marking their contributions as distinct from women's writings. Many Black men compartmentalized manhood and womanhood as separate from one another in friendship albums, summarily maintaining visual authority within these spaces. Frederick Douglass explicitly described his attention to gender roles in the friendship album. Writing, in June 1850, "I never feel more entirely out of my sphere / Than when presuming to write in an / Album," Douglass positioned masculinity as incongruous with, or outside of, album writing. Douglass congratulated Cassey on the "beauty, elegance, and refinement" that typified such albums but excluded his own contribution from the space based on his "habit of life, passed history, and present occupation." Slavery, as much as manhood, made Douglass an unlikely contributor. Douglass considered masculinity marked by the "sterner qualities" of his "head," inducing within him greater pleasure at the experience of "rocks" than at the "gazing upon the most luscious flowers." Finally, Douglass scribes an apology to Cassey for "not writing something becoming the pages of [her] precious album," as manhood limited his ability to partake in ladies' popular culture.[29] Much like Wood Forten, Douglass remained acutely aware of gendered decorum even within the supposedly safe space of the album. His pronouncement of masculinity as incongruous with the friendship album was also meant for display. Although many brothers, husbands, and men affiliates read and extended contributions to this "womanly" artifact, these contributors also maintained a panoptic masculine gaze over the pages of the album and rendered Black women's femininity as a foil for men's intellect. Douglass's contribution explicitly addresses the album as a specifically gendered space, and one where he negotiated his inclusion with a textual performance of masculinity to shore up his position within the parlor and its visual culture.

Friendship albums helped Black women move creatively within the precepts of respectability and develop visual practices to contend with the exigencies of emancipation. Album contributions reveal Black women reframing the misrecognition of their femininity in public culture with this other way of seeing, while also cultivating critical viewing practices. Free women marshaled an optics of respectability as a coping mechanism and a means of relating to one another as commonly engaged in "interlocking systems of oppression."[30] From this vantage point, they could see through the oppressive conception of Black women as coarse and unwomanly—as utilitarian bodies worthy of enslavement—but also through oppressive gender ideologies that buttressed a still burgeoning free community.

Sentimental Bodies

It was with this critical visual practice that free Black women amended sentimentalism—the literary and epistemological convention that emphasized feeling as distinct from reason and as a marker of morality—and its derivative popular cultures. Middle-class Black women existed within an aperture during the slave era as privileged compared to most African descendants in the United States, but still outside dominant notions of womanhood. Many of them enjoyed the privileges that defined the "cult of true womanhood," but slavery's vision of the Black body continued to circumscribe the way in which free women could display freedom. Free Black women had the means to participate in sentimental consumer cultures, like friendship albums, but they also lived outside of sentimentalism's emphasis on White affect. Accordingly, their unique ways of seeing one another and seeing Black womanhood distinguished free Black women's sentimental print cultures from those of White women. Black women's participation in sentimental amusements were part of a project of reconstitution, connecting them to dominant notions of womanhood and developing new versions of Black selfhood. Only with a polyvalent mode of seeing, then, could free women participate in sentimentalism's exclusionary popular cultures.

Black women writers employed sentimental literary conventions in a multitude of ways. Both free-born and formerly unfree women used appeals to feelings and rich description of Black women's experiences to write for diverse audiences; these writers wrote across different genres, producing essays, autobiographies, and poetry that explicitly called on affect. Gabrielle Foreman argues that African American women used sentimentalism's conventions as "camouflage" so that presuppositions about thinking and feeling would mask the intersectional critiques levied in works like Harriet Jacobs's *Incidents* or Harriet E. Wilson's *Our Nig*, for example.[31] Like White women, Black women writers used sentimentalism for politics, as well as for fiction and fictionalizing. The itinerant preacher Jarena Lee and her contemporary, sister preacher Zilpha Elaw wrote spiritual autobiographies of their conversion experiences that detailed common encounters with servitude and gender prejudice in Black churches.[32] Spiritual autobiographers such as Lee and Elaw were among the earliest of African American women writers to explicitly engage sentimentalism, using this convention to "buttress their texts against white contempt and dismissal."[33] Black women writers employed sentiment to speak for themselves and to lobby for abolition just as sentimentalism gained traction among White abolitionists.

Sentiment in African American women's friendship albums was altogether different from, even if connected to, other forms of print. First, Black women scribed album contributions for a smaller, and somewhat secluded audience. These items did not circulate in the uncontrolled manner of a newspaper essay or a spiritual autobiography. Sentiment in a friendship album was an explicit demonstration of feelings for either a specific individual or the select group of individuals who had access to the album. Second, and more importantly, sentiment in the form of a friendship album provided Black women with tangible experiences of commodity forms of affect. Similar to the material culture produced for White women sympathizers against slavery, Black women's friendship albums "scripted" performances of sentiment, inviting contributors to feel and portray affect in their interactions with the album.[34] These friendship albums did not just reveal the sentimental feelings among friends; they also served as recitals of sentiment to be displayed in the parlor, inviting Black women readers to perform sentimentality upon reading an entry. Black women who consumed sentimental popular cultures inserted themselves into the "scripts" of feminine performance by receiving albums, doting on notes from their friends, appreciating their tokens of affection, and carefully illustrating images or writing poems in return.

Sentimentalism, in the form of the friendship album, replicated sentimental emphases on White women's bodies. "American sentimentality" as a "national project" in the nineteenth century, connected "the nation's bodies and the national body," implicitly marginalizing Black women at the same time. Sentimentality's "double logic" of power and powerlessness imprisoned middle-class White women as sentimental icons, empowered by the "home" and excluded from the public, but still gave language to White women's power.[35] Too fragile for harsh labor, the White woman's body gave way to her internal goodness. Sentimental popular cultures appealed to middle-class White women of the parlor who "involuntarily" portrayed delicacy through "swoons, illness, trances, ecstasies, and, most important, tears," who then absconded to the parlor to evade "the harsh social realities of expansive industrial capitalism."[36] Over time, a burgeoning White middle class relied on capitalism's polarization to develop itself and mounted sentimentalist discourses that thrived on White womanhood but included White men as well. Sentimentalism mitigated the deleterious impacts of competitive markets by constructing an ideal of the compassionate essence of the genteel person. This discourse allowed for the accentuation of feeling, which, in the place of material reforms, seemed to diminish in the unfair labor practices and the expanding distance between laborer and owner of production.

When White women expressed feelings about problems of race in this rubric, such writings often pertained to the lives of enslaved Black women. White women writing on behalf of early abolition turned this gendered ideology of women's power into a site of counterpolitics that compelled national social movements.[37] Although women reformers took risks, they also moved within a context where sentimental White women appeared morally compelled and persuaded others with their emotions. Sentimentalism facilitated a concept of the emotive female Other that could speak without overtly staking claim to rational faculties. Such logics applied to White women, exclusively. Sentimentalism allowed White women to make evaluations within the dictates of a moral rationalism that perpetuated notions of White women as purely feeling. Their use of sentimentalism relied not only on constructions of White womanhood but also on the ability of White men to respond to women's feelings—to identify with White women's emotions and to desire to calm and protect them. However, where sentimentality expanded White women's expressions of power through Black women's bodies and experiences, this discourse only reiterated slavery's rubric of racial authority and White women's control over Black women's lives.

Sentimentality's emphasis on White affect emerged in close relationship to slavery. Coming out of the early eighteenth century and the Enlightenment's reliance on rationalism, Western philosophers turned to theories of moral evaluation or judgment that prized sentiment over reason as a basis for political action. The valuation of sentiment, and especially sympathy, as central to human judgment emerged in a context that conveniently rationalized the maintenance of chattel slavery. Sentiment rendered slavery as morally permissible in that it organized wealthy persons as moral agents who could still lay claim to ethics despite their unscrupulous lifestyles.³⁸ At the ideological level, sentimentalism created distance between capital's benefactors and capitalistic exploitation, but in everyday life, sentimental popular cultures provided a philosophical justification for the comforts of the parlor—emphasizing sensitivity, nature, and beauty. Although sentiment in ethics and popular culture appear distinct, the consumer culture of sentimentality serves as an important counterpart to this line of thinking, and both occur in an Atlantic world context that fostered the flow of human chattel. Consequently, sentimentality did not apply to all feelings, just White feelings. White women's feelings for the enslaved would matter more than the feelings of unfree people of African descent. Again, this was because sentimentalism rationalized affect as well as organized people of African descent as capricious and teleologically outside the bounds of appropriate sentiment. Slavery's construction of Blackness refuted Black people's emotions. Their expressions of pain, grief, terror, and sorrow were not recognized or respected, despite sentimentalist notions of moral compulsion. If Black women were to exist within the realm of sentimentalism, it would have to be through slavery and through sentimental appeals to abolish slavery.

The imbrication of slavery in sentimental popular cultures complicated free Black women's participation. Whereas the enslaved woman of African descent provided a site of sympathy for White women, privileged Black women had no proper place within this relationship. Slavery organized the Black female body as rife for exhibition and exploitation; modes of cultural production reiterated this "entitlement" to black women.³⁹ Popular cultures buttressed a climate in which European cultural producers envisioned Black female bodies in scenes of "colonialism, scientific evolution and sexuality."⁴⁰ White people's prerogative over the unfree Black woman's body translated to visual culture, which also consistently re-presented enslaved women's bodies on a regular basis. Conversely, existing outside this power relation, free Black women became invisible. Sentimental representations did not include free women because mainstream White audiences did not relate emotionally to the free Black female body.

The body as a point of departure in sentimental culture is also the distinguishing feature between Black women's and White women's albums, even where album content and construction suggest much similarity. Both Black women and White women used tropes of affect and gentility in their writings. Black women employed "sentimentality as a vehicle to engage invited contributors," much like White women, but also to archive those instances of grief, loss, joy, and love that informed free Black life in the antebellum city.[41] Amid this chaos, free Black women of the middle class wrote to each other in albums with a clear awareness of the period's turmoil by expressing sentiments of remembrance. Latent within their works of art and poetry, free women shared concerns of not seeing each other over lengths of time, and even acknowledged the possibility of never seeing each other ever again. For instance, in an entry initialed "A.H.H." for Ann Howell Hinton, the author gifted an image of flowers along with a poem to a friend (figure 2.3).[42] In this addition to Martina Dickerson's album, Hinton offered a painting of clustered flowers with a note, "A mark of friendships pleasing power / In this small trifle see / And sometimes in a lonely hour / View it and think of me."[43] This undated entry, tidily offered in the frame of an embossed page, referenced the way in which albums among Black women enabled the maintenance of friendships across distances as this author intended to give her friend a reminder of their relationship. Forget-me-not flowers were also a popular inclusion among Black women who wanted to symbolize remembrance in their album contributions. Sarah Mapps Douglass signed her initials "S.M.D." on a painting of forget-me-nots (figure 2.4), pictured as sparse branches of red and lavender flowers in Martina Dickerson's album.[44] Likewise, Margaretta Forten added a poem about memory and loss to another album, explicitly addressing movement as a strain on women's friendship: "What this the wave with ceaseless motion / Protracts the union of our lot." She concluded, though, "Our hope's the rock which stands Time's ocean, / Our love's the flower, 'Forget me not.'"[45] The title of her offering explicitly signified commemoration to her friend and pupil. Each of these entries references a widespread concern for separation among free Blacks, and their purposeful archiving of the self and of relationships. Within the space of personal albums, free Black women maintained their support networks with a purposeful eye toward the fleeting nature of their existences. These discussions again call on the inherently fugitive nature of Black freedom in the slave era and the ways in which homelessness and illegibility haunted freeborn Blacks as well. Even though albums signified a parlor to which they belonged, they also circulated to a community of album contributors who moved around in pursuit of opportunities or because violence and political change forced families to relocate. The persistence of slavery, which meant the constant threat of kidnapping, enslavement, and sexual victimization without legal recourse, loomed over the lives of freeborn Black women. In practicing the artistic crafts of flower painting

Figure 2.3. "A mark of friendship's pleasing power . . . ," 1840, Martina Dickerson Album. (Courtesy of The Library Company of Philadelphia)

and poetry writing, not only did these women pass time alone, but they also expressed the importance of remaining in touch with one another across space.

Alternatively, while White women also used their albums to archive themselves and their memories, middle-class White women's bodies were not under the peril of enslavement. Instead, Catherine Kelly argues that sudden death and moving from place to place strained White women's friendships; their albums were primarily concerned with "vanishing"

Figure 2.4. "Forget-Me-Nots," 1843, Martina Dickerson Album. (Courtesy of The Library Company of Philadelphia)

in the future, and acknowledging the precious nature of friendship.[46] Although White women's albums reveal the period's concern for mortality, White women's bodies were not subject to the institutionalized threat of slavery. For example, a White woman of Trenton, New Jersey, Amy Ann Abbott, began her friendship album in 1832. Her meticulously crafted calligraphy, so fine that it is nearly impossible to read, circulated among friends who lived in her vicinity, with all of her entries coming from other

New Jersey women.[47] Like most friendship albums, Ms. Abbott's artifact illustrated sentiment, but from a much tighter network of women located within her vicinity. Unlike African American women's scrapbooks, which traveled long distances, Abbott's album reveals an intimate network of like-minded friends in close proximity to the owner. Moreover, while politics, such as the abolition question, were not an inherent part of White women's albums, these same materials circulating among literate African American women of the early nineteenth century reveal the extent to which the issues of slavery and social advancement were intertwined.

The permanent specter of Whiteness inscribed in friendship books serves as a more evidentiary distinction between Black women's and White women's artifacts. For example, albums such as Mary Wood Forten's keepsake mixed gifts from Black contributors alongside prefabricated illustrations of White women included by the manufacturer. This woodcut (figure 2.5) shows a White woman, lavishly dressed in a gown with jewels, and facing forward, with title, *Just Seventeen*, indicating her age. The image reveals that Wood Forten's friendship album was produced for a White woman consumer, and that the manufacturer anticipated the album's display as representative of White womanhood.[48] Images like these were common and appeared in Abbott's album as well. Media producers manufactured friendship albums for Whites to gift delicate nature metaphors and images of gentility to one another. Album manufactures often produced preprinted pages in friendship albums that depicted sentimental scenes of flowers, White children, and White women. Sentimental illustrations of White women symbolized feeling to potential album consumers and evoked sentiment from album readers. These depictions contrived the White female body as an affected space, as well as a means for inducing sentiment in others. They left free Black women with little choice about the appearance of White raciality in their friendship albums. Albums inherently invited Whiteness into African American personal spaces, both the scrapbook and the homes where Black women displayed these materials. If ever images of Black bodies appeared in White friendship albums, it is unlikely that such depictions were preprinted into the artifact, or that the image represented a *free* person of African descent. Free Black bodies could not double as sentimental bodies, even in Black women's own friendship albums.

The bodies of color that appear in African American women's albums were sentimental gifts by a male contributor. Robert Douglass, the artist and brother of Sarah Mapps Douglass, called explicit attention to the

Painted by Sir Thos Lawrence P.R.A.   Engraved by J Cheney

JUST SEVENTEEN.

Published by Gray & Bowen Boston

Figure 2.5. Just Seventeen, Mary Wood Forten Album.
(Courtesy of Moorland-Spingarn Research Center,
Howard University)

political nature of his artwork with depictions of affected figures. Douglass commented on indigeneity in Martina Dickerson's album with a pen-
and-ink drawing of two Native Americans on a rock, in anguish, reacting
to the "first steamboat on the Mississippi" (figure 2.6). Additionally, Douglass copied a popular poem about White men's power and the steamboat's
destruction of Native American territories to correspond with the illustration.[49] Indigenous men are suffering and worthy of sentiment in this
combination of text and image. In a second token, Douglass contributed
a sentimental gift of racial politics to the Mary Anne Dickerson album
with a poem and pencil drawing, titled *Booroom Slave* (figure 2.7). Douglass created his own version of this popular image of a woman of African

Figure 2.6. First Steamboat, 1841, Martina Dickerson Album. (Courtesy of The Library Company of Philadelphia)

descent with her hands clasped, as she kneels before a stormy landscape. It combines the submissive posture of the "Kneeling Slave" image that was quickly coming to represent the transatlantic antislavery movement, along with the controversial dress and style of the Cinque portrait banned from exhibition in Philadelphia. Douglass narrated this image with excerpts from an abolitionist poem: "When the grim lion urged his cruel chase / When the stern panther sought his midnight prey / What fate reserved me

Figure 2.7. The Booroom Slave, 1841, Martina Dickerson Album. (Courtesy of The Library Company of Philadelphia)

for this Christian race? / A race more polished, more severe than they?" He signed this entry "Shenstone" for the author and then initialed "RD" with a note to acknowledge that this poem was "copied."[50] Together, the image and the verse construct the enslaved black body as worthy of sympathy, with a strong but suppliant posture.

Conversely, Black women rarely, if ever, depicted the Black female body in their own albums, neither free nor enslaved. An eye on respectability meant that free women understood the importance of suppressing Black women's corporeality, and they may very well have desired to maintain this limited status of visibility. Although album contributions like "Fuchsia" and "Good Wives" made comment on Black women's bodies, these visions did not translate to the imagery of the album. While Black women contemplated corporeality, they simultaneously avoided drawing the eyes of others to the Black female body. Their alternative ways of seeing one another and their willingness to participate in mainstream print cultures did not undercut Black women's concerns for respectability and slavery's peculiar organization of race and visibility. Across four friendship albums, the only scene with bodies drawn by a Black woman is the colorless image entitled *Residential New York Street* in the Amy Cassey album (figure 2.8). In accord with the title, the home is the focal point of the image, shown as large and centered, prominent in the background. The artist created a setting that appears quite deliberate, surrounding the home with a fence and including a cut tree stump to suggest that this scene represents a real space. Within the yard of the home, a traveling man on horseback converses with another person, possibly a woman, in front of the home.[51] The gender indeterminacy of the bodies in the scene add to Cassey's deemphasis of bodies in the image, choosing instead to make the residential occupation of a New York space the central concern of the image. Here, the people on the property, like the smoke that emanates from the chimney, indicate that this space belongs to actual people, even if the individuals are difficult to discern.

Instead of emphasizing corporeality, Black women used flowers to represent the free female body. Flowers helped these women connect to one another and acknowledge their common experiences—their similar relationships to Black men and their middle-class approaches to womanhood. Whereas early-nineteenth-century print so heavily intertwined the body and text, constructing White women's bodies as emblematic of White women's print cultures, free Black women may have been disinterested in depicting Black female bodies in a print culture that only obscured or

Figure 2.8. Residential New York Street, 1838, Amy Cassey Album. (Courtesy of The Library Company of Philadelphia)

objectified Black women.[52] Sentimentalism's floral metaphors were a perfect stand-in, because not only did flowers have a significant symbolic value among Black women but floral motifs are also a common component of the friendship album. In African American women's albums, the flowery language and illustrations of sentiment were not just metaphoric; they were also a visual grammar for the optics of respectability. Black women personified flowers in their friendship albums. For a contribution to the Wood Forten album from Philadelphia, one unidentified writer distinguished flowers as most special, describing them as "fleeting," affected by the weather, which "will mar their fragrance" and "rob them of their blood."[53] A similar gift from Sarah Mapps Douglass to the Cassey album began, "I love a flower if it ever brings / A warmth of feeling to my heart," adding with exuberance, "Oh they are eloquent/ They speak when life would still be dumb."[54] Flowers indicated Black women's familiarity with sentimentalism, in accord with true womanhood and respectability, and could stand in for everything else they may have wanted to imply about their unique circumstances as free women. By softening their observations through the language of gentility, Black women made their critical faculties more palatable to the diverse audience of the friendship album. Elite women used their albums for personal and public purposes. While album writing presented free Black women with a chance to empathize with one another, albums also helped them demonstrate familiarity with mainstream notions of womanhood and display investment in sentimental parlor discourses.

The flower and nature metaphors used in sentimentalism also paired well with Black women's symbolism. In fact, nature remained an important sign to enslaved African Americans as well, who understood the unadulterated wilderness as preferable to the "gardens" of the plantation that fit into a larger system of Black exploitation.[55] Although Whites attempted to make association between Blackness, nature, animality or the lack of civility, nature metaphors have been central to Black women's communication with one another.[56] Flowers also remain relevant over time in Black women's discourse. Even as late as the twentieth century, Black women poets of the Harlem Renaissance used floral romanticism in a media climate not very different from the antebellum era, with the Klan-inspiring *Birth of a Nation* appearing in 1915 and the expansion of racial entertainment. These women also seemed to be acting outside the contours of Black racial difference. The literary critic Maureen Honey describes African American women's desire to distance themselves from cruel realities, thus "nature offered an Edenesque alternative to the corrupted, artificial environment created by 'progress,'" even as such metaphors resembled a Western writing tradition and not an "identifiably" Black cadence.[57] Thus, the trajectory of flowers in Black women's literary and cultural production exists from the preemancipation-era friendship albums, up through the twentieth-century appearance of flowers in African American women's stage productions.[58]

Black women writers used floral motifs even though they could not find themselves in mainstream notions of womanhood and consumer cultures of sentimentalism. Similar to other forms of print, the earliest volumes on the language of flowers first targeted White women, specifically, and did not attend to Black women as consumers. International writers in England and France created popular interest in the "language of flowers" by the 1820s, producing books that listed flowers by names and by meanings. The first flower dictionary appeared in the United States in 1829, offering narrative definitions for various flowers and details on the precise art of flower painting as a masculine practice.[59] When a London publisher printed Mrs. E. E. Perkins's *Elements of Drawing and Flower Painting: In Opaque and Transparent Water-Colour* in 1835, she addressed this shift in the foreword, explaining that the "'mind has no sex,' yet the usual and necessary forms of society restrain females from many pursuits which are open to the competition of the other sex."[60] Transforming from its connection to botany and the "accurate" capture of nature, the vogue inclusion of White women in flower discourses made room for femininity through the accentuation of delicacy. Books like *Elements of Drawing* or the *Language of Flowers: The Floral Offering: A Token of Affection and Esteem* provided readers with anecdotal definitions of flowers and instructions on women's etiquette.[61] While mainstream media markets made direct appeals to White women as a "new" audience for sentimental flower paintings, Black women improvised and cultivated their own media cultures to attend to gender ideologies.

The sentimentalist symbols of the friendship album enabled free Black women to participate in mainstream notions of womanhood, all the while reformulating practices of perception and figurations of the free female body. Albums provided a meeting place for free Black women to commiserate over shared social concerns and to collectively engage the ideologies of domestic space, such as the album and the parlor. Although public life excluded Black women from tropes of feeling and delicacy, leisure and disposable income still enabled middle-class women's participation in album culture. Privileged free women like Cassey enjoyed literacy and an elite social network but still experienced exclusion from moral and emotive discourses. Among sympathetic friends, these women showed themselves as "true women" by dominant standards even as sentimentalist discourses still had not made room for free Black women consumers. Conforming to the demands of the parlor, free women used flowers and sentimentalism as tools, as magnifying glasses to help gain appreciation from Black men and from Whites. Album literatures were a part of Black women's acculturation into dominant cultural mores. Learning sentimentalism meant learning the discourses of the U.S. mainstream and the broader Atlantic. These fluencies were just as important as formal education in that they provided familiarity with gender norms, as well as a means for subtle cultural significations. In a climate in which the fragile, fainting woman symbolized domesticity, Black women participated in sentimentalism even as its philosophies were not easily mapped onto the free woman or her Black female body.

Black Parlors, Black Albums

African American friendship albums functioned as textual extensions of the architectural spaces of the free middle class. Albums, then, do not just represent privilege but are also privileged spaces for contact, dialogue, surveillance, and for illustrating social belonging. Together, the albums limn economic, social, and spatial activities among elite Black life in private contexts. The parlors of free Blacks were spaces for political action, as well as for the structuring of men and women's gender identities. However, even as Black men experienced domestication in home interiors, especially in the closets, cabins, and small rooms of the literary imagination, men also enjoyed the actual space of the masonic lodge as an iconographic place *outside* the home for "(re)constructing" masculinity.[62] Men of the free community could use the parlor and places outside the parlor to anchor their masculinities, but Black women needed to rely on the parlor for both personal and social space. The parlor functioned as a place for free Black women to represent womanhood to friends and supporters, as well as a semiprivate space for Black women to support one another. The household was constitutive, in part, of a national identity for elite Black people in the antebellum period, such that Black women were also responsible for establishing homes that benefited their communities. Middle-class Blacks in particular believed that "a stable black body" emanated from "a stable black household."[63] Accordingly, Black women's personal spaces—the parlor and the album—replicate much of the complexity of White women's domesticity—where the White woman's home and body were sites for imagining nationhood and respectability—but Black women also needed to indicate domestication through these spaces. African American friendship albums represented other sites of Black interiority besides the body, and Blacks' ability to participate in domesticity and domestication on another kind of terrain.

Like a friendship album, a middle-class parlor was a unique attainment for a free Black woman in the early nineteenth century, since most free women remained destitute and in "continued service in the households of others" rather than in their own homes.[64] Additionally, the majority of Black women who were born free or reached freedom remained impoverished. Whereas slavery imagined Black women as always already available to the needs and desires of White society, Black women's bodies also existed as implicitly public after slavery. Black women were without private interiors, quite literally. The Black woman's body remained open to unwanted sexual advances and available for the reproduction of an exploitable labor force of Black children. Over time, the perpetuation of critical discourses against Black women negated the markers of privilege that emerged among free Black women. All women of African descent, whether fair-skinned or free, remained marred by the legacy of enslavement and pigeonholed in slavery's false dichotomy of the Black woman as either hypersexual or asexual.[65] When slavery rendered the Black female body and the Black home as open to White intruders, friendship albums represented personal spaces that free women could control. Although they displayed these items, free women regulated the interior of the album by inviting specific friends to contribute to its pages. Parlors were also invitation-only spaces.

African American friendship albums are shorthand symbols for the labor-intensive development of personal space for free people in the slave era. The Dickerson albums represent the social location of the Dickerson family, and the various kinds of privilege afforded to Mary Anne and her sister Martina. Spatially, the Dickerson parlor sat among other important structures, near one of Philadelphia's identifiably Black neighborhoods, on Locust Street, below Eleventh Street. Living in close proximity to two Black churches, a school, and an African lodge, the Dickersons navigated a geographical terrain that put the girls in close proximity to important figures within their communities.[66] Working as free people, the Dickerson parents used their incomes to support their children. Family patriarch Martin Dickerson "was a self-freed slave who worked as a male nurse" until his death at the age of fifty in 1838. His wife, Adelia, also worked as a bartender in the Walnut Street Theater at Eighth and Walnut Streets before her death in 1877.[67] With the fruits of their work, the Dickersons paid to formally educate all five of their children, including their three daughters. Mary Anne and Martina Dickerson studied penmanship and free womanhood under the tutelage of Douglass, each recording her lessons in personal albums. Mary Anne received her New York–manufactured scrapbook as a gift in 1833, when she was just eleven years old, as indicated on an engraved title page. Martina likely received her album around the same time as Mary Anne, but this London import remains undated until 1840. Although Martina's album included a greater number of entries, Mary Anne's album featured writings and paintings from Philadelphia's most influential people.

Such albums also portray the way in which the middle-class interior of the African American home was often a place for political thinking and acting. Black women's friendship albums welcomed White abolitionists, much like African American homes in which Black women hosted White activists for antislavery conventions.[68] William Lloyd Garrison, the abolitionist leader and editor of the *Liberator*—an antislavery weekly that also published Black women's writing—contributed his opinion on the "Abolition Cause" to the Cassey album. Garrison praised Black abolitionists who exhibited courage against the "ridicule, anger, and reproach" meant to "Blacken their character," facing threats of jailing, assassination, and physical violence along the way. Garrison lauded the work of Black abolitionists who risked peril to "save their country, and abolish the bloody system of slavery."[69] Garrison's gift did not discuss womanhood or marriage; he saved the promotion of gender norms for the pages of the *Liberator*. Instead, he used the occasion of writing for Cassey's album as a chance to display his support for abolition—a commitment that also signaled Garrison as a friend of the free Black community. Moreover, while Garrison's friendship with women like Cassey permitted his entrée in the space of the album, his explicitly political offering also suggests that, as a White man, anger and indignation toward slavery were the most appropriate expressions of feeling for Garrison to share in Black women's personal space. Perhaps sentimental feelings toward Cassey or free Black women communities would have seemed inappropriate.

The diversity recorded in Black women's friendship albums is emblematic of the preemancipation African American parlor. Both albums and parlors were symbols of middle-class aspiration—places to exhibit signs of class ascendancy—as well as places for privacy and publicity. Both spaces excluded outsiders but also welcomed a diverse network of friends and activists. More importantly, both places were stages for free Blacks to display proper performances of womanhood, freedom, and middle-class status. Album manufacturers created these token gifts of friendship for "socially conscious middle-class women," who placed their albums where they might be appreciated, in "places of honor on hundreds of parlor tables."[70] These fine materials were meant to portray opulence and prestige, whether open or closed; items like the Amy Cassey album were for exhibition. The significance and uniqueness of the Cassey album is made clear by its appearance. The ornate album features intricate embossing on the cover (figure 2.9) with a centered lyre framed by ovals and a rectangular floral border, and quality, heavy-gauge paper. Emerging around 1825, mass-produced items like gift books (ranging in price from about two dollars to five dollars) were "placed beside the Bible and the hymnal

Figure 2.9. Cover of Amy Cassey Album. (Courtesy of The Library Company of Philadelphia)

on the center table in the parlor" to represent the gentility of the lady of the house.[71] Many of the albums, gift books, and similar materials were produced to mimic handcraft, but with technological developments like the steam-powered printing press, lithography, the availability of paper in rolls, and cloth binding, newer items could mimic the old quality while appearing on the market faster than ever before. The move from stamped bindings pressed by hand with a woodcut, to embossed covers, which used a steel or brass plate to engrave an entire cover in one maneuver, made albums like Cassey's very fashionable and too expensive for most folk markets.[72] Cassey's volume represents her access to a material culture that many White women could not have afforded during the early nineteenth century. Amy Cassey refuted the prohibitions levied against Black women consumers with the fine quality of her album and filled its pages to reveal the cultural currency of her large social network.

Inserting themselves into middle-class leisure activities was also part of a complicated process of claiming national belonging. Although mass-circulated prints often objectified Black bodies to advertise runaways to White viewers, media producers overwhelmingly ignored Black people as media consumers. To acknowledge Black audiences was to suggest they had "won citizenship" and the right to participate in mainstream cultures.[73] The production of albums, novels, and later on the trade card constituted a larger national media culture focused on the White woman consumer and her possessions, even as this construction only emerged out of a direct comparison to the Black woman as a preindustrial domestic.[74] Elite Black women's enjoyment of friendship albums illustrated the manner in which their middle-class privileges of leisure and literacy were also part of their claims to national belonging. Just as White women's domesticity connected them to the home, the exclusion of Black women from parlor ideologies was indicative of their larger omission from a burgeoning U.S. national identity. Black participation in parlor cultures enacted a "radical critique of whiteness" by ignoring "white exclusivity" and paradoxically embracing "genteel rules and commodity forms."[75] Free women consuming materials and prints not issued for Black audiences were still able to participate in nationalizing popular cultures, but over time, these practices became part of an *outsider within* organization of African American identity—the fugitive nature of Black raciality was also becoming the character of Black national identity. I say more about the concept of nationhood in chapter 4; however, it is worth noting here that middle-class pursuits and the organization of a parlor space were also about claiming a national identity in the antebellum North.

Albums circulated between and within parlors at the same time that racist caricatures circulated around northern U.S. cities. Libelous images of free Black women Philadelphians were already popular in the transatlantic sense by the mid-nineteenth century. Sold as an individual image, and in

Figure 2.10. The Lady Patroness of Alblacks, 1834. (Courtesy of The Library Company of Philadelphia)

series, the popular image *La Belle de Philadelphia* (figure 2.10) or the *Lady Patroness of AlBlacks* ridiculed African American women of Philadelphia for the pleasure of viewers in the United States and Europe. This image of a charcoal-toned "Black" woman preparing for a night at a ball inside her cluttered and chaotic boudoir offered comment on Black femininity as well as on Black private spaces. La Belle has thrown clothes about in a tumultuous manner, including an ostentatiously pink plaid gown and a large yellow hat with pink bows all over. She prepares to don this garish ensemble, combing her hair in a mirror and admiring her own appearance. The captions reads: "I tink I shall gage de tenshun ob all de gentlemen, to night at de ball. Hope, my dear, Casius Antonius, wont be jealous." Although La Belle perceives herself as stunning, the pandemonium of her private space helps secure the punch line and confirm her misperceptions. While the *La Belle* cartoon suggests that La Belle cannot interpret her own image, "Fuchsia," on the other hand, pointed to a perceptive approach to freedom, visibility, and respectability as lens. Caricatures like this hostile portrayal offered comment on Black women's spectatorship and visibility practices, representing them as visually illiterate. Inside La Belle's busy room, viewers of the image can see a frightened cat that watches in terror on the floor, a mirror that does not reflect beauty back to the woman, and corresponding images on the bedroom wall confirm La Belle's confusions. The cat shown at the bottom right corner of the picture recognizes La Belle as gruesome, indicating that an animal can see more accurately than this free woman. The cat's inclusion in the image guides readers and indicates that La Belle is so terrifying that the cat arches its back and raises its tail at the sight of her, underscoring the woman's inability to understand her impropriety and the visual horror she purportedly inflicts on the viewer. The person La Belle perceives in the mirror when looking at her own reflection is more attractive than the "real" individual, indicated by the smoother complexion free of lines and wrinkles shown on the "real-time" woman on the other side of the mirror. This disparity of perception is the reason La Belle believes she has the right to occupy a boudoir, fill it with costly trinkets, and adorn her body for attracting male attention at the ball. The cartoon connects the "right" to occupy private spaces to visual literacies, organizing a peculiar relationship between proper dress, domestic interiors, and national belonging. The image pictures Black women's freedom around a faulty self-perception, a way of seeing that would be negligible for her public conduct. The final signpost for this message is the "metapicture" embedded in the illustration in the form of three pictures centered on La Belle's bedroom wall.[76] The artistic works in her home portray a similarly dressed woman, now in a public encounter after her private preparations. This foreshadowing version of La Belle now receives a proposal from her companion, who is kneeling on bended knee to ask her hand in marriage. This self-referential portrait of La Belle's future engagement suggests that her private room preparations result in the success of matrimony. Framed in a bedroom, such illustrations warned about the risk of undisciplined Black domesticity producing reckless public behaviors. Moreover, the image suggests that Black women's private spaces are precursors to sexual liaison, the implicit counterpart to a marriage proposal. Such images were part of a transatlantic visual climate picturing freedom in hostile ways. While slavery continually subjected unfree women to harsh labor and sexual violence, popular culture imagined free Black women as abrasive and licentious in order to maintain slavery's peculiar notion of an untamed Black interiority.

Contrary to these visions, however, free Black women's parlor interiors provided some degree of refuge. These spaces fostered engagement, where free women cultivated new visual cultures and honed literary skills. Women contributors to African American friendship albums already lived in a world that hypersexualized the Black female body and where, for the most part, imaging technologies worked to intensify these practices. Albums, like parlors, provided space for free Black women to meditate on how to visually convey the attributes of freedom. Through friendship albums, Black women expanded their personal spaces but also lived within them and furnished them with their own concerns. In the process of experimenting with mainstream ideas about womanhood, Black women used sentimental discourse to create personal spaces that conformed to their own unique needs and revealed their familiarity with relevant ideas of home.

Free Femininity

Free women often explicated their involvement in the parlor's projects of domesticity through emphasis on marriage, activism, and friendship. These themes connected elite Black women to one another and remade the parlors of politically influential homes into places for rehearsing free visibilities. Being seen as a woman of the parlor or as a woman who socialized in important homes of the Black elite would have also helped free women navigate their social networks. Maintaining a friendship album was a crucial aspect of Cassey's demonstration of respectable freedom, and it allowed her continually to renew her display of domesticity through the album's circulation. Likewise, being seen as a contributor to Cassey's album or having a diverse network of powerful Black elites and antislavery activists to read one's contributions would have helped Cassey's friends as well. Cassey's album served as a management tool, helping Black women handle scrutiny from Black men about women's sexuality and diminish suspicions about Black women's comportment.

Matrimony was chief among the ways in which free Black women achieved access to the parlor and demonstrated fidelity to its ideals. Marriage was integral in free Black women's lives during the slave era because it signified respectability to the larger free community and contributed to one's overall stability in a still tumultuous time.[77] Amy Matilda Cassey maintained two parlors in conjunction with two marriages to powerful men who also engaged in racial uplift work. Cassey settled in Philadelphia when she married the businessperson Joseph Cassey in 1826. Mr. Cassey, a widower twenty years senior to Amy, earned wealth from his work as a hairdresser, perfumer, moneylender, and real estate owner. With his income, he hired help to assist Mrs. Cassey in managing the home and their six children. While Mrs. Cassey tended to her own parlor, her help (likely a lower-class woman of African descent) would have answered the door and cleaned other parts of the home.[78] When Mr. Cassey died in 1848, Amy married another prominent abolitionist, Charles Lenox Remond (brother of the world-renowned Black activist woman Sarah Parker Remond) and moved with him to Salem, Massachusetts.[79] In her second marriage, Cassey continued to socialize and organize with other abolitionists in the area, participating in Salem's antislavery community. In her successive marriages to Cassey and Redmond, she maintained her membership in a circle of elites who enjoyed the comforts of middle-class life in the early nineteenth century.

Cassey amassed some of her power through marriage, not because her husbands empowered her, but because matrimony made it easier for her to maneuver in a larger geographic space and with the support of a Black male counterpart. Though she avoided the brutality of bonded labor and working-poor occupations, Cassey still needed to do the "race" work of expanding literacy and assisting runaways. Working as a married woman, Cassey's home served as a meeting place for abolitionist organizing and the development of the local free community. Although Cassey's life and its privileges distinguished her from her domestic servant, Cassey never securely distanced herself from the ideas about Black womanhood wrought in slavery. Even for Black women of privilege, feminine designations of domesticity were fragile and required constant vigilance. Comparatively, employing a servant bolstered Cassey's middle-class femininity. Nevertheless, neither the help nor the woman of the house could permanently embody the designation of "lady." Cassey's claims to true womanhood remained tenuous, like those of many other Black women in the antebellum period.

Cassey's album was a place to promote the ideals of marriage to a diverse cadre of readers. Cassey's friend Sarah Forten contributed a sentimental gift wishing her companion well on her first marriage in a poem that hoped the love Joseph "then pledg'd may he never depart."[80] In the polite venue of her friend's album, Forten's good wishes for the Cassey marriage hoped for a joyous union and a secured sense of respectability for Mrs. Cassey. Free matrimony was a prized possession as marriages among Black couples within slavery were continually disrespected through the sale of family members and the need to steal away from enslavement. Marriage among free African Americans was politically significant to the extent that the law recognized these marriages, unlike non-legal, but ceremonial, marriages among the enslaved.[81] Although marriage had a symbolic value in the lives of free Black women, these unions also resulted in material gains. By marrying Cassey—a man who could afford to contribute to mutual-aid efforts in Philadelphia—and then later marrying Remond, Amy ensured that she, too, remained involved in a social network of persons with the means (either money and/or time) to participate in antislavery political culture. In Philadelphia, she initiated the first mixed-gender reading society for Black Philadelphians, the Gilbert Lyceum, with Mr. Cassey. In Boston, she filed suit against a theater for ejecting her in 1853.[82] Her marriage choices ensured the maintenance of her lifestyle by keeping her relatively free from the constraints of domestic labor both in her own home and in the homes of others. Marriage helped Cassey maintain middle-class privilege and respectable visibility, buffering the inevitable hostile encounters in spaces where Whites either ignored or rejected free Blacks outright. She earned an elite social standing in the free Black community through her work as a wife and her demonstrations of middle-class femininity. Cassey's marriage, her mutual-aid efforts, and her maintenance of a friendship album collectively satisfied middle-class expectations about free Black womanhood.

Antislavery activism also served as the connective tissue among elite Black women's friendships. Sarah Forten and other women of her prominent family of antislavery activists all contributed to the Cassey album. Forten's parents, James and Charlotte Forten, had three daughters and one son, all of whom participated in some form of abolitionist organizing. Mrs. Forten, her three daughters, and two granddaughters contributed to the antislavery cause by "acting as hostesses for important antislavery gatherings," writing for antislavery papers, and working in mixed-race antislavery organizations.[83] Of this second generation of Fortens, Sarah was perhaps the most prolific writer, contributing to Cassey's album several times, while also adding a contribution to Mary Anne Dickerson's album. In addition to these semipublic contributions, she regularly contributed to the *Liberator*, served as an initiating member of the Philadelphia Female Anti-Slavery Society (PFASS), and actively participated in a host of other clubs and organizations. Forten's activism may have been a necessary part of being a member of her prominent family. With parents and older sisters so heavily bound up in the abolitionist movement, Sarah might have been required to participate in these forms of work. At the same time, activism also served an interpersonal function for women of this community. Forten and her friends used these instances of political organizing to cultivate writing skills in the safe space of intimacy. As a reputable woman in the abolitionist community, Forten participated in social uplift opportunities, but these activities also provided her with the chance to spend time with women like Cassey. Abolitionism inadvertently created spaces for Black women to build and maintain community with one another. Forten, Cassey, and other esteemed Black women met regularly to do the work required by their churches and literary organizations. Marriage facilitated these opportunities by creating powerful families and expanding activist networks.

However, these ties also added to the sense that free women's album contributions and life choices were under a great deal of scrutiny. Sentimental notes on love, and even death, appear in friendship albums, but there remains an overt silence around childbirth and its impact on free women's relationships to one another. Album notes on love and marriage thus speak to what Darlene Clark Hine terms a "culture of dissemblance," masking the inner lives and traumas connected to Black women's sexuality.[84] While the practice of marriage among free communities variously facilitated Black women's social lives, pregnancy as a counterpart to these domestic duties effectively crushed many women's political participation. Elite Black women managed a delicate balance of matrimonial labor and communal labor to retain access to elite parlors and friendship albums. Women such as Sarah Forten navigated this complex set of demands for as long as possible in order to remain in contact with other women of her circle. Forten's life and eventual marriage revealed the fragility of middle-class womanhood associated with the parlor, as an unexpected pregnancy might have displaced her from the social circles of her friendships. Marriage was a means of policing free Black women's bodies that also interfered with other commitments. Coordinating the labor of marriage as a

responsibility to one's family and spouse, along with other social obligations, sometimes removed Black women from the productive space of the
parlor and the friendship album. Regrettably, marriage to young Joseph
Purvis curtailed Forten's social and political life in the antislavery movement. Unlike her sister Harriet, who enjoyed a long courtship before marrying Robert Purvis Jr. of the prominent Purvis family of abolitionists,
and her elder sister Margaretta, who elected a career as a teacher rather
than marriage, Sarah made a choice that ended her activist career. Julie
Winch speculates that Sarah's short engagement to Joseph was most likely
due to an early pregnancy that would have "delegitimized" their first
child.[85] More importantly, proof of premarital sex would have discredited
Sarah's respectability within the free community, a still-fragile charac-
terization that her foremothers consciously cultivated through emphasis
on chastity and education. Forten may not have intended to marry a man
with so little activist ambition (Joseph was very much unlike his brother),
but the choice would surely make her participation in abolitionist activities more difficult. With marriage, Forten's work changed from activism
to caring for her eight children without hired help on the outskirts of Philadelphia (Bucks County). Unlike Cassey, Forten's choice to marry caused
the demise of her activist life by literally removing her from the parlor
spaces of her elite friends. Although her opinions on abolition and racism appeared in albums and newspapers of the period, her appearance in
public virtually disappeared by the end of the 1830s, concomitant to her
marriage to Purvis.[86] Unable to harmonize two different kinds of labor,
Forten's activist career took a subordinate role to her duties as a wife and
mother on a farm outside the city. Although she was once an internationally renowned author and activist whose writing was read among abolitionist audiences in England and France, Forten's international career as
a poet and news contributor was curtailed by marriage. The once-open
space of the Atlantic world and the bourgeois parlors of her friends quickly
narrowed with her removal from the city. Whereas marriage provided
entrance to designations of respectability, some Black women needed to
succumb to the institution just to make the expression of sexuality more
acceptable, even if that choice removed them from close contact with other
powerful families and friends. The end of Forten's activist career suggests
that Black men were especially vigilant about free women's womanhood.
A pregnancy and family might have produced demands that made it
necessary for Forten to terminate her work outside the home. Marriage
helped to shroud her sexuality and sexual desire, but at the expense of

her political career. Black men's vigilance over free women's decorum and gender roles implicitly meant surveillance of Black women's bodies. In the visual culture created within the albums, Black men presented hurdles to women's participation in parlor cultures and semiprivate spaces of African American women's politics.

It is perhaps this complex web of race, place, and work that made Sarah Mapps Douglass so reluctant to marry, putting it off until her forties—an uncommon act for free women of this period. Douglass remained "free" from the responsibilities of a nuclear family of her own until the age of forty-nine while she pursued her other interests. In fact, Douglass's friend Sarah Grimké encouraged her to marry Rev. William Douglass—a widowed minister with twelve children. Douglass and William married in 1855, and the reverend died six years later. Douglass remained ambivalent about her unhappy marriage, calling it a "school of bitter discipline" that seemed less enjoyable than her husband's intellect, something that might have initially attracted her to marriage (even if reluctantly).[87] A writer, teacher, and antislavery activist, Douglass expressed her opinions in materials that document friendships among women in the Female Literary Association and the Minerva Literary Association. A free woman, Douglass befriended other middle-class women of antebellum Philadelphia, educating their children and working in mutual-aid organizations within the city.[88] The first Black woman to attend the Female Medical College of Pennsylvania in 1852, Douglass also enjoyed a career promoting hygiene among women with the help of "imported 'manikins.'" Although she is best known for teaching at the Institute for Colored Youth, as well as for her "public lectures on anatomy and physiology, presented to mixed audiences of women and men," her many achievements traversed the expectations proscribed for Black women during the slave era.[89] While Douglass managed her own school for more than fifty years and educated both children and young adults, this work was distinct from her work as a wife and stepmother. Her highly political and often subversive writings that appeared in various media of the 1820s and 1830s relied on parlor access for reflecting on Black women's experiences, whereas her marriage did not.

Douglass enjoyed access to spaces of influence without getting married because she came from an esteemed family. Born free in 1806 to Robert and Grace Bustill Douglass, Sarah belonged to a generation of African Americans who began to reap privileges from earlier generations of unfree Blacks, even as slavery persisted. Black abolitionists throughout the North were already familiar with Sarah's more prominent brother Robert Jr., who worked as an artist. Sarah studied under private teaching in a school organized by her mother, Grace, and family friend James Forten before taking over as teacher at the school at the age of twenty-one. Her maternal grandfather, Cyrus Bustill, owned a bakery, while her mother managed a Quaker millinery store next to the bakery. Additionally, Sarah's father, Robert (from St. Kitts), "was successful as a hairdresser, wigmaker, and perfumer."[90] Her imbrications in the tight-knit web of Philadelphia's free middle class granted Douglass and her four brothers the chance to study rather than work in common labor arenas, such as food and clothing trades. Whereas a number of free Black women in the city remained illiterate and impoverished, Douglass and her friends enjoyed the social benefits of the parlor as well as the cushioning of its literary and material cultures—its books as well as the carpets and lamps.

Recitals

Black women used friendship albums to confront material, literary, and visual conventions about womanhood. Albums reveal print as useful beyond the act of reading, as Black women combined tactility, display, as well as a multimodal literacy to engage freedom and the transformations of emancipation. With a critical reflexivity, Black women practiced seeing themselves anew, as free women in a climate still focused on unfree Black bodies. Free women's friendship albums do not suggest a bifurcation of public and private visibilities; instead, they reveal the still-public nature of Black women's private experiences in the early nineteenth century. Dominant expectations about chastity and middle-class womanhood influenced how free Black women related to one another and how they pictured freedom for others. Privacy remained a privilege for Black women in the early nineteenth century, one to which middle-class women retained access by buttressing ideologies of respectability and republicanism as values of the free community. In complex gifts of love and recognition to one another, Black women critically developed a conscious sense of spectacle, a way of perceiving one another within and without the terms of mainstream concepts of womanhood.

Black women's albums instructed other Black women to see Black womanhood as misrecognized by outside viewers, but also as far more visually complex than portrayed in other media contexts.[91] Contributions to personal albums made Black women's looking practices visible to one another. The optics of respectability resisted and retained some of slavery's problematic visions of the Black female body but enabled free Black women to express reflexivity about the restrictions placed on free women's visibilities. The optics of respectability also enables us to discuss the multitude of relationships between Black women of the early republic and the objectifying gaze of normativity: these women were familiar with it (knew its constructions), interacted with it (accommodated its vision), and critiqued it (watched with detachment). This other looking position complicates the possibility that even when caught in the gaze and presumed not to be looking *back*, Black women enjoyed other ways of seeing that were critical of dominant culture even while they remain objectified as racial spectacles. With this viewing practice, free women writing in albums intimated an analytical awareness of respectability politics, performing its visual demands of nondescript Blackness all while sharing an analytical posture toward its ideals. With the optics of respectability, free Black women watched their exclusions from dominant notions of womanhood among Whites, and the strict scrutiny of womanhood among Black men. At the same time, by using flowers instead of bodies to establish identification with a closed community of readers, Black women retained some of slavery's peculiarly enforced tactics of invisibility. At times, album contributions worked within notions of Black visibility as problematic, perpetuating the obfuscation of free female bodies within the pages of Black women's own artifacts. However, Black women's choices to remain opaque in this period make sense; they lived among the persistent danger of kidnapping or rape, and the residual fugitivity that still defined Black experiences.

Black women's album contributions complicate simplistic notions of floral motifs and saccharine sentiment with the unique details of Black freedom in the early republic. Albums document parlor conversations among women like Douglass and her friends who ruminated on ways of presenting themselves within the confines of respectable visibility. Albums became part of the larger display of respectable womanhood among middle-class and elite women of African descent who needed the intimate space of the album for community but simultaneously recognized the theater of the parlor as a place for putting on acceptable portrayals of domesticity. Black women were hyperaware of being looked at, and albums became spaces for Black women writing to one another to acknowledge the persistence of White-supremacist and masculinist gazes.

They also shaped a looking practice unique to free Black women's evolving experiences of freedom and domesticity. While public life on the street intimated an increasing sense of antagonism toward free Black women, these women used the parlor and its media to prepare one another for the public hostility that free people faced outside of their homes.

Figure I.1. Portrait of an unidentified woman from the Dickerson Daguerreotype Collection, ca. 1850. (Courtesy of The Library Company of Philadelphia)

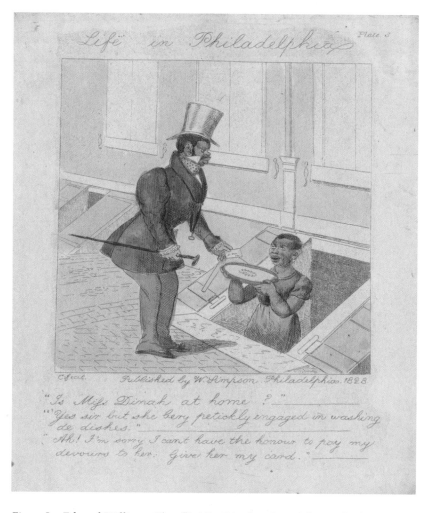

Figure I.2. Edward Williams Clay, *"Is Miss Dinah at Home?,"* 1828, "Life in Philadelphia" series. (Courtesy of The Library Company of Philadelphia)

Figure I.4. Sarah Mapps Douglass, *"A token of love from me, to thee,"* ca. 1833, Amy Matilda Cassey Album. (Courtesy of The Library Company of Philadelphia)

Figure 1.1. Elizabeth "Mumbet" Freeman, 1811. (Courtesy of the Massachusetts Historical Society)

Figure 1.2. A bracelet of gold beads made from Freeman's necklace. (Courtesy of the Massachusetts Historical Society)

Figure 2.2. Drawing accompanying the poem "Fuchsia," ca. 1841, Martina Dickerson Album. (Courtesy of The Library Company of Philadelphia)

Figure 2.3. "A mark of friendship's pleasing power . . . ," 1840, Martina Dickerson Album. (Courtesy of The Library Company of Philadelphia)

Figure 2.4. "Forget-Me-Nots," 1843, Martina Dickerson Album. (Courtesy of The Library Company of Philadelphia)

Figure 2.6. First Steamboat, 1841, Martina Dickerson Album. (Courtesy of The Library Company of Philadelphia)

Figure 2.10. The Lady Patroness of Alblacks, 1834. (Courtesy of The Library Company of Philadelphia)

Figure 3.4. Destruction by Fire of Pennsylvania Hall. On the Night of the 17th May, 1838, 1838. (Courtesy of The Library Company of Philadelphia)

Figure 3.6. Edward Williams Clay, *"How do you like de new fashion shirt . . . ?,"* 1828, "Life in Philadelphia" series. (Courtesy of The Library Company of Philadelphia)

BALL DRESS.   EVENING DRESS.

shed for the Lady's Book Jan.y 1833 by L.A.Godey &Co. Athenian Buildings Franklin Place Philadelphia.

Figure 3.8. "Philadelphia Fashions," *Godey's Lady's Book,* January 1833.

Figure 4.5. Angelina Grimké's wedding purse. (Courtesy of Clements Library, University of Michigan)

Figure 4.13. Edward William Clay, *A Five Points Exclusive taking the First Steps towards the Last Polish,* ca. 1833. (Courtesy of The Library Company of Philadelphia)

Figure 5.1. Edward Williams Clay, *"Shall I hab de honour to dance de next quadrille . . . ?,"* "Life in Philadelphia" series, 1828. (Courtesy of The Library Company of Philadelphia)

Figure 5.2. William Summers and Charles Hunt, *"Shall I hab de honour to dance de next quadrille . . .?,"* 1831, "Life in Philadelphia" series. (Courtesy of The Library Company of Philadelphia)

Figure 5.5. Life in Philadelphia: The Cut Direct, Or, Getting up in the World. (Courtesy of The Library Company of Philadelphia)

Figure 5.6. "Vues d'Amerique du Nord." (Courtesy of John Nicholas Brown Center for Public Humanities and Cultural Heritage, Brown University)

Figure E.1. "Obama Delivers Remarks on Iran," 2009. (Pool/Getty Images News/ Getty Images)

3

"Look! A Negress": Public Women, Private Horrors, and the White Ontology of the Gaze

Free Blacks in the preemancipation North meditated on freedom in their parlors, but they also expressed autonomy on city streets. Visible distinctions in dress, labor habits, social practices, and social interactions with Whites revealed that free people, and free Black women in particular, held self-concepts in conflict with the visual logics of slavery. A transforming Black visuality, signaled by habits of free Black communities, also carried daily implications for White northerners. Parlors became important sites of respite for Whites confronted with Black freedom. Just as free Black women employed print to manage the exigencies of emancipation, Whites also turned to print and the visual to cope with the erosion of slavery. Thus, White viewers retreated to the parlor with illustrations meant to reorganize racial codes of seeing threatened by the emergence of free Blacks. The parlor signified the middle-class White woman's domain of virtue and protection. Popular magazines like *Godey's Lady's Book* represented a genre of publication targeted toward White women consumers and the parlor as their proper setting. The rise of a small but powerful Black middle class represented a threat from which the parlor provided protection. Print media for White parlors invited viewers to take up practices of looking at free Blacks and to rethink the crucial reformations happening on city streets. Parlors served as places of retreat where Whites coped with the changes of gradual emancipation; Philadelphia in particular represented anxieties of space, personal and public, that increased alongside growing numbers of free Blacks in the North.

Freedom by the Numbers

Black freedom, as both a popular idea and a socially relevant phenomenon, directly confronted White ways of seeing race and seeing the self. Black people who were free in the preemancipation North faced hostility and violence from both poor and middle-class Whites because each group perceived free Blacks as a direct threat to slavery's visual culture and to White superiority. Philadelphia represented an especially fertile space for interracial contact, and for subsequent forms of White violence in response to the perceptible transformations associated with free Black communities. Northern laws for gradual emancipation produced noticeable results by the late 1820s, and Philadelphia became home to a diverse free population that included northern-born Blacks, West Indian migrants, and fugitive free Blacks from the South. Northern free and migrant Blacks who made homes for their families in the city also brushed up against "nearly 9,000 runaways [who] entered Philadelphia through various ways." By 1830, Pennsylvania's entire Black population had reached approximately thirty-eight thousand, with fifteen thousand of those individuals residing in Philadelphia County.[1] White Philadelphians were unhappy about the rapid growth of the city's Black population, even without regard to the specifics of the free community's makeup. In 1831, Nat Turner's Rebellion in Virginia felt dangerously close for Pennsylvanians who feared droves of Blacks flooding northern cities. One petitioner made explicit their concern over the "penal enactments" to expel Black populations in Maryland and Virginia, which would result in an "influx" of some 123,000 "ignorant, indolent and depraved" Black people infringing on "liberties of the citizens." Throughout 1831 and 1832, Whites offered similar kinds of petitions to the state government, asking lawmakers to restrict the mobility of free Blacks already within its boundaries and to suppress further migration of new Blacks into the state.[2] Whites justly feared a growing Black population as Pennsylvania represented a thoroughfare for Blacks moving into the North; a combination of births, migrations, manumissions, and escapes from slavery drastically transformed Philadelphia's demographic makeup.

In addition to the increased numbers of free Black Philadelphians, hostile Whites remained attuned to the perceived prosperity of free African Americans. Elite middle-class Black women like Sarah Mapps Douglass and her friends were part of a diverse and remarkable community of free people in Philadelphia who made their freedom known to Whites and others outside the space of Black parlors. All of free Black Philadelphia would have seemed looming to Whites in the 1810s and 1820s, even though the majority of free people in the city were not middle-class. Within this diverse group of born-free and formerly enslaved Blacks, wealth distributions were severely imbalanced. Black Philadelphians "owned approximately $1 million worth of property" and paid "$167,000 in rent."[3] With these internal disparities, this combination of newly free, middle-class, and working poor people constituted a Black Philadelphia that was visually distinct from slavery. White onlookers of this Philadelphia would have seen Blacks leaving their own homes, no matter how destitute, and patronizing Black establishments. Whites of the colonial city had enslaved people of African descent since 1684, but they now faced the emergence of free Blacks and the visual, structural, interpersonal, as well as affective consequences of freedom.

White people turned to pictorial ridicule, imagining Black freedom in hostile ways in order to manage anxieties about sharing northern spaces with free Black people. Racial caricature provided a means to cope with the threats to slavery's racio-visual order. In 1828, the White Philadelphian Edward Williams Clay developed his wildly popular "Life in Philadelphia" cartoon serial to mock the growing number of formerly enslaved, newly freed Blacks who now shared his city.[4] In addition to images like the cellar scene discussed in the introduction (figure I.2), Clay portrayed sightings of Blacks about town with the illustration of fourteen colored lithograph sheets, packaged in brown paper, for viewers to enjoy in sequence. "Life in Philadelphia" expressed distaste toward wealthy free Blacks by ridiculing their speech, dress, and what Clay deemed as free Blacks' unwarranted sense of self-importance. Clay mocked the possibility of a Black middle class with scenes that revealed an inherent incongruence between Blackness, refined taste, and social mobility. Using darkly colored figures in outlandish dress, Clay illustrated free women as unwomanly and outside of middle-class definitions of womanhood. In sheet after sheet, Clay incorporated scenes of Black women consumers who were able to buy ruffled gowns and jewelry but were unable to overcome their inherent lack of refinement. Representing Black freedom in the White imaginary, Clay argued that Blacks who migrated north and occupied Philadelphia as a new sustainable locale were a ridiculous lot. "Life in Philadelphia" emerged to teach White readers that free Blacks knew nothing about decorum or social mobility and thus were unprepared to experience freedom or succeed in U.S. society. Hostile pictures of freedom such as the "Life in

Philadelphia" series presented opportunities for White viewers to reformulate slavery's visual culture and racial ways of seeing, turning hostile
illustrations into tools of recuperation for Whiteness as a viewing position, which emancipation seemed to threaten. Clay emerged as a major
figure in U.S. cartooning to join the ranks of the English-born graphic
artist Henry Dawkins, who brought his cartoons to Philadelphia during
the 1750s. Dawkins engraved plates for booksellers and mapmakers, with
his cartoons peaking in popularity from 1790 to about 1810, when "prints
were hung in book sellers' windows and sold for from fifty cents to three
times as much."[5] Given the expense of this relatively new form of entertainment, it became customary to "rent portfolios of them from barber
shops and other places for a nominal sum" to entertain one's guests at
home with graphic prints. Renting allowed viewers to enjoy prints tem-
porarily without paying the high cost of purchasing them. However, with
the advancement of printing technologies, Dawkins's engravings gave way
to other kinds of printed materials, such as lithography, which made it
possible to mass-produce cartoons in higher volume.[6] By 1825, artists like
Clay and David Claypool Johnston, "who began with etched and engraved
cartoons," started using lithography to lower the cost and increase the
availability of cartooned entertainment. Now with the designer and the
engraver or lithographer as separate entities, one person could design the
cartoon while various others reproduced it for sale. This wider circulation increased the price of amusement until new technologies emerged
in the late 1870s, and the lithography process was superseded by that of
photoengraving.[7] With this drastic reduction in costs, viewers with less
disposable income could actually possess their own prints. Cheap prints
now appeared in even the more modest parlors of working-class viewers.
During his most prolific period, from 1819 to 1837, Clay produced popular
entertainment that could satiate the needs of lower-class Whites. He created affordable materials that helped the masses (re)interpret the lives of
free Black women who challenged slavery's visual logics via ownership of
their labor and their bodies. With an analytic eye for the happenings in his
city, Clay also portrayed White Philadelphians with a critical hand, drawing prints to lampoon pretentious Whites who overtook Philadelphia's
Washington Square Park (figure 3.1). Clay was the most prolific social and
political cartoonist of the Jacksonian era and up through 1857; he started
at a firm illustrating images for clothing advertisements and documenting scenic attributes of Philadelphia with drawings of the Delaware River
and Roper's Gymnasium on Market Street.[8] However, it was Clay's robust

Figure 3.1. Edward Williams Clay, *Promenade in Washington Square Park,* 1828, "Life in Philadelphia" series. (Courtesy of The Library Company of Philadelphia)

narrative of Black "Life in Philadelphia" that made him most popular; his graphic hostility served as an important counterpart for organized White violence orchestrated by mobs that fixated upon Black socioeconomic security and destroyed Black institutions.[9]

Scholars often cite Clay's unflattering caricatures of Black women as proof of the hostile public culture that free people navigated in the antebellum North.[10] And they are correct to do so because many free Black women who lived in Philadelphia became the subjects of ridiculing representations. However, taken up as cultural practice, not just historical evidence, Clay's method of picturing freedom illustrates the ways in which White viewers in the antebellum North used printed images of free Blacks to deal with their own problems of identification. In this chapter, I explore the ways in which the "Life in Philadelphia" series would have been helpful for White viewers who were engaged in their own processes of identity (re)production prompted by the question of Black freedom, and the way representations of free people of African descent helped to reconstitute

Whites' own racial, class, and national identities. In their moment of circulation, Clay's derogatory pictures provided White consumers with the opportunity to rethink issues of ocularity and ontology as structured by slavery and disrupted by the changes associated with freedom. Clay's caricatures became increasingly popular in the early decades of the nineteenth century, and circulated throughout other northern cities that were also dealing with the dissolution of slavery's visual cultures. Images such as those in the "Life in Philadelphia" series were sold in local print shops and cultivated a spectacular concept of Black freedom—creating a "social relationship" between individuals through mediation, "objectifying" and materializing a worldview of Blackness as hypervisible.[11] I argue that these items satisfied White viewers who needed to compensate for the visual threat of interracial encounters and Black demonstrations of freedom. Racial caricatures such as those in the"Life in Philadelphia" series circulated to recuperate the White ontology of the gaze, as cultivated in slavery and jeopardized by the emergence of emancipation.

Central to my argument is the explication of the visual impact of Black freedom on White people. Free people of African descent distinguished themselves from slavery by comporting themselves as free and by making noticeable changes to the city. Black Philadelphians altered the geography by anchoring a free community with churches and schools. Clay, in particular, watched a small free Black population share in many of the same privileges that he enjoyed. For example, Clay had no formal training in the arts like the Douglass family; however, Clay remained solidly upper-middle-class and was preparing for a career as a lawyer before a leisure trip to Europe changed his path. Moreover, Clay's well-to-do family—many were educated, active in politics and religion, and married into "families of equal education, influence, and wealth"—lived within several blocks of a niche of elite Blacks in a home located near Third and Arch Streets.[12] Accordingly, Clay experienced the visible and spatial impact of emancipation firsthand through his own physical proximity to free Blacks. This kind of privilege and proximity is cause to unpack the disruptive force of Black freedom on Whiteness and visuality. Drawing on existential theories of the "look," I treat the philosopher Frantz Fanon's personal experience of the White gaze, captured in the phrase "Look! A Negro," as a practical observation to linger in the moment of White sight and to consider the effect of Blackness on Whiteness. Whereas canonic theorizations of the look have typically focused on the impact of the White gaze on the Black self, I use these same theories to think through the impact of the Black gaze on the White self. It is through this critical turn that I read Clay's body of work. It represents a space wherein he used his power and access to respond to freedom and retain slavery's racio-visual logic. I reveal the way in which Clay's racial caricatures rejoined noticeable transformations in Black life, especially those that challenged the idea that middle-class status was available to Whites only.

Free in Public Places

The slow erosion of slavery and the development of free Black communities had a visible impact on the city of Philadelphia and only became more noticeable with each passing decade. Philadelphia's Black community featured a diverse group of freeborn, manumitted, and unfree people from the seventeenth century forward. Their places for living, working (in shops, on farms, at the wharfs), and socializing (with liquor available) in the colonial city were closely scrutinized, and managed with "black codes" that governed the movement of the free and unfree alike.[13] Accordingly, people of African descent were a visible presence in Philadelphia even before emancipations changed the demographics. In 1780, the Pennsylvania legislature passed "An Act for the Gradual Abolition of Slavery," which set terms for slowly emancipating unfree Black people. The first and most severe of its kind, Pennsylvania's law suppressed the importation of new unfree Blacks into the state and required masters to register their human property with the county. However, the law also allowed *owners* to recoup the expenses of slavery by retaining people in bondage for a specified period. Black people born into slavery before March 1, 1780, remained enslaved for their entire lives, but their children born after this date lived in bondage until the age of twenty-eight. Slavery in Philadelphia dissolved in advance of the provisions set forth by the law as the passage of this decree undermined the legitimacy of slavery. Increased numbers of Black people freed themselves, many refusing to work and others reporting their owners' failure to adhere to the law.[14] While the number of unfree Blacks decreased, the size of the free population increased well into the nineteenth century.

The demographic changes to Philadelphia's Black population came along with cultural and structural changes to the city. City streets in the North became the stage for free Blacks to enact new approaches to the self and to social interaction with Whites. The increased numbers of free

African Americans may have seemed disturbing to Whites, who would have seen conspicuously free people engaging the gaze as an affront to slavery's peculiar ocularity. Many Whites were unaccustomed to seeing free Blacks as autonomous and openly visible, returning rather than avoiding White surveillance. Black freedom signaled self-possession. In particular, revised approaches to labor and to personal comportment revealed that free Blacks were developing new self-perceptions and that they expected different, more respectful, treatment from Whites. Although some free people opened their own businesses, many others continued to do physically grueling work but moved out of White homes, even if they continued to labor as servants for their former White owners. African American labor in the earliest years of emancipation remained circumscribed by racism, but it also became more varied in terms of the spaces where work occurred and the tactics of resistance that Black laborers employed.[15] Similarly, monetary income enabled free Blacks to participate in popular enjoyments like dancing, as well as fashion themselves as self-governed individuals through dress choices.

Black women and the matter of clothing underscore the visual transformations associated with freedom in the preemancipation North. Taken up as an area of commerce, clothes represented a central part of Black people's paid labor in the era of slavery. Free Black women participated in various forms of garment work, taking pay and making conscious decisions about their labor with the same skills that went uncompensated during slavery. Wilma King reveals the ways in which freedom meant the right to decline work, especially for Black women who exercised this choice often, even as they continued to labor in many of the same jobs for Whites. For example, the number of Black women who worked in style trades as dressmakers, tailors, and millers continually increased from the turn of the century and moving toward the 1840s. Although many Black women continued to labor in some of the same jobs organized by slavery, now, in freedom, Black women also laundered or ironed and folded clothes in their own homes and then delivered clean clothes back to their customers.[16] A White onlooker watching an evolving Philadelphia would have seen Black women doing garment work from their own homes rather than in White homes, and working in both creative and perfunctory positions. Over time, Whites began to deny "respectable women of color" dressmaker work, even when there was an advertised need, to instead usher Black women into housework as cooks and cleaners.[17] Such grievances reveal that Whites attempting to reconcile the slow dissolution of slavery continually regarded free Black women's labor, especially in clothing and style work, as politically salient. Clothing or style labor in particular represented the capacity to control one's personal appearance, as well as that of others, on top of turning a profit. Different from other forms of work that also facilitated consumer power, clothing labor satisfied both social and political needs for African Americans who wanted to demonstrate their free status. Clothing mattered to free Black women, both middle-class and poor, for both income and adornment.

Wearing fine clothes helped freeborn and fugitive free Blacks communicate their status to the broader society. People of African descent who once wore handed-down clothing now signified regard for their bodies through making and purchasing clothes in the transition to freedom. Runaway notices that recount fugitive flights to freedom often report that Black people stole fine garments from their masters in order to dress themselves as free. Where the "exposure of the slave woman's body" through the deprivation of clothing translated to concepts of Black promiscuity, clothing and the entire issue of personal appearance emerged as a characteristic that distinguished freedom from enslavement.[18] This visible change would be markedly different from slavery, when Blacks had less governance over their self-presentations. In the earliest emergence of free communities in the decades after the gradual emancipation law, the right to cover one's body represented a new entitlement for women of African descent. Although slavery stipulated Black female bodies as open to touch and scrutiny, the practices of making and wearing clothes offered a unique opportunity to self-define one's personal appearance, as dress provided an opportunity for Black women to cover themselves and to avoid unwanted sexual advances.

Prerogatives about clothing and the body are among the complex media that Black women deployed to convey their freedom. Whereas albums helped women cultivate a visual practice among groups of women within Black homes, dress further intimated a practice of spectatorship at work among free people and a way of interacting with hostile gazes on city streets. Decisions about how to appear in public indicated a regard for one's personal appearance and demonstrated preparation for interacting with other people as well. As with print, Black women's public appearances remained in conversation with White and mainstream concepts of women's fashion. Just as class privilege enabled some Black women to participate in album culture, consumer power allowed free women to partake in dominant concepts of womanhood constituted in dress. For Whites hostile to the visual changes of freedom, emancipated Blacks committed what Monica Miller terms "crimes of fashion" as they appeared conspicuously free and used dress to symbolize "a self-conscious manipulation of authority" via "racial and class cross-dressing."[19] Free Blacks used clothing to transgress norms relating to civil status as well as socioeconomic privilege. Dress portrayed entitlement to respect, and it offered a pleasure that was no longer accessible to Whites only. For free Black women, clothing meant an opportunity to "wear" respectability and to make it visible for others. Black women especially focused on adornment because class determined dress and dress garnered respect in the early nineteenth century, leading African American women to make even more stringent and calculated fashion choices.[20] Dress was yet another method that free Black women used to demonstrate mainstream concepts of womanhood in the early republic. Many African American women were somewhat conservative in their dress choices because constant scrutiny from Black men and from Whites compelled Black women to regulate their bodies. With Whites judging Black women's comportment, and Black men watching to ensure that they properly represented the free community, dress offered another way to make visible the obligations of freedom to a dominant culture—to appear in ways most flattering to the entire community. Constantly under the gaze of their partners, and of Whites looking to either ridicule or instigate violence, free Black women's clothing choices were consistently in conversation with the larger social context.

Dressing the free body was a politicized act, and styles of dress further conveyed political values. Clothing helped free women signal their distance from the hand-me-downs of slavery, but the specific styles of clothes also addressed other kinds of involvement. Privileged Black women wore styles that signaled their social commitments but avoided "the drabness of plain dress" and "the hoops, bustles, and ruffles" of fashionable White women.[21] While free women took up numerous occupations in the early republic, elite women who lectured or worked as activists gave considerable forethought to dress. Women preachers in the African Methodist Episcopal tradition donned "plain" dress to show piety, using their consumer power to protest slavery by abstaining from flashy purchases; instead, many used money to help the poor. Conversely, women journalists and activists elected to wear "respectable" dress—clothes with stylistic flourish and patterned fabrics that accentuated curves but always covered the flesh.[22] While "fashionable" dress in the early nineteenth century invoked extensive use of decorative embellishments, such as ballooned sleeves and large, ribboned hats, Black women of the elite and middle class dressed themselves according to their public stations. Fashion was not simply a choice between antislavery activism and trend for free women but also a demonstration of wealth, social commitments, and freedom. In selecting specific kinds of dress for different occasions, even for showing membership to particular groups of free Black women, they also revealed themselves as discerning about public presentation.

Free Black women tailored their public appearances to directly counter slavery's visual culture, to reclaim rights to covering and to sacredness. Clothing provided free women with the means to demonstrate ideas about the entitlements of freedom, and decisions about dress evidence a consciously honed visual practice. Self-styling introduced the private ruminations of the parlor to encounters on the street. Amid the various changes to life in the urban North, both clothing and clothing work represented an evolving Black visuality.

Increased numbers of free Black Philadelphians also effected the built environment of the city, demonstrating a structural response to the impact of Black freedom. Free communities organized around physical institutions such as schools and churches that African Americans established with their own money. When Absalom Jones and Richard Allan founded a separate church for Black congregants, Mother Bethel African Methodist Episcopal on Sixth and Lombard Streets in 1794, they ignited the creation of sanctuaries and businesses in Philadelphia that catered to African Americans specifically. Various other religious denominations, like Shiloh Baptist, established a building nearby, along with a number of banks and schools. Although separate churches like Mother Bethel emerged in response to White racism and racial segregation within the city's churches, Whites recognized separate churches as signs of vanity and viewed these institutions as signs of Blacks demarcating social spaces that excluded White people.[23] Images like the 1829 lithograph titled *Bethel African Methodist Episcopal Church* (figure 3.2) illustrate how some Whites viewed the church—as a large edifice, taller than the surrounding buildings, with Black men and women entering for worship.[24] Most of the women are well dressed with parasols, but one Black woman wears modest clothing, and the Black men wear top hats. Importantly, a few Whites appear in the image: a White woman and a White child appear in front of the church but stand as barred from entrance by a fence, watching the worship that happens inside from outside on the sidewalk. Although the image is not a caricature or intended to ridicule Black religion, the artist

Figure 3.2. Bethel African Methodist Episcopal Church, Philadelphia. (Courtesy of The Library Company of Philadelphia)

portrayed the space of Mother Bethel and the African American patrons as unwelcoming to Whites. This illustration represents an overarching sentiment among Whites about Black churches like Mother Bethel, as well as schools and orphanages for Black children. Collectively, these structures signaled Black entitlement to the physical space of the city. While Whites perceived Black churches as problematic, free Blacks imagined the church as an epicenter of social and class mobility. To White onlookers, Black churches represented a new public visibility that allowed well-dressed men and women of African descent to flaunt their economic prowess through church attire and church buildings.

To be fair, churches were fraught symbols of changing self-perceptions among Black communities, as well as spaces that free people understood as representative of African American life. Churches were central to disseminating notions of propriety and decorum, where various religious denominations and different church congregations organized by class, color, and the number of generations removed from slavery.[25] In these practices, churches in Philadelphia's Black communities revealed the intrarace diversity among free African Americans and prevailing ideas about how to improve the lives of Black people. In relation to this, the church also represented a panopticon for respectability. It facilitated a watchdog approach to Black life with a "collective female gaze"; churchwomen settled civil disputes, offered family services, surveyed personal conduct among church constituents, and rendered Black men and women as "constantly on display" to make sure that no one's personal behavior detracted from the reputation of the larger Black community.[26] Whites who felt threatened by Black freedom often ridiculed the practices of Black religion, incorporating the church into visual narratives meant to problematize emancipation. Conflicting assertions about the nature and impact of Black visibility represented a conundrum for free people, and churches were places for denying negative allegations against free Blacks, and preparing constituents to deal with these charges.

Churches were essential to an overall view of Black freedom in the eyes of Whites. For example, in 1830, John Fanning Watson, the Philadelphia historian, offered vivid details about the appearance of free Blacks and firsthand accounts from Whites who watched these changes unfold. Watson argued that the "dressy blacks and dandy *colour'd* beaux and belles" [*sic*] seen leaving their Black churches were a recent phenomenon; adding that at the turn of the century "they were much humbler, more esteemed in their place, and more useful to themselves and others."[27] Watson argued that freedom and gradual emancipation changed Blacks for the worse, and he found testimony from other Whites to corroborate his position. Watson cited an unnamed but "discerning" White woman, familiar with the "olden time" when White domestic comforts were not "every day interrupted by the pride and profligacy of servants." This woman's testimony supported Watson's central idea, that enslaved Blacks treated Whites better than free Blacks and for the most part "felt themselves to be an integral part of the [White] family to which they belonged."[28] In this account of a changing Philadelphia, churches were a structural indicator of the social and cultural vicissitudes associated with free Black communities.

The destruction of property associated with Black freedom was another kind of White response to the significance of these transformations. Beginning on May 14, 1838, Black and White abolitionists convened to dedicate the establishment of Pennsylvania Hall, a meeting place for lectures and discussions located at Sixth and Haines Streets. The depiction

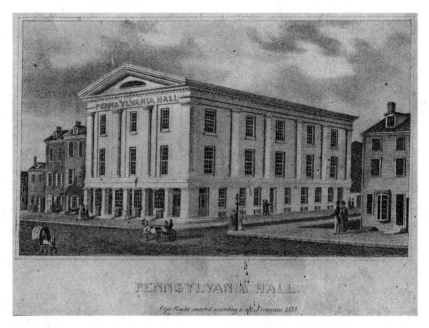

Figure 3.3. Pennsylvania Hall. (Courtesy of The Library Company of Philadelphia)

of this conspicuous building in figure 3.3 shows its looming presence in the mind of the artist. A number of well-dressed Whites and Blacks are portrayed walking past the building but not interacting with one another. This before-picture suggests that Whites believed that Pennsylvania Hall was an imposing structure where mixed-race socializing took place among well-to-do people. An organized mob of Whites, however, viewed the antislavery meeting convened at the hall as a celebration of "miscegenation" as well as women's-rights activism, and responded with organized violence. On the night of May 17, 1838, suspicions of "the fraternal commingling of the races and the sexes in and around" Pennsylvania Hall resulted in its destruction, along with that of the "Shelter for Colored Orphans on Thirteenth Street near Callowhill," and a three-day streak of organized anti-Black violence began that threatened the AME church. Popular perceptions of prosperity among Philadelphia's burgeoning Black community led to anti-Black violence and victimization as White mobs started fires, committed murders, and chased free Blacks out of town, intending to diminish community wealth "wrongfully" perceived as

Figure 3.4. Destruction by Fire of Pennsylvania Hall. On the Night of the 17th May, 1838, 1838. (Courtesy of The Library Company of Philadelphia)

"growing" economic prowess.[29] Figure 3.4 portrays the thrill of destruction at the site of the hall before a crew of Whites who raise their hats in celebration and the negligent fire department that hosed water away from the blaze. This event represents the extent to which it was not only the autonomy of individual free persons that upset Whites in the city, but also the entire set of visible changes associated with abolition—free Black people and the institutional structures that supported their communities.

Ironically, the perception that free Blacks were becoming too wealthy and gaining too much stability was a shared notion among pro- and antislavery advocates alike. Poor Whites recognized freedom as frightening to the point of inciting rage and acts of destruction, while free Black and White abolitionists saw the advancement of the free community as delicate but stable enough to continually acknowledge and cultivate. Both anti-Black mobs as well as purported friends of free Blacks, like the Pennsylvania Abolitionist Society and local Quakers, viewed the *appearance* of free Blacks as meaningful to the reformation of the early republic. Abolitionists used the 1837 census of the "free-Negro" population to argue for their progressive roles in society, as compared to enslaved Blacks. Activists circulated political pamphlets to publicize the "good" of abolition and to refute disenfranchising legislation that targeted the Black community.[30] Although the free community made important contributions to its own advancement, via money paid in taxes, fund-raisers to support abolition, and care for underprivileged African Americans, abolitionist propaganda overstated these successes. Most freeborn Blacks were not as financially successful as Black men runaways. While these abolitionist efforts failed to persuade legislators—since Blacks remained disenfranchised until the ratification of the Fifteenth Amendment—or rioters about the upstanding character and contributions of Philadelphia's free population, they also pinpoint the peculiar perception of Black freedom that continued well after the passage of gradual abolition laws. Whereas slavery produced and demanded a permanent state of destitution for people of African descent, it also ignited a permanent association between Blackness and poverty. Blackness was to function as a class signifier in conjunction with slavery. Accordingly, in these earliest decades of the nineteenth century, Black freedom problematically connoted prosperity, as the path of antislavery. Many Whites understood that Black freedom was not simply liberty from bondage but also access to economic privilege. This concept persisted, even as the overwhelming majority of the free Black population remained impoverished. Worse, yet, in the eyes of many White northerners, Black freedom necessarily meant the end of White prosperity, and, potentially, White enslavement.

Whiteness and the Gaze

Whites who encountered the black gaze might have felt both terror and disruption, in an ontological sense; at the very least, free Blacks who took up the right to look back often appeared threatening to Whites. The realization of a black gaze in the context of slavery would have seemed like a danger to the primacy of Whiteness and to White people's self-concepts in the preemancipation North. Whereas slavery constructed Whiteness in practices of surveillance and disembodiment, a growing free Black community organized opportunities for interactions across race that also disrupted prevailing assumptions about the right to look, and the right to not be looked at in return. Free Blacks who variously expressed autonomy with regard to themselves and their communities unsettled White assumptions about personhood. Likewise, while slavery empowered Whites with the ability to observe Black people's behaviors, free Blacks with access to print also publicized their judgments about Whites. For these reasons, White northerners may have experienced dismay, in addition to annoyance, at the realization of a transforming Black visuality. This is not to say that the emergence of Black freedom happened steadily or without repercussions; incidents like the destruction of Pennsylvania Hall illustrate how discernible changes associated with Black freedom intensified White violence. Instead, changes in Black visuality and the large-scale resistance of the peculiarly ocular institution created a threatening environment for the norms of White ways of seeing, and by consequence, White subjectivity.

By the early 1830s, African American thinkers were documenting their concepts of Whiteness in literature and in news stories about White racism. Mia Bay reveals the prevalence of Black ethnologies of race and racism, where prominent figures like the Black Nationalist physician Martin Delany argued for African American superiority through the disparagement of White raciality. Appealing to classic ethnologist rubrics of environmentalism, religion, and science, nineteenth-century African Americans appreciated distinctions in skin color, intelligence, and morality along a spectrum of race.[31] Bay's intellectual history of Black thought provides a body of evidence that illustrates critical considerations of White people. This archive of writings and speeches on racial difference predominantly represents the work of Black men, many of whom were educated, and proves that people of African descent, both free and enslaved, were ruminating on White raciality, just as Whites like Thomas Jefferson authored works on Black racial distinctions.[32] Connected to this, however, is the issue of free Blacks *looking* directly at Whites, subjecting Whiteness to the scrutiny of a Black gaze. What remains difficult to discern, despite the robust nature of this archive, are the day-to-day practices of surveillance among African Americans as they were meaningful to White people, especially as these ways of seeing *did not* find their way into literature or the historical record, explicitly.

Here, thinking about Black women's specific experiences with the gaze offers an important reorganization of racial spectatorship and canonic theories of looking and race. Frantz Fanon's important description of racio-visual trauma, captured in the phrase: "Look! A Negro!" offers an important starting point for discussing racialist gazing. When a White child announces Fanon as "Negro" on a train, Fanon's incapacity to return the look and his internal coping processes prove that hostile stares perpetually reinvigorate slavery's vision of a savage Black raciality.[33] This theory of Black visuality heavily relies on misrecognition as a determining factor in the terror Fanon feels about his subjection by the White gaze. However, Nicole Fleetwood offers important insight on the "Fanonian moment," pointing out the way in which Fanon's theorization attends to the terror of being marked visually as black, but also reinscribes "the black female subject as unintelligible." Fanon's experience of scopic violence, in part, results in the fact that he holds the body in permanent definition, as externally defined. Fanon's confrontation with the White gaze is fraught by his organization of an insurmountable Black corporeality that maintains a permanent imbalance in visual encounters between Whites and Blacks. Fleetwood offers a Black woman's gaze as a corrective, which integrates the gaze *and* the body to reveal the racial gaze as performance, and reveals Fanon's retreat as one that "fails" to dissolve the "troubling vision" of Blackness.[34] Again, it is this Black feminist turn in the context of visual objectification that offers another valence for hostile encounters. For Fanon, the Black body is problematized in the sight of the White gaze; for Fleetwood, the Black woman's body is the bearer of its own look, which undulates in relationship to hostile gazes. It is in this other, or third space of seeing—where Black women presume their own omniscience—that results in another way of treating the gaze. A black feminist gaze engages the visual with a lens—an added layer of scrutiny.

The preoccupation with recognition in Fanon's discussion is meaningful for White bodies as well, making theorizations of White scopic violence against Black people useful for thinking about the White gaze as both a practice and a personal experience of whiteness. "Racist interpellation" of Black raciality "reveals whites to themselves" and discloses the processes of the White gaze.[35] Jean-Paul Sartre's discussion of the visual is useful for thinking through the interconnectedness of this scenario, especially because his experience of "White indifference" toward African Americans during a 1945 visit to the United States—where he witnessed how Whites rarely looked at and often looked through Black people as "machinery" for labor—is an important element of his conceptualization.[36] Sartre both recognizes White people's refusal to acknowledge Black humanity as well as accentuates the role of recognition in the development of a White gaze.

His example is unpacked through the anecdote of a self-centered masculine subject who pleasurably walks through a park, taking in his surroundings as though they occur for his enjoyment. The green of the grass, the empty park benches are all "objects" for this viewer to notice—in fact, they primarily exist from, and within, *his* point of view. The serenity that Sartre describes in this way of seeing is disrupted when the objects on display now appear for another "man" who cannot be qualified as object, like the benches and the grass because these things are fixed in space, are acted upon, and have no history. In Sartre's account, the presence of this second man represents "an object [that] has appeared which has stolen the world from me" as the only one who sees.[37] Different from the bench and the grass that have a determined distance from Sartre as *the* seeing subject, different from the bench that he moves toward (and that cannot move toward him), the appearance of another "man" is specific. The appearance of a second seeing entity creates the possibility that objects such as the bench now exist for the other as well. Now, everything that once appeared for Sartre as the primary subject—the trees, the benches, and the statues in the park—also has a spatial relationship to another person. In Sartre's theorization, all the things that exist around this Other person have infringed on his sense of possession as the original subject. Where all objects were once "made with *my space*," unfortunately "there is [now] a regrouping in which I take part but which escapes me, a regrouping of all the objects which people my universe."[38] In the Sartrean sense, looking is a subject practice that enables the objectification of others, and if another can "look," then "he" can objectify with his gaze. These realizations can maintain this new "man" in the position of "Other" because for Sartre, "everything still exists for me," however they now mean "everything is traversed by an invisible flight and fixed in the direction of a new object."[39] Thus, anyone who thought "he" owned the park must now question what he believed about all of the objects within the park. Now he must even reconsider the greenness of the grass. One must now entertain questions about the self, and the idea that if one could be wrong about the purpose of things, then "he" could also be wrong about everything. Worse still, he could be seen as an object in the eyes of another seeing subject. Catastrophically, "the appearance of the Other in the world corresponds therefore to a fixed sliding of the whole universe," because that whole universe was initially perceived as existing for one point of view.[40] Sartre's experience of the look unfolds problems for one's own credibility in terms of his entire perception of the world, within which these new possibilities unravel.

For Sartre, one does not just relish in the power to see but also basks in being the only one who can see. Sartre's visual subject avoids seeing the self being looked at by others. This avoidance of the "look" supersedes the presence of eyes, or "two ocular globes," but is *felt* as an awareness that Sartre denotes can arise from the rustling of branches or the appearance of a farmhouse standing alone at the top of a hill. "The bush, the farmhouse are not the look; they only represent the *eye*,"—and the eye is the support for the look.[41] The "look" is not just the existence of eyes that can confront other people (not just the appearance of another), but also the presence that objects exude. It is the sense that something is occurring *at me* or in my direction, with the probability that someone else is causing the occurrence. For Sartre, the feeling of a "look" actually requires not seeing the eyes, because "if I apprehend the look, I cease to perceive the eyes."[42] The feeling of the look is cognizance of being looked at, and it transcends the experience of seeing the eyes of the onlooker. Sartre's theory of "the look" organizes a distinction between having the ability to see and being seen by another—"we can not perceive the world and at the same time apprehend a look fastened upon us; it must be either one or the other."[43] In this approach, the whole premise of looking is bound to a belief in one's solitary existence. Looking at others and "being-seen-by-another" have a difficult time existing simultaneously. The experience of being looked at overcomes one's ability to look and only conjures the realization that "I am vulnerable, that I have a body which can be hurt"—that when branches rustle behind me, "I am seen" by another.[44] In this order, being seen places the body and the idea of the self in peril.

Both Fanon and Sartre offer linear constructions of visual interaction that coincide with the racio-visual logic of slavery, even in the twentieth century. Neither theorist can account for a sighted subject who arrives at the scene of subjection with a critical lens through which to engage hegemonic notions of Black visibility. The seeing subject of these linear theories either looks or is looked at, and he remains ill prepared for his own objectification. Fanon's *experience* of the *phrase* "Look! A Negro" resonates with Sartre's detail of "the look" as troublesome. Each theory imagines that "oppressed groups are constituted by the gaze of a 'master' or oppressor," resulting in an imagined "concreteness and historical ladenness of the gaze."[45] Although the persistence of race consciousness, the awareness of one's self as Black, is a significant point of departure between Sartre's and Fanon's larger projects, Fanon's preoccupation with the past and with the body as a hindrance to a revolutionary present is yet another instance where bodies show up in a limiting way in Fanon's invaluable discussion of the visual.[46] Inside Fanon's feelings about White interpellation, however, is also his ethnographic witnessing of White reception, or his empirical account of a White child seeing a Black man and issuing an utterance in response. In this rubric, the statement "Look! A Negro" might also be thought of as an offensive tactic—a preemptive strike where the White child avoids having to say, "Don't look at me!" For that reason, the assumptions of dominance and normativity that undergird Fanon's theory might also apply to the Whites who issue racializing gazes.

We can think of the existential disruption and fright that characterizes each of these theories as latent in *dominant* experiences of being seen by others, and as notions that would have also corresponded to the earliest visual encounters between Whites and free Blacks in the early republic. For Whites privileged to believe the gaze to be their racial dominion, the possibility of Black surveillance directed toward Whites would have been an unsettling prospect. In a context that imagined vision as a tool of capture and control—via the runaway notice, for example—spectatorship among people of African descent also meant the power to make Whites vulnerable to the gaze. Worse, when free Black people dressed in ways that garnered stares from Whites, they also undermined the disempowering matrix of visual culture in the context of slavery. Free Blacks who dressed themselves in splendid ways or garnered public attention further disrupted peculiar visual logic of slavery by commanding the gaze, rather than retreating from White stares. The power of the White gaze would seem somewhat demystified if free Black people, and Black women especially, willfully accepted or invited stares from others.

This alternate vantage point on this instance of terror is productive for thinking through the undocumented visual encounters across race that happened in the preemancipation North. Existentialist theories of the gaze can correspond to a White seeing subject, no longer able to fantasize about White solitude in the presence of free Black communities. Whites in antebellum Philadelphia might have found their lives disrupted by interracial encounters or might have worried about the implications of Black freedom on White visuality. Whereas slavery's peculiar ocularity shrouded Whites from the experience of the gaze by legislating against Black looking, freedom and emancipation threatened to disentangle the protective cover of the ocular institution. Coterminous with the emergence of Black freedom, free people issued gazes as well as received them and, in the process, disrupted the shroud of invisibility in which Whiteness existed under slavery. In a context rife with paranoia about a changing visual culture, Whites were subject to an existential terror—a complex mix of fear, shame, objectification, perhaps even a loss of freedom experienced in the captivity of the look. This anxiety circulated widely among Whites who feared the impending changes of gradual abolition and Black emancipation. In the context of visual culture as a zero-sum game, with only one person properly visual and present in any interracial encounter, the public sphere became more frightening and unpredictable. It demanded the existence of the parlor as a place for White refuge. Within the parlor and parlor literatures, slavery's visual culture could remain intact. Whites retreated to parlor entertainment and consumed pictures that countered the displays of freedom visible on city streets. Such enjoyments helped Whites retain slavery's visual order, and also to cope with growing free Black communities. Pictures that rendered free Blacks as objects to look at helped Whites manage the danger realized in Black visuality. Political caricatures that emphasized the significance of racial difference in social encounters enforced visibility as a tool for managing anxieties about place, power and nationhood. Caricature removed the White looker from the page and thus removed Whiteness from the threat of a piercing look.

Clay's Philadelphia

Clay recast the lives of free people through caricature and asserted powerful control over the image of Black freedom. He depicted "Life in Philadelphia" in such a way that developed and maintained social distance between free Blacks and free Whites, even as they lived within close geographic contact. Clay's method of picturing freedom portrays a sense of threat, but of a particular kind experienced among middle-class Whites who were not in danger of losing their jobs or their financial stability to free Black people. Much of White discomfort and "fretful complaint" with freedom in the preemancipation North had to do with the conduct of free Blacks on city streets, which Clay portrayed through illustrations of Black "dandies" and "dandizettes" to uphold a connection between Blackness and slavery.[47] Clay's images agonized over the supposed privileges of Black freedom, such as shopping, working, and organizing, to illustrate a sense of entitlement among free African Americans. He used contemporary occurrences in his cartoons to ridicule the entire population of free Blacks, emphasizing free Black women in particular, and to frame the visible changes among Black communities in a hostile manner.

A newcomer to the City of Brotherly Love, Elizabeth Willson made her migration to Philadelphia from Georgia, and with her brother Joseph, joined Philadelphia's Black middle class by the early 1830s. While Joseph interviewed free Blacks for his book *Elite of Our People*, Elizabeth made friends and married Frederick Augustus Hinton, who was about ten years her senior (Elizabeth was approximately twenty-four years of age at the time). Hinton was a well-established activist and self-employed entrepreneur who made a life in Philadelphia after migrating from North Carolina. Although the Hintons shared the experience of migration to the North, beliefs about gender roles in the free Black community helped distinguish the Hinton's communal obligations and popular enjoyments from one another. Frederick Hinton funded abolitionist organizations and newspapers, promoted expatriation to Trinidad and Liberia, and supported his family with money earned from his own operations. Similar to many free Blacks of the city, Frederick was in the style business. He owned the "Gentleman's Dressing Room" (a hairdressing salon and barber shop) at 51 South Fourth Street. While Frederick set about an explicitly public and political life, Elizabeth managed the domestic relations. Widowed with two children, Hinton married Elizabeth, who helped raise his family. In constructing a social life, Elizabeth probably participated in parlor cultures with other elite Black women. Elizabeth Hinton's younger sister, Emily Willson, contributed to the friendship album of Philadelphia activist and freeborn woman Amy Cassey, as did Frederick's first wife, Eliza Ann, who offered sentiment to Mary Anne Dickerson's album, also a freeborn woman of Philadelphia's Black elite.[48] Women like Hinton would have demonstrated high regard for tropes of respectable visibility, perhaps more so than men like her husband, who could call on their institutional "works" in uplift organizations and Black-owned businesses to represent them. Together, as prominent members of the free community, the Hintons represented observable changes among free Blacks in the preemancipation North. They were part of a much larger group of free people who owned their labor, purposefully changed their geographic locations, and developed some degree of economic stability in the earliest decades of the nineteenth century.

With attention to detail, White media producers variously mobilized the Hintons' visibility. Announcement of the Hintons' wedding on January 11, 1837, appeared in the January 21, 1837, edition of the *Liberator*, and

William Lloyd Garrison thus suggested the event as relevant to his abolitionist readers.[49] Similarly, the Hintons' nuptials were also represented in
popular lithograph form as part of Clay's satirical work. Although Clay
may not have known the Hintons personally, he could have encountered
reports of Frederick's second marriage to Elizabeth just about anywhere
after the *Liberator* had announced their wedding. In Clay's pictorial
response to their union (figure 3.5), he "documented" a free Black couple
shown in a scene suggestive of a spectacular existence, but he attempted
to define the reception of free Blacks taking up residence in Philadelphia.
The figure Clay describes as "Frederick Augustus" appears well dressed
and somewhat jarred by the stare of an onlooker. While Frederick tries
hard to see the spectator, this would-be "Elizabeth" (the character isn't
named) seems hardly to notice. Clay represents this woman as either fixed
in her pose and unconcerned by the gaze, or as uncertain about foreign
stares altogether. In the image, the bride asks her companion: "What
you look at Mr. Frederick Augustus?" The verbal exchange helps to portray either Elizabeth's ignorance or her nonchalant demeanor about their
spectacle. Frederick Augustus responds to her request for clarity by lift-
ing his monocle to answer: "I look at dat White loafer wot [sic] looks at
me," rationalizing, "I guess he from New York." Clay created *Philadelphia
Fashions, 1837* to show the Hintons commanding attention through their
visibility, even as they are both too "ignorant" to comprehend the strange
impact of free people of African descent occupying northern territory and
enjoying consumer power. At the same time, Clay's depiction suggests
that the Hintons might have brazenly faced the White gaze, electing not to
look away and even querying the White right to stare at free Blacks.

In Clay's vision of Philadelphia, Black women expose a host of perceptual problems, and so his satirical cartoons re-presented free Black wom-
en's visibility as folly. Hinton's migration to the North and her marriage to
Frederick expanded her social network and her popular enjoyments; however, Clay printed Elizabeth's privileged life as humorous. Clay's reception of the Hintons as real people and his depiction of their class mobility
countered the stringent efforts of middle-class Black women to portray
upward mobility. Women such as Hinton and her friends monitored the
conduct of free Black women from the South, and policed one another
toward respectable habits in the interim.[50] These reformers intended to
protect their economic gains and their attempts at gaining citizenship
by regulating "attire and public conduct" among other African Americans, hoping to increase the value of Black womanhood and to redefine

Figure 3.5. Edward Williams Clay, *Philadelphia Fashions, 1837.* (Courtesy of The Library Company of Philadelphia)

mainstream concepts of "Black morality."[51] However, Clay's rendition of Hinton's notoriety peculiarly reflects the way in which Black people's attempts to censor one another's visibilities and performances of freedom (especially in terms of class and culture) failed to distinguish free Blacks from one another in the eyes of White onlookers. Whites who opposed emancipation also resisted changes in visual culture. Clay and other antagonistic Whites contested the conduct of free Blacks and expressed hostility at the possibility of the Black gaze confronting and objectifying a White subject. Whites judged privileged women like Hinton just as harshly as they judged poor Black women because, after slavery, the concept of Black womanhood knew no distinctions across class in the dominant imaginary. Essentially, slavery sanctioned sex and labor as signifiers of Black femininity, and this continued even in freedom. Accordingly, U.S. viewers struggled to reformulate the old picture of a supposedly enslaved lascivious Black woman into a new, progressive picture, that of the free, upwardly mobile "respectable" lady. For Clay, this picture meant a mix of material goods used to decorate an individual not far removed from slavery. Although the Hintons' relative wealth could buy them fine clothes, and perhaps even education, it could not raise their class to the level of Whites like Clay. Moreover, women like Elizabeth may have possessed their freedom and money, but they had no purchase on a credible visual practice; Hinton did not know how to appear properly in public, according to *Philadelphia Fashions*. Clay pictured free Black women as unable to perform "middle-class" belonging because they were really lower-class women in "drag." He imagined free Black women as dressed up but without any legitimate claim to middle-class identity or polite decorum.

Whites like Clay who watched a changing Philadelphia saw a number of free Black women selling their own labor and using the profits (no matter how meager) to change their individual lives and their communities. Clay produced the "Life in Philadelphia" series in order to reimagine these forms of progress. The colored lithographs inside marked by the vibrancy of aquatint used vivid shades of pinks, yellows, and blues to clothe the densely Black skin of Philadelphia city dwellers in jovial scenes of ignorance. With their money and their freedom, Clay pictured free Black people engaged in dance and leisure, outfitted in fine and elaborate clothes. Capturing their social interactions, Clay depicted formerly enslaved Blacks shopping for more garments and joining social organizations. Prints throughout the series invoked absurdity as the punch line for pictures of free people in scenes dissimilar to their "nature." Underscored by malapropic speech, this early serial Black caricature argued that free Blacks were crude and foolishly unable to see the incongruence between their race and their class aspirations.

The emergence of Clay's illustrations coincided with the popularization of Blackface minstrelsy in U.S. theater culture of the early nineteenth century. The often comedic, but sometimes tragic, stage performances of Black raciality, featured White actors donning painted Black faces to portray African Americans as lazy buffoons, much as they appeared in Clay's caricatures. Dale Cockrell offers a long historiography of Blackface minstrelsy that includes performances such as *Othello* in 1751, arguing that a countless number of Blackface stage shows entertained a primarily elite, educated, White audience of theatergoers up through 1843.[52] Although diverse audiences of nonelite patrons also grew to enjoy Blackface performances by later in the nineteenth century, nevertheless, this clientele may have had more access to leisure and disposable income than the consumers of Clay's cheap prints. The popularity of mimicking Black raciality quickly spread throughout the United States with performances like T. D. Rice's 1828 "Jump Jim Crow," the gesturing Black figure who "jumped just so"; Edwin Christy's 1843 troupe known as "Christy's Minstrels," and Stephen Foster's minstrel music for the parlor.[53] Clay's illustrations appeared in a growing context of White audiences' preoccupation with the objectification of Black racial difference as a form of entertainment; Clay contributed to these theatrical musings with his own illustration titled *Jim Crow*.[54] Each of these offerings made innovations in the representation of Blackness for popular consumption, standardizing the performance of Blackface as a genre through methods of voice, gesticulation, and narrative organization.

However, Clay's method of picturing freedom existed at the intersection of racial mimicry as an idea, and minstrelsy as a form of popular culture. His depictions ridiculed *specific* people such as the Hintons, inviting local Whites to poke fun at real people in their communities, all the while commenting on White concerns about free Blacks impersonating White privilege. Clay's materials served a seemingly benign need for popular enjoyment but also responded to anxieties about intimate public contact with free Black people. Marvin McAllister unpacks the "extratheatrical" practice of Whiteface minstrelsy, where African Americans assumed presentations of Whiteness through speech, dress, and "social entitlements."[55] These performances were not limited to theater venues because free Blacks in preemancipation New York also staged Whiteness and "White

privilege" on the street; "stylish Negro promenaders" dressed fashion-
ably for "social performances" that both annoyed and terrorized Whites,
particularly those who were not so well dressed.[56] Clay and his White
contemporaries worried about these instances where African Americans
assumed a posture of entitlement. Clay's body of work commented on the
belief that Blacks were involved in the racial mimicry of White people but
then also invited White parlor dwellers to mimic Black performances of
Whiteness in their own homes. Professional White actors who blackened
up for the stage were distant professionals, but Clay's cheap prints placed
the ability to mimic Black mimicry in the hands of White consumers.

Clay emphasized Black women as aspiring to White womanhood in his
caricatures, problematizing their demonstrations of class and sexuality as
impediments to freedom and integration. The "free" Black women shown
in four of the fourteen lithographs of "Life in Philadelphia, are purchasing
items, displaying items, or commenting on the purchased items of their
partners. In one scene from the series (figure 3.6), Florinda, dressed in an
elaborate yellow gown with a large headpiece, fans herself while compli-
menting her mate on his newly popular striped shirt, claiming that it made
him look like "Pluto de God of War." In this and every other scene in which
Black women appear, their presence in the image addresses some aspect of
vanity, or what Clay seems to understand as an unwarranted demonstration of pride. Either through their physical existence (always fully orna-
mented with fans, parasols, handkerchiefs, bright dresses, and headpieces)
or through their conversations, Clay's depiction of Black women is fixated
on their consumer power as it related to their visibility in stores, at parties,
and on city streets. In another image (figure 3.7), a much-decorated Black
"Madame" enters a stocking boutique, garishly dressed in a pink dress and
wearing a large blue hat with feathers and ribbons attached. She asks the
French sales clerk for a pair of "flesh coloured silk stockings," to which the
"young man" responds with an accent, to offer her "von pair of the first qual-
ite!" The comedy here is that she would want a pair of stockings that match
her "sooty" complexion, as well as the fact that this free Black woman dares
to waste her money on ornaments that do nothing for her attractiveness.
Clay portrayed "flesh"-colored items for Black women as laughable, suggesting that Black women forget/deny their distance from Whiteness and
White beauty when they use these standards to shop. Clay reinforced this
attitude with the inclusion of the disproportionately large hats that connote
the "big heads" or inflated egos of the Black nouveau riche. Similarly, those
who accommodate Black freedom are equally ridiculous. The Frenchman

Figure 3.6. Edward Williams Clay, *"How do you like de new fashion shirt . . . ?,"* 1828, "Life in Philadelphia" series. (Courtesy of The Library Company of Philadelphia)

who entertains this Black woman's patronage, as well as her loudly dressed sister who watches the transaction from the doorway, seem equally ridiculous. This scene pictures a free woman with purchasing power who cannot mitigate the built-in deficiencies of her appearance; social aspiring and consumer power do not suppress the problems inherent to Blackness. In Clay's concept of Philadelphia life, Black women's labor and their efforts to gain education translated to scenes of overindulgent self-importance that spilled over into obtrusive public appearances.

Figure 3.7. Edward Williams Clay, *"Have you any flesh coloured silk stockings . . .?,"*1828, "Life in Philadelphia" series. (Courtesy of The Library Company of Philadelphia)

Visual Differences

Racial caricatures like those portrayed in the "Life in Philadelphia" cartoons were a unique and powerful venue for Whites to contemplate the meaning of Black freedom. These items were unlike those found in any other print genre in circulation. Illustrators of the early nineteenth century depicted other kinds of differences that were also popular among audiences, but these works were distinct from attempts to *picture freedom.* Not yet deemed White, Irish immigrants also faced satirical depiction in U.S. and British print cultures during the early nineteenth century. In fact, the disparagement of Ireland's race, class, and religious identities was a specifically transatlantic phenomenon throughout the nineteenth century; British print media emphasized a hierarchal relationship to the Irish, who were personified in the caricatured figure of "Paddy," identified as "a Celt, a Catholic, and a peasant."[57] With the rise of Irish nationalism, U.S. audiences became increasingly interested in the "Paddy" figure, and by the 1860s, the pictorial representations of "Paddy" had changed from a harmless whiskey drinker to a gorilla-like rebel. These illustrations stereotyped Irish immigrants and characterized them as unfit for U.S. citizenship.[58] The unsavory rendering of Irish persons in print circulated in lithograph sheets and underground cartoon markets, but it also received national attention in major magazines like *Punch* (a British weekly) and *Harper's Weekly*. The image of "Paddy" portrayed Irishness as problematic, but illustrators also mobilized this character to comment on race at large with phenotypical comparisons to Blacks in charts that assessed head shape and size of facial features. According to these images, Irish immigrants and people of African descent represented difference that could be accounted for "scientifically." Cultural producers have used satirical graphics to lampoon various ethnicities throughout U.S. history; the Irish were among the earliest of European immigrants to see negative portrayals of themselves in early U.S. print culture.[59] This hostile reception of the Irish resembled the treatment of free middle-class Blacks, but the undermining of Irish efforts to assimilate into U.S. national belonging eventually started to decline late in the nineteenth century.

While racial caricatures helped create boundaries around what did not count as White, illustrations also introduced viewers to images that actively intertwined Whiteness and "Americanness." Through the "construction of vernacular heroes" in popular representations of Davy Crockett and Yankee Doodle, U.S. popular culture developed a racial dramaturgy that flourished within the era of Jacksonian politics.[60] In a period driven by an ideological division of the labor force across racial lines, Whiteness became pronounced in the production of White characters. Images of racial "types" served a social function by producing narratives of difference that were legible even to the illiterate. Images of difference became popular signifiers of U.S. culture in that these images circulated within the context of a burgeoning mass media, as sense-making demonstrations about the cultural changes happening within the developing nation.[61] In fact, the media industry emerged in a climate attempting to understand racial and ethnic variety, becoming an active vehicle in the early U.S. conceptualization of difference. This context cannot be divorced from explicit racialization that happens through media culture. Image producers helped to make the Whiteness of "Americanness" explicitly clear to viewers through popular culture and the circulation of racial attitudes. Regardless of which racial type appeared on the page, these items together helped cultivate the sense that difference is salient, even when not explicitly focused on Black people.

Caricature, then, as a way of familiarizing the public with social difference, addressed gender distinction as well, something that White women's-rights activists discovered when they sought inclusion in the public sphere.[62] Caricaturists ridiculed White women like Lucretia Mott and Frances Wright (who befriended free Black women of Philadelphia). The behavior of white women activists who organized and participated in women's conventions and assumed prominent public roles as speakers and debaters was often regarded as inappropriate by men and women outside their activist circles. Lecturing may have been especially problematic as an overt demonstration of "looking" or critiquing others from a podium, and thus White women, too, threatened a visual culture invested in the notion of an invisible seeing subject, figured as White, middle-class, and male. Accordingly, illustrators reacted by repositioning these women on cheap pages in unflattering positions. Caricatures derided both the political platforms and physical appearance of poltically active White women.

Despite these negative examples, White women still saw a number of positive representations of themselves circulating in nineteenth-century print culture. Media producers constructed White women as the prototypical woman and as the audience for parlor literatures. In addition to hostile illustrations, White women appeared in another distinct set of depictions as printers targeted them as a niche market. For example, Godey's Lady's Book, produced in Philadelphia in 1830 by Louis Antoine Godey, circulated monthly as a magazine intended specifically to entertain the growing group of literate White women. In addition to biographical sketches and articles on hygiene, handcrafts, and mineralogy, Godey's prominently featured descriptions of fashion accompanied by "colored plates." Editors paired vivid illustrations with short suggestive commentaries on lady's attire, so that viewers could see and create dresses of "rich emerald green" and "blue gaze St. Vallier" (figure 3.8).[63] Often, women in these depictions ignored the image spectator with "empty expressions" and distant gazes that relegated them to "a closed society or separate sphere."[64] In plate after

Figure 3.8. "Philadelphia Fashions," *Godey's Lady's Book,* January 1833.

plate of what Godey titled "Philadelphia Fashions," White women "modeled" clothing for readers, affectionately detailed in descriptions of the various promenade dresses, walking dresses, and so on. Isabelle Lehuu argues that *Godey's* was a significant popular material because it printed women on the page, whereas previously they were absent. Issuing images of "elegant and delicate ladies," *Godey's* disseminated a feminine aesthetic that many White women so enjoyed that they examined the pages, then tore them out "to decorate middle-class homes."[65] Thus, *Godey's* provided White women with opportunities to consume flattering portrayals and hands-on experience with representations of White womanhood that differed from satirical caricatures. This monthly magazine depicted White women as figures for decoration but also issued images of White womanhood as adornment for the parlor. *Godey's* valued White women's bodies, and under the editorship of Sarah Josepha Hale, the magazine became a place for "syncretic, multivalent embodiment," allowing Hale and other White women to negotiate their own "public corporeal presence" through the magazine's materiality.[66] White women's encounters with print culture were distinct from those of Black women because of the existence of items like *Godey's*—such items actively addressed White women consumers, acknowledged their centrality to the parlor, and even empowered White women like Hale to design parlor literatures.

Racial caricatures that ridiculed free Black women represent an important outlier in a print climate focused on White women. White parlors featured images of Black women as sources of amusement and mockery, not as decoration or as beautiful muses for the latest fashion. Black women provided White viewers with a canvas for working out various anxieties and White fears about the power of looking. Clay's cartoons depicted Black women in styles that mimicked *Godey's* ladies, with dresses drawn in detail to relay the particulars of the fabric and the embellishment. Different from *Godey's* ladies, however, Clay's "colored women" wore clothes that undermined gender conventions among free Black women and suggested their lack of sentiment. He placed free Black women outside the burgeoning United States by illustrating African American women as figures who demanded attention with ostentatious appearances. Clay's cartoon *Philadelphia Fashions* (figure 3.5), discussed above, takes its title from *Godey's* to depict a focused and well-dressed Elizabeth Hinton but uses malapropic Black dialogue to distinguish Hinton from the White women of the ladies' magazine. Similarly, while *Godey's* printed more than fifteen colored plates of "Philadelphia Fashions" between 1830 and 1836, the White women depicted in the drawings rarely face forward on the page or offer up their gaze directly to viewers in the manner of Clay's representation of Elizabeth. Clay mocked the Hintons and free Blacks of Philadelphia by suggesting that their version of "Philadelphia Fashions" was unlike *Godey's* idea of style in the City of Brotherly Love.

The simultaneous occurrence of Clay's *Philadelphia Fashions* and *Godey's* "Philadelphia Fashions" reveals the extent to which images about

Black freedom were contextualized in a larger visual culture from the onset. Clay's "Philadelphia Fashions" called upon consumers to know the difference between the styling of a free Black couple who had trouble seeing how they appear to others, and the styling of White women in *Godey's Lady's Book*. Popular political cartoons resonated with audiences through their use of enthymematic form to reflect the values and attitudes of the viewers.[67] Racist caricatures succeeded in gaining popularity because they accounted for a wide array of audience concerns. Picturing Black freedom becomes important among all of these other portrayals because people of African descent represent the Other within the early nineteenth century, distinct from ethnic immigrants. While caricature represented a rite of passage for all people marked as different in the early republic, U.S. viewers were also accustomed to representations of African descendants appearing in prints that undergirded slavery. Different from "foreign" newcomers, people of African descent had lived in close proximity to White Americans for more than a hundred years by the 1820s. Moreover, whereas the printing business represented an entrepreneurial opportunity for early Americans, ethnic immigrants also took up the business of printing and circulating hostile images of African Americans—a business Black people would not get into until the twentieth century.[68] Accordingly, racist images of free African Americans were special in an unflattering manner. Black freedom seemed to upend slavery's peculiar ocularity, and thus, in an era of unrest with regard to defining a national political culture, U.S. popular culture experimented with ways of seeing itself through developing new ways of seeing people of African descent.

Picture and Perception

Picturing freedom helped Whites retool dominion over the visual in response to their fears of Black emancipation. Clay's materials represent the anxious need to reclaim the power of "looking" through the deployment of lowbrow entertainment. With advances in media technologies, Clay's depictions of Black freedom circulated across a wide and diverse swath of viewers, satisfying the needs of both middle-class and less affluent Whites. Since graphic humor is undeniably critical in nature, using satire to portray depicted figures as unlike the illustrator, racist caricatures offered an opportune site for middle-class Whites to cope with anxieties about the end of slavery.[69] Clay's caricatures taught White viewers that free African Americans maintained unlearned and insurmountable racial deficiencies that would permanently bar them from national belonging. In agonizing over emancipation and the potential of a Black middle class, Clay's narrative of African American women's visibility created a unique position for them in White parlors. Clay moved African American women into parlors as objects of ridicule in print. Clay's work offered middle-class Whites the opportunity to share the space of the parlor with African Americans, but not with Black women who read, kept albums, and wore fine garments. These illustrations maintained slavery's visual hierarchy and its organization of White superiority just as gradual emancipation seemed to threaten this order. In the "Life in Philadelphia" cartoons, Blackness became something to look at and compensated for experiences on the street where free African Americans could return the gaze. These cheap amusements circulated a narrative of free Blacks as overreaching their racial essences. In an effort to maintain the drawing room as a space for Whiteness and for middle-class refinement, Clay's curriculum on the meanings of Black freedom emphasized free women's lack of sophistication as the basis for their inability (lack of right) to occupy the parlor. While northern state governments contemplated how to move out of a slave economy, the preponderance of Black women seeking privilege and comfort meant that the parlor was a permeable barrier. Domesticity, as symbolized by the parlor, seemed threatened with expansion of free Black communities, and by free Black women who ignited questions about the nation as a home for Black people, and about domesticity as the sovereign domain of White women.

Clay's works were part of a larger social fabric coping with the evolution of Black visibility and a growing free Black population some thirty years before the national abolition of U.S. slavery. The "Life in Philadelphia" series countered the visual tactics of middle-class Blacks, showing African American women as unladylike. While women of the free community worked to educate one another, Clay used the details of their lives for pictorial ridicule. Some of Clay's images documented actual occurrences in antebellum Philadelphia, but he skewed them in order to restore the significance of Whiteness in visual culture. His cartoons portrayed Black women as devoid of any kind of self-consciousness or purposefulness about their appearances. Despite the strenuous efforts of free Black women, Clay issued images that excluded these women from concepts of middle-class identity. His representations taught viewers that Black women were purely visible, incapable of complex or critical relationships to public perceptions. More, his illustrations suggested that the visible changes among free people exemplified all the ignorance and caprice that warranted their enslavement. Clay's caricatures undermined the idea of Black spectatorship by contributing to a visual culture that cleaved to institutionalized dynamics of slavery. Clay's images, much like the friendship albums, represent another tangible manifestation of looking practices that made ways of seeing palpable and teachable for others. His images expanded throughout other northern cities and became national representations of Blackness at a crucial moment in a fraught political climate. These caricatures in particular inspired additional parodies of Black freedom. Collectively, these items confronted and assuaged White concerns over the visual logic of race that slavery helped to institute. Just as the unwelcome sight of free Black communities became increasingly consequential, cultural producers found ways to maintain these linkages and to skew the mainstream perception of Black freedom at the same time.

The very simple fact that a free Black woman could curtail the birth of new unfree people made her freedom and her security of greater significance within the U.S. landscape. The class positions occupied by Black women were all the more relevant to an uncertain political and economic climate. Elite Black women combined both freedom and the means to control their own appearances, refusing the visual and socioeconomic organization of race in the early republic. Black women in the North now commanded gazes in public simply by being free, even as slavery continued throughout the country. Whereas the peculiarly ocular institution hinged the economic fate of Whites on a "slave" class, Black women saw few, if any, progressive renditions of pictures of freedom in media circulation. In response, Clay's materials appeared as one of the first and most poignant portrayals to use class to problematize Black freedom in the U.S. popular imagination.[70] In response to their unflattering portrayals, African Americans invoked what became a double-edged sword to ensure their detractors that Blacks were safe and trustworthy. Many Black writers and purveyors of the Black press sought to demonstrate the community's worthy character to White detractors by documenting free people's involvement in building the nation. External to their segregated enclaves, free middle-class Blacks worked together with White abolitionists to reframe the derogatory discourse about Black freedom. Free Blacks in the antebellum North remained caught in a quagmire, imagined as having too much material gain to live peacefully on the one hand, and yet lacking the political advantage to live autonomously on the other.

4

Racial Iconography: Freedom and Black Citizenship in the Antebellum North

Ruminations on the abolition of slavery and increased numbers of free Black people in northern U.S. territories hastened White concerns about the national home. A changing Black presence in the North inspired anxieties about the meaning of U.S. citizenship, even as many people of African descent contemplated emigration to other locales, such as Mexico and Liberia. The parlor as a nation space represents the cultural boundaries around people fit for belonging in the United States as a home interior. Many free and elite Blacks engaged ideals of citizenship through honing literacy skills and forging media platforms. Conversely, Whites against Black national belonging accelerated negative portrayals of freedom, increasing the number of hostile caricatures in circulation. The parlor as nation space speaks to the ways in which audiences envisioned Black national identity in parlor literatures. Domesticity in this parlor meant questions about Black citizenship—about comportment, middle-class aspiration, literacy acquisition, and access to the justice system. While many African descendants addressed these questions by using education and print, many Whites portrayed Black freedom through images of improper decorum. Black people emphasized argumentation, while Whites continued to fetishize Blackness as hypervisible. The parlor as a home, then, became host to an array of methods for picturing freedom, many of which buttressed one another.

Black Visibility in the North

Set in a New York "police office," a group of White men watch over a quarreling trio of free Blacks in a court-like scene (figure 4.1). Elevated above the Black characters, White men in the image manage books and writing implements, even while their eyes remain fixed on the disagreement. One white onlooker grabs a lapel to hold back the complainant, a Black man who waves his fist at the other. Facing his opponent, the first man exclaims, "my name is Antonio Ceasar de Wilson, I have been paying a visit to Miss Araminta Arabella Towson in de oyster celler where she live, where Massa Sambo came in and say 'you have no business here.'" Wilson's malapropic diatribe muddles Sambo's title, the second Black man on the page, but his cry is a clear indication that Minta has been entertaining more than one visitor in her basement dwelling. Part of a series of eight prints titled "Life in New York" issued by the French-born lithographer Anthony Imbert, these images portrayed self-important free Blacks in various city scenes. Illustrators indicated the swaggering and pompous nature of Black freedom with subtle details like the exaggerated shirt collars in this image, which appear in sharp contrast to White men's dress, as well as with Black men's confrontational postures.[1] Wilson goes on to explain that he looked "at Miss Minta and she say I have [the right to be there]," before he and "this gentleman," the other Black man, "have a tussle." The melee that ensues between Wilson and Sambo is both an argument over Minta and a disagreement about a token of her affection. The stand-in for a more explicit description of Minta's sexuality is a handkerchief, which Wilson argues "is not his [Sambo's], but one Miss Minta made a present of it to me." Although Miss Minta is the catalyst for this disagreement, she has no words on the page to explain her own position. Instead, her other suitor fills in the narrative and even speaks for her. Sambo explains, "I can ensure you that Miss Araminta did give me the witching glance, which told me as plain as eyes could speak that I was the more welcome visitor." Miss Minta's "witching glance" welcomed Sambo's affection, and thus he understands that the "handkerchief it is Miss Minta's" and that he has "a better right to it than this other gentleman," since Sambo has "presented to her a scissor, a thimble and a lock of my hair."[2] Miss Minta stands idly by, with a fan and parasol in tow, watching her lovers quarrel in the police station. This squabble about Black "Life in New York" put Black women at the center of conflict among free Black men, as the central impediment to Black men's assertion of civic participation.

Hostile racial caricatures about free Black people pictured freedom in scenes of illegitimate social practice, excluding African descendants from belonging to a still-coalescing U.S. national identity. Imbert's image suggests that Whites believed free people of African descent in

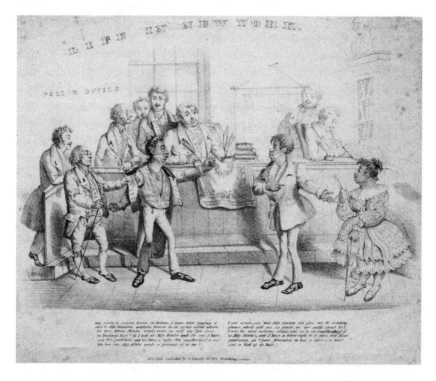

Figure 4.1. My Name Is Antonio Ceasar . . . , by Dominico Canova, ca. 1830, "Life in New York" series. (Courtesy of the Library Company of Philadelphia)

preemancipation New York used public institutions to resolve petty grievances. While the White men in the background deliberate over important documents and serious matters (one White man in the far right corner cannot be bothered to watch), the troupe of free Blacks in the forefront squabble over promiscuity. Moreover, although this Black woman is present in the image, she is nonverbal and of no assistance—her presence is merely ornamental. Cartoon images like this New York scene joked about Black popular culture, but they also featured many serious symbols of national identity including the legal system, all of which coincided with notions of statehood. The composition of these images organized a comparison between free Blacks and free Whites. Imbert employed various artists to illustrate similar scenes for his "Life in New York" series, where free Blacks engaged in ridiculous scenes of polite social activities and duplicated the failures of their Black friends in other northern cities. Illustrations in the set ridiculed free Black New Yorkers for imitating the social appetites and forms of dress associated with White high society. Images portrayed middle-class Black New Yorkers in fitted coats and military-style hats to distinguish themselves as well-off, setting themselves apart from lower-class Blacks and poor Irish immigrants. Black women caused conflict among free men in multiple "Life in New York" plates where they render Black men cuckold in simultaneous courtship with multiple suitors. Like their sisters in Philadelphia, Black women of New York frequently betrayed their lovers at social gatherings as they pursued the affection of other men; in fact, Black women cultivated their feminine wiles specifically to deceive male suitors. In terms of space on a page, determined through the mass of the image or the lines of text, Black women make up a significant portion of visual commentary in the "Life in New York" series, even in instances where they are not the focal point of the story line.[3] Through picturing Black women as fixated on public occurrences and life on the city street, these racial caricatures positioned free women as central to much of Black impropriety and to the failure of free people of African descent to integrate into the domestic space of a national home.

This chapter explores Black visibility in public culture to think through picturing freedom as a means of conceptualizing nationhood. Federal law did not address the legality of Black citizenship until 1857, with *Dred Scott v. Sanford*, but political and popular cultures circulating around the 1830s collectively built on the same sentiment: some Black people might be free, but none of them qualified as citizens with protection under the U.S. Constitution. Here, I show how seemingly disconnected materials like racist caricatures, Black newspapers, and abolitionist material cultures aligned through an inability to elide slavery's visual culture. Common ideas about the public are central to this discussion, especially to the extent that these concepts undergirded gender norms in the free Black community. The Black public sphere of the early national era revered institutions as vital to mounting a prolific literary tradition and promoting a collective, self-determined Black consciousness against "white appropriation."[4] Whereas these choices were decisive, over and above an "individualistic artistic vision," I want to take up the implications of such a public as relevant to picturing freedom. I am interested in the scant number of visual appeals to freedom produced by free Black people, particularly when the social relationship between Whites and Blacks was "mediated by images," and caricatures reported free Black bodies as spectacular.[5] The relative success or failure of a Black "counterpublic," steeped in institutional organizations and print culture, is a related, but not central focus of my discussion.⁶ While scholars recognize rigid notions of the "public" as a fallacy, derision of free Black people in the early republic often emphasized their lack of literacy, rationality, and ability to own property when so many people of African descent remained the property of Whites. Myths of the public were important for Whites who were hostile to picturing freedom. Ridiculing images of free Blacks such as the "Life in New York" caricatures pretended the existence of a Habermasian "public sphere" to emphasize dialogic exchanges among literate, rational men of the White middle class as well as "commodity exchange and social labor."⁷ Ideas about the public were also ideas about domestic belonging, making comportment in social scenarios central to ideas about Black people's national identities.

Hostile illustrations of freedom emphasized Black women's domesticity as a hindrance to Black national identity. In what Martha Jones has termed "African American public culture," women made claims to political rights, but the most acceptable demonstrations of "female influence" happened when Black women portrayed free people's investments in self-improvement.⁸ In the first section, I explore women's visibility and the largely argumentative approach to picturing freedom that prevailed in early African American public culture. Although Black women's labor as organizers and teachers was central to the establishment of Black institutional life, inhibitions about the Black body, and women's bodies in particular, diminished efforts to *illustrate* freedom. Black women's engagement with public and print cultures of the early nineteenth century represents the multivalent management of visibility. These women needed to be visible in ways that served the free Black community but avoid public recognition at the same time. Accordingly, I argue that Black women's visibility in public culture was also indicative of attitudes about racial visuality at large, in both Black and White communities, and unfortunately, curbed the power of a prolific antislavery press.

I connect ideas about visibility in African American public culture to the propaganda of the U.S. antislavery movement. These items perpetuated slavery's construction of the Black body as susceptible to touch and visual scrutiny. Moreover, although they intended to suppress chattel slavery, antislavery imagery did not offer any clear pathways toward imagining Black people as free or as citizens in the aftermath of abolition. Antislavery images were less successful at picturing freedom than were anti-abolitonist images, which I describe in the third section. While Black and White activists issued texts against slavery, printers like Imbert circulated images against freedom. While Black abolitionists used print to ruminate on national belonging, caricatures portrayed a "black upside-down world" and an illiterate "nonbourgeois community" of people of African descent.[9] When abolitionists sought to familiarize Black freedom with emphasis on education and civic participation, illustrators hostile to emancipation successfully linked unfavorable pictures to a language of illiteracy. In the fourth section, I discuss the way in which anti-abolitionists seized the image of Black freedom, rather than Black enslavement, to marginalize free Blacks from domestic belonging. "Anti-abolitionist" media targeted Blacks in the urban North "who shared the same space with northern Whites and sought the same things—jobs, housing, opportunity."[10] These cultural producers were successful because they combined print and visual cultures in complementary ways, and they portrayed Black freedom as a spatial problem with which Whites needed to contend. In the final section, I describe picturing freedom across the North, to illustrate the way in which elements of caricature, such as malapropic speech, created an indistinguishable mass of free Blacks, serving to both mimic the efforts of specific free communities, but also to cultivate a general idea about U.S. Blackness.

Picturing freedom as contrary to the nation, and to the justice system in particular, communicated Black freedom as extralegal and outside the realm of citizenship. The legal system was central to the evolution of Black-White relations in the North, and African Americans in New York City frequently sought legal redress in their grievances with Whites. Some of the most significant demonstrations of Black freedom appear in the historical records of New York "police offices," in which White New Yorkers often felt perplexed by the ways in which both free and unfree Black people interacted with the law. For example, records indicate that Blacks in New York complained about violent owners to the police, arrogantly ignored the law when committing crimes of theft and arson, shrugged off judges' prison sentences, and sued Whites for unpaid wages.[11] Even for free Blacks in New York who lived in the interstice between slavery and citizenship, the law figured into civil status. Lawmakers ratified an uneven schema of gradual emancipation in the state, following the Pennsylvania example, so that by 1827, Black men and women born after July 4, 1799 were free at the age of twenty-eight and twenty-five, respectively.[12] Accordingly, the Black population of New York City, "which was never very large," represented a number of concentric circles of free and unfree people, growing in size from the turn of the century through the 1840s.[13] Whether enslaved or free, Blacks had been taking up their issues with the courts for decades before emancipation came to the state. African descendants explored institutions of national belonging, with real and imagined interactions with the law figuring prominently in popular perceptions. Illustrations such as the "Life in New York" scenes acknowledged the real occurrence of Black people appealing to public institutions, but they minimized these significant acts by suggesting that Black people remade symbols of citizenship into trivial emblems of self-importance.

Collectively, image makers for and against abolition organized a visual culture in which viewers rarely, if ever, saw images of free Blacks behaving as U.S. citizens. By 1830, images like the "Life in New York" caricatures were appearing in major cities throughout the northeastern United States, especially in cities with prominent populations of Black activists. The founding of the American Antislavery Society (AAS) in 1833 marked the institutionalization of immediatism as a relevant, but still radical, position among U.S. antislavery activists. Although many Black abolitionists, especially women, were advancing radical calls for immediate, not gradual, ends to slavery in the late eighteenth century, the organizational promotion of immediatism in the 1830s carried with it a highly prolific propaganda machine that spread this message throughout the Atlantic world.[14] The publicity efforts associated with abolition added to the visibility of free Black communities, even as White antislavery activists often marginalized Black abolitionists and tried to define the tone of Black activism. Nonetheless, hostile Whites in cities with identifiable Black neighborhoods, Black institutions, and Black protest rhetorics circulated images meant to undermine a burgeoning African American identity. In New York, Boston, and Philadelphia, for example, free African Americans established reading groups, orphanages, debate societies, homes for the indigent, private schools, and other kinds of institutions to support poor Blacks. These establishments helped to anchor identifiable Black enclaves in the North and to constitute a notable African American public culture that emphasized literacy and mutual-aid efforts to support newly free Black people. In the establishment of this public sphere, people of African descent also flooded northern cities with paper. The landscape of early-nineteenth-century print culture is one wherein Black visibility is at once a marker of progressive values among White abolitionists and the impediment to Black national belonging.

"Educate Your Children—And Hope for Justice"

African American public culture displayed a curious attitude toward visibility and representations of the body in the earliest decades of the nineteenth century. In the creation of their own print media, few people of African descent incorporated depictions of the body in their antislavery tracts or political documents. In particular, members of the free middle class typically promoted verbal, not visual, arguments for the end of slavery.[15] After more than one hundred years of seeing the Black body printed in advertisements for slave auctions or fugitive capture, Black people printing their own documents may have felt that the proliferation of texts that accentuated the Black body would have only compounded the rampant problems of representation. When the popularity of racist caricature accentuated the Black body as key to excluding free people from U.S national identity, what role could the Black body play in African American print culture? Uncertain of the answer, many writers diminished Black corporeality in the pages of the Black press and in other forms of print media, promoting freedom in ways meant to distance themselves from slavery's vision of Blackness as pure embodiment. Deemphasizing the Black body represented a new prerogative of the free person who could exercise autonomy in ways denied to the enslaved, by covering the body with clothes or by deemphasizing the body as a counterpart to Black publicity. Emancipation, in part, meant that free Black people could exist as selectively public, rather than forcibly public.

Although African American public culture emphasized language and literacy over images, the speaking body and Black oratory were central elements of the antislavery lecture circuit. Formerly enslaved African Americans were popular speakers because they could recount firsthand experiences of slavery. For example, Sojourner Truth, the Black abolitionist and women's-rights activist, famously bared her breasts on the public speaking platform, authenticating her womanhood and her enslavement to proslavery attackers in the audience.[16] Similarly, other abolitionist speakers like Henry Bibb offered a sense of authenticity at the lectern with the live recounting of personal experience with slavery, combining the affects of eloquent speech and the pained body for antislavery audiences.[17]

However, this coupling of the body and the spoken testimony did not translate to early Black print culture, which largely maintained an aversion to reproducing free bodies on the page. Instead, many early free African Americans considered English literacy and argumentation as primary modes of civic engagement. Free Black people of the middle class welcomed language as a barometer for gauging one's fitness for civic inclusion because they could hone rhetorical agility through literacy and debate education. Toward these ends, free African Americans institutionalized efforts to improve literacy through the establishment of schools, reading clubs, debate societies, and venues for publication. Elite and free Blacks publicized literacy as a way to advocate for the abolition of slavery. Working on language skills was also a response to a set of material circumstances. African American rhetoric in the early nineteenth century was undoubtedly "about the problems of speaking," as the processes of transatlantic slavery problematized African dialects and outlawed the full acquisition of English literacy.[18] Black speech was politicized by way of (en)forced dispersal and (en)forced ignorance through the middle passage and the proliferation of slavery. Thus, many free Blacks attended to literacy as a means of dealing with the consequences of enslavement. Free African Americans valued speech acumen and literacy for the ways in which these skills prepared them to advocate for the abolition of slavery, as well as for the experience of living as free. Blacks of the middle class heavily invested in educational opportunities, believing that social and political advancement of the race depended upon a well-educated gentry.[19] Many of them treated education as an uplift strategy to coincide with organizations that addressed poverty and destitution. Elizabeth McHenry argues that African American literacy societies were essential to the promotion of activism and the creation of Black citizenship. These societies provided spaces to develop the literacy skills necessary to advocate for national belonging, as well as the opportunity to demonstrate preparedness for U.S. citizenship as a concept steeped in language and argumentation.[20]

Print culture was a necessary counterpart to these educational efforts because it provided a medium for disseminating ideas about politics and helped characterize the development of national identity for Black people. Publication venues enabled free African Americans to contemplate the nature of citizenship with one another and to disperse those conversations across a wider swath of territory. Such discussions were important because many free Blacks were uncertain about staying in the early United States, even as hostile Whites imagined Black freedom to mean an overarching desire for permanent residency. U.S. national belonging seemed like a complicated possibility to many Black people, and "Africa," as a concept, remained central to how many Black elites imagined U.S. citizenship. A commitment to African ancestry appeared in various kinds of institutional practices, especially churches, which took on names such as the African Episcopal Church or the African Methodist Episcopal Church. Similarly, African Americans in New York included African cultural traditions in their funeral practices, and in parades to commemorate the close of the transatlantic slave trade. Black New Yorkers acknowledged African heritage as early as 1809, when they discussed Pan-Africanism and spectacularly declared a separate kind of freedom with Fifth of July celebrations.[21] African culture was a value that marked a distinct experience of the United States for Black people but also fueled discussions of emigration to other places in the Diaspora, such as Mexico and Haiti.[22] Over time, however, many elite Blacks considered commitments to Africa as counterproductive to their claims for national belonging. The idea of leaving the United States had become increasingly controversial by 1816 in the face of colonization schemes mobilized by the American Colonization Society (ACS) to send Black people "back" to Liberia.[23] African Americans continued to debate the possibility of emigration, but these discussions also became opportunities to express verbal commitments to the United States as a permanent homeland. African American public culture became an important tool for combating organizations like the ACS, as well as for contemplating emigration as a real possibility. However, the nefarious reputation of the ACS created suspicion around relocation to Africa, making Blacks who favored emigration appear unaware of the implications and traitorous to the larger Black community.[24]

Black men were at the helm of nationally circulating print culture in the free community beginning in the late eighteenth century, as they regularly used publication opportunities to speak on behalf of Black communities. Free Black men publicized their claims to freedom in "petitions, speeches, pamphlets and broadsides" that cited founding documents like the Declaration of Independence, revealing familiarity with tenets of U.S. nationalist ideologies and threatening White supremacy at the same time.[25] David Walker's *An Appeal to Colored Citizens of the World*, written in four "articles" with a preamble, mimicked the format of the U.S. Constitution.[26] Walker's *Appeal* emerged in a context comprised of literary societies and reading groups that provided free Blacks "with opportunities to practice and perform literacy" and the chance to "experiment with voice and self-representation" for the development of national identity.[27] African Americans who independently printed their seditious claims to freedom simultaneously asserted ties to the nation with petitions to the First Amendment. A number of prominent free Black men were expressly active in the production of literatures that promoted the abolition of slavery, confronted the U.S. legal system, and questioned notions of nationhood. In fact, "between the 1790s and 1860s," African American men issued a prolific "Black protest culture," taking advantage of new technologies to print their speeches, sermons, and arguments in pamphlets and newspapers.[28] Men of means such as Frederick Hinton of Philadelphia and Charles Lenox Remond of Salem funded papers and created their own prints. Similarly, James Forten Sr. used his influence and education to protest legislation prohibiting migration among free Blacks throughout the state of Pennsylvania in 1813.[29] With the wealth earned from his sail-making business, Forten also helped to finance the startup of both the first nationally circulated African American newspaper, the *Freedom's Journal*, in 1827, and the radical abolitionist periodical the *Liberator* in 1831.[30] Free Black men in particular represented the separate, but simultaneous, existence of a Black public with the development of several U.S.-based Black newspapers including the *Colored American, National Era*, and Frederick Douglass's *North Star*, each serving as a platform to rally against slavery, to contemplate national identity, and to publicize Black literacy. Free African Americans founded more than forty newspapers before the Civil War, although most of these ventures failed thanks to insolvency, harassment, infighting, and illiteracy.[31] Some papers were short-lived, such as the *Aliened American*, while others, like *Frederick Douglass' Paper*, produced more than two hundred issues.

Despite amassing such a robust platform of publicity, most African American newspapers avoided illustrations altogether, but especially depictions of Black bodies. The *Freedom's Journal* largely eschewed images of African Americans, instead printing images that connoted education and self-improvement. The image of sheet music propped up in a scene of leaves and musical instruments (figure 4.2) identified the poetry section of the newspaper and appeared in the paper on a regular basis.[32] Similarly, items like a crest that appeared in the *Aliened American* with the caption "Educate Your Children—And Hope for Justice," vaguely illustrated bodies at work. The poor quality of the image makes it difficult to discern racialization in it, although the paper's stated purpose— "To furnish News: To favor Literature, Science and Art: To aid the development, Educational, Mechanical and Social, of Colored Americans"—makes it likely that the editors intended to represent African Americans with this illustration.[33] To some extent, cost might have determined these printing choices because images added to the expense of producing a periodical,

Figure 4.2. "Poetry," *Freedom's Journal,* February 22, 1828.

with wood engraving being the cheapest choice.[34] Newspapers such as the *Freedom's Journal* regularly printed images of objects, such as clocks or other items taken from stereotype books, but illustrations related to the body remained noticeably absent.[35] Papers such as the *Colored American* eventually published images of people, including representations of other ethnicities. One complex scene, *Britannia Giving Freedom to Her Slaves* (figure 4.3), depicts people of African descent on the verge of freedom, showing an unfree Black man set among other unfree Black women and children. Although his head is bowed, the man stands to face "Britannia," who wears warrior clothing and decrees Black freedom.[36] The image accompanied a story recognizing the coming emancipation of enslaved people in the "British West-India Islands," and the end of apprenticeship.[37] The African American news circuit paid close attention to abolition in the Caribbean, and this writer wanted to emphasize the productive outcomes of focused agitation and to refute stories of "disorder, or evil effects of any description" that may have circulated. Although this image did not offer a vision of Black freedom divorced from slavery, the illustrator managed to represent the symbolic process of emancipation without reiterating the submissive or suspicious cues in the kneeling slave emblem or the runaway notice. In general, the images that appeared in Black newspapers

BRITANNIA GIVING FREEDOM TO HER SLAVES.

Figure 4.3. Britannia Giving Freedom to Her Slaves, in *Colored American*, May 9, 1840.

were rarely images of free Black bodies and were rarely representative of the people who produced the papers.

African American opinion leaders pictured freedom in ways that often perpetuated slavery's curious organization of Black visuality. An emphasis on print publicity and deliberation avoided the Black body in ways that reasserted slavery's peculiar construction of Black corporeality. Rather than illustrating the free body speaking at the lectern or stenciling portraits of the prominent Black abolitionists of the time, print producers instead often focused on disseminating powerful words. This trepidation on the part of Black editors and writers was entirely warranted as the advancement of printing technologies in the early nineteenth century also increased the number of negative depictions of the Black body in circulation. Lithography advanced the circulation of caricatures as well as newspapers and advertisements for runaways, such that appeals to the visual in this climate might have seemed most problematic for free African Americans. Visual representations of free African Americans could call the body into peril by putting free people on display in the dangerous context of slavery. In a visual culture that readily enlisted Whites to search for Black people, free African Americans focused on the printed word as a primary tool for political change to follow national practices of publicity.

At times, cultural producers compounded notions of racial hypervisibility by diminishing the free Black body in protest literatures. Representations of the free Black body would largely have to wait for the advent of the daguerreotype, when artists could create re-presentations of freedom without the overt prejudice of the hand. Frederick Douglass considered representation and lamented the inability of White artists to produce "impartial portraits" of African Americans "without most grossly exaggerating their distinctive features."[38] Douglass shared the period's hopefulness about depiction and investment in photographic technologies—a value he revealed by sitting for numerous portraits. However, Douglass remained skeptical about the possibilities entailed within print images of Black people. Sarah Blackwood points to an important comment in the *North Star* masthead, where Douglass offered an explicit critique of the runaway icon. Blackwood explains a revision in the form of a free Black man, replete with stick and bundle; Douglass references the fugitive icon "only to explode it" by showing the figure with his back to the reader and his arms spread open toward the North Star.[39] The layout of the image reveals Douglass using his paper as a direct confrontation to the visual constructions of Black freedom in circulation. This instance did not stand as the permanent masthead, however, Douglass and many other African American media purveyors rarely illustrated free Black people in the pages of their papers.

When so much of public culture emphasized the Black body as a major impediment to national belonging, African American opinion leaders turned to verbal agility and argumentation to make claims to citizenship. Efforts to promote literacy were, in part, measures for deemphasizing the body as an insurmountable distinction. The body represented a site of difference that education and abolition could not easily mold into new conceptions of national belonging. The body—the highly ridiculed marker of racial difference—remained threatened by enslavement, and many African Americans did not want to draw additional attention to it through illustration.

This problem with the visual might have tailored the ways in which Black women contemplated citizenship in print. Arbiters of African American public culture considered Black women as vital for companionship to Black men, and essential to instilling education and religion in children.[40]

Although the nation struggled with the idea of women's public speaking, across race, Black women faced unique limitations on their activism and their writing. Slavery rendered Black women's domesticity inconsequential, so that in freedom, many elite African American men overemphasized the need for Black women to work within mainstream gender norms. At the same time, whereas slavery threatened both free and unfree Black communities, Black women's activist labor was essential to its eradication. African American communities needed Black women "within" the home, conceptually, to suggest a commitment to true womanhood, but also needed them in organizational roles outside the home. Such conflicting attitudes made political participation difficult for prominent women such as Maria Stewart, who lectured to mixed-gender audiences in Boston before reproach toward her as a public-speaking woman forced her from the city.[41] Uncovering the literary history of African American women writers and their contributions to antebellum "black resistance movements," Carla Peterson argues that Maria Stewart "specified" the cultural work of Black women who were already excluded from Black men's social institutions and White women's organizing efforts by the 1830s.[42] Pigeonholed within social institutions "constructed to deny women access to power," Black women of the middle class experienced a "double bind" in antebellum public culture.[43] White racism, even in abolitionist circles, suppressed Black women's contributions to antislavery conversations, while elite Black men overinvested in the politics of respectability to diminish Black women's involvement in political conversations.[44]

Such prejudices compelled some Black women to seek alternate avenues of publicity. Many women turned to literacy and debate organizations such as the Female Literary Association (1831) in Philadelphia, or mutual-aid associations such as the African Dorcas Association in New York (1828), where they discussed problems with education but also prepared for formal education.[45] In addition to informal opportunities for learning, Black women teachers studied "religion and philosophy, literature, writing, basic mathematics, Latin and French, and the mechanical arts," in preparation for teaching Black children, who also began learning in formal school settings by 1830.[46] These efforts were essential to Black women's involvement in the public campaign to represent Black freedom as viable and nonthreatening. Many freeborn Black women like Sarah Mapps Douglass, who contributed to friendship albums, also used their literacy skills to eradicate slavery. These women were pioneers of immediate abolition, writing protest literature to antislavery periodicals in advance of the AAS.

Their poems and essays are yet another way that free Black women used mainstream print cultures in transformative ways.[47] Similarly, Jarena Lee and Zilpha Elaw published their spiritual autobiographies using their own funds after facing controversy about women in the pulpit.[48] Women like Lee, Elaw, and Stewart faced criticism for their approaches to public discourse because Black men imagined them as trespassing beyond the boundaries of the woman's sphere. Even with optics of respectability at work among elite free African American women, they could not overhaul reservations about the body in public culture with this critical viewing practice. Even as free women understood Whites to experience complex feelings of envy and distrust about free Black bodies, the reality of peril during the antebellum period meant that elite African Americans often publicized freedom without further exposing free people to surveillance or visual scrutiny. Although free Black women produced a set of coping mechanisms for ways of seeing one another within the parlor, slavery's organization of Black visibility required continued trepidation, especially in public encounters outside of Black homes. While African American editors of the Black press limited coverage of women to stories that dispelled "unsavory images" of free people, Black abolitionist women used inventive approaches to communicate about freedom and slavery in other spaces.[49]

These production choices left the practice of pictorial representation of the Black body up to White producers of abolitionist propaganda. Problematically, whereas images function as shorthand cues, legible even to the illiterate, African American print culture did not educate a national readership on how to visualize Black activists or free Black people. Black newspapers promoted a progressive picture of citizenship with an overemphasis on literacy and other disembodied tactics. Middle-class African Americans alternated between predetermined notions of acceptable appearances and invisibility, each as a measure used in service of framing freedom as a positive event for the nation. This is not to say that an emphasis on literacy was unimportant or apolitical in the antebellum era. Instead, elites of the free Black community used words to create an image of African American citizenship.

Free Blacks made choices about visibility that coincided with the philosophies of visuality developed in their parlors. Printing their own protest literature allowed Black abolitionist men to distinguish their opinions from integrated antislavery organizations like the AAS, which relegated them to tertiary leadership roles (instead of higher-ranking positions) even as Black capital played a vital role in organizational development.[50] The "separateness of Black publicity," expressed in new institutions and mass demonstrations, made a notable impact on national politics in the early republic by revealing a noticeable practice of self-segregation from White exhibitions of nationhood.[51] These acts of publication and publicity in Black culture blatantly disregarded the concerns of Whites that Blacks were out of control and feeling self-important. Though the collective speaking and writing about slavery may not have induced immediate emancipation, these efforts began to instantiate ideas about African "Americaness." Words and texts became important elements of national identity as an African American rhetorical tradition solidified. Different from personal print materials circulating among a few homes of the Black elite, African American newspapers exposed observations on prejudice and slavery to national audiences. Although African American public culture revealed new ways of seeing the Black self, it neglected publication as an opportunity to demonstrate new methods for picturing freedom.

The Black Body in Antislavery Prints

White antislavery organizations mounted an image-rich propaganda program—in the form of petitions, broadsides, and pamphlets—to suppress slavery, problematically promoting Black freedom via pictures of enslavement. Despite their good intentions, "abolitionist" and "antislavery" print cultures failed to really picture freedom or contemplate Black citizenship.[52] Transatlantic abolitionists sought to reveal slavery as horrific through images of captive bodies and the crude tools of enslavement, circulating propaganda to create a sense of witnessing for viewers.[53] The AAS issued a prolific print campaign, printing annual *Antislavery Almanacs* that depicted enslaved Blacks sold at auction, stripped from their children, and even committing suicide to escape slavery. Although these items offered powerful revelations about slavery, Black freedom served a curious role in this agenda, as emancipated Blacks often appeared bereft and forsaken to support this antislavery schema (figure 4.4).[54] Although Black abolitionists on both sides of the Atlantic were central to efforts to abolish slavery, antislavery visual culture rarely depicted free Black people to balance these other portrayals. Antislavery literatures increased the manner in which the bonded Black subject appeared ubiquitously in print cultures of the Atlantic world. These media disseminated a splintered message—a

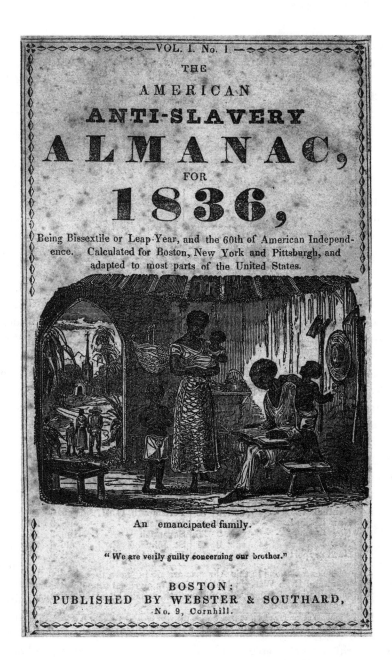

vision of the enslaved Black body as an enthymematic argument for the promotion of emancipation.

Many antislavery illustrations emphasized the pained and subjugated Black body. Coming out of the late eighteenth century and British anti-slavery conversations, U.S. abolitionists took up three very important portrayals to develop an iconography of antislavery activism. Images such as the "famous" cross section of a slave ship overloaded with bodies, as well as the series of pictures produced in clusters "depicting whippings and other punishments of slaves" or atrocities, represented antislavery's "journalistic" approach to portraying the Black body in print.[55] The British potter Josiah Wedgewood offered the third and most powerful emblem, intending abolitionists to wear his "Kneeling Slave" ceramic cameo as a sign of support for this cause.[56] This item quickly became the icon of transatlantic antislavery activities. The "Kneeling Slave" made its print culture debut in the United States when it appeared in the *Genius of Universal Emancipation*, but the image continued to appear throughout various antislavery newspapers and served as a moniker for abolitionist organizations throughout the North. This prominent item alerted White social movements to the symbolic value of the Black body. Within the domestic dealings of the home, the supplicant harkened sentiment and reflected a sentimental interiority back to parlor dwellers. In the realm of political activism outside the home, activists who adorned themselves in the iconography of abolition displayed themselves as radical agitators with a tangible commitment to the antislavery cause.

The "Kneeling Slave" was perhaps the most reproduced symbol of the abolitionist movement and extended to material and print culture items in the parlor. The image of a subjugated man or woman promoted the end of slavery by showing people of African descent in an unthreatening manner. Much of antislavery propaganda employed this iconography to question the morality of slavery by displaying the inhumanity and brutality of the peculiar institution. At the same time, the supplicant's question, "Am I Not a Woman, and a Sister?" implored sympathetic Whites to promote abolition without simultaneously increasing White fears about Black insurrection.[57] The image of the "Kneeling Slave" spread throughout the parlor, appearing on "furnishings and fabrics, depicted on transfer-printed china on the tables," as well as "portrayed in illustrated books" shelved in the parlor, "printed on stationery for the mistress's writing table and even worn on the body itself."[58] In these other reproductions, the "Kneeling Slave" referenced the Black body, but interpellated White

Figure 4.5. Angelina Grimké's wedding purse. (Courtesy of Clements Library, University of Michigan)

activists to understand themselves as the ones to grant humanity and bestow abolition. White women abolitionists used the "Kneeling Slave" to imagine themselves as "empowered, sanctified uplifters" coming to the aid of a "helpless debased [Black woman] victim."[59] For her wedding to the abolitionist Theodore Weld, Angelina Grimké adorned herself with a wedding purse that featured antislavery images (figure 4.5).[60] One side of the purse displayed the well-known "Kneeling Slave," but the opposite side of the bag featured a lesser-known depiction of a grieving Black mother. The woman sits in a tropical setting, with mountains and a palm tree in the background, and a hut on the horizon. She holds her head and looks down at what appears to be a deceased infant. The abolitionist nature of the image is rather curious since the image does not clearly indicate the woman is in bondage with common cues such as shackles. Moreover, because the woman sits in what might be thought of as a kind of "nativist" setting, it is not clear that she has been stolen from a homeland or placed into captivity. Instead, the image evokes sentiment by commanding grief for mothers of African descent, employing the Black mother as worthy of sympathy. Read as the reverse side of Grimké's antislavery handbag, this image of transatlantic Black motherhood is part of her sentimental ensemble. It does not indicate where in the Diaspora this woman exists, but shows that she is worthy of White sympathy. In the act of wearing the purse, Grimké put her sentimental White hands on the bereaved Black mother and the shackled supplicant. Wearing the purse at her wedding, Grimké displayed her sentimental commitments to abolition as she took her wedding vows, symbolizing White women's virtue by wearing the Black woman's body. Materials like these enhanced the sensory experience by combining print's impulse of circulation and visuality's inherent representability into a tangible form.

These material interactions between White women and antislavery imagery reveal the complicated existence of the Black woman's body in the context of transatlantic abolition. Rigid notions of a "woman's sphere" demanded that women remain invisible from the public, although White and Black abolitionist women pushed these boundaries with antislavery fund-raisers and fairs.[61] However, whereas the concept of a "woman's sphere" as outside the public remained a popular notion, the widely circulated "Kneeling Slave" image of a bare-breasted Black woman in chains traveled throughout the Atlantic world, further publicizing the Black female body. While this body served as a means of gaining "rhetorical force" and invited White women into antislavery activism, this representation in particular contributed to two specific problems for *free* Black women in abolitionism.[62] First, although the "Kneeling Slave" represented antislavery activism among both Blacks and Whites, these images often circulated alongside texts of African American public discourse. The combination of pictured slavery and voices of Black abolitionists created a problematic synergy through associating the words of Black protest with an image of imploration. Where African American abolitionists were quite vocal within the pages of the antislavery press, White editors illustrated this rhetoric with the image of a kneeling supplicant who inquired about his or her humanity rather than asserting it as fact. For example, papers like the *Liberator* coupled Black women's abolitionist rhetoric with the "Kneeling Slave's" beseeching question: "Am I not a woman and a sister?" African Americans throughout the North frequently contributed abolitionist writings to the *Liberator*, especially Black abolitionist women, like Sarah Forten of Philadelphia, who wrote entries for the *Liberator*'s

LADIES' DEPARTMENT.

'Am I not a Woman and a Sister?'

☞ Our word for it, there are few young white ladies who can prepare an essay for the press with more accuracy in regard to orthography and punctuation, or written in a more beautiful hand, than the following, by a young colored lady. We beg for other favors.

For the Liberator.

UNNATURAL DISTINCTION.

I have often thought of the distinction made in places of *Public Worship* between white and colored persons, and have wondered that the latter should humble themselves so much as to occupy one of those seats provided for them.

A reverend gentleman who addressed the audience at Franklin Hall on Monday evening last, in speaking on this subject, said, ' If such seats were pointed out to *white* persons on entering a House of Worship, they, instead of occupying them, would instantly leave the house.' It is reasonable to suppose they would. And why should we submit to

Figure 4.6. "Ladies' Department," *Liberator,*
July 28, 1832.

"Ladies' Department."[63] However, for the nineteenth-century reader specifically looking for contributions by Black women abolitionists, identifying the supplicant, unclothed Black female body on the page also became the way in which to identify Black women authors within a field of other writings (figure 4.6). The abolitionist seal as a moniker imprisoned *free* Black women in chains through the verbal and visual tropes that left the power of advocacy in the hands of Whites.[64] Amid rampant anti-Black racism in the antislavery movement, African American women barred from organizations such as the Boston Female Anti-slavery Association remained politically active despite hostility from groups that claimed to act on their behalf.[65]

The second, and perhaps most troubling, consequence of this means of representation was that free Black people and Black abolitionists found themselves without the support of pictorial representations that had already proven so central to transatlantic conceptions of the Black body by the 1830s. Readers who consumed prints by Black abolitionists rarely enjoyed the words of their favorite writers alongside depictions of the individual. The absence of corresponding pictures of freedom meant a blow to publicity efforts for Black freedom campaigns because activists often relied on slaving imagery. Middle-class and literate Blacks who acted in communities, whose words readers could easily find in print culture, appeared in public discourse without any kind of representative illustration. Forten and her activist friends combined women's concerns for education and religious worship with explicitly political questions about emigration and immediate emancipation in the *Liberator*. However, neither the likeness of a Black abolitionist woman nor a generic image of freeborn Black woman ever accompanied their writings. White abolitionists like the *Liberator* editor William Lloyd Garrison duplicated the aversion to the free Black body that appeared elsewhere in popular culture so that the visual practices taking shape within the folds of antislavery media venues blurred the image of freedom.

A few prominent images of free people of African descent circulated in transatlantic print culture, and in correlation with Black-authored abolitionist texts, but these materials often represented remarkable individuals rather than a compendium of Black freedom fighters. Generally, frontispiece portraits of slave narratives functioned to verify the authenticity of the account, while also calling pointed attention to the contrast of an unwieldy enslavement and the formality of portraiture.[66] Frontispiece portraits demonstrate the poise and status of the author, but they also reveal the way in which slavery's peculiar visual culture demanded that people of African descent authenticate or verify themselves by offering up their bodies for examination. Phillis Wheatley, the poet and first published woman of African descent, would have her likeness attached to her book *Poems on Various Subjects, Religious and Moral* in 1773, as an engraved frontispiece. The artist, perhaps Scipio Moorhead, an enslaved man of African descent living in Boston, depicted Wheatley as seated at a writing desk, with implement in one hand, and the other hand to her chin as if in contemplation.[67] Wheatley's portrait served as a confirmation of her ability to think and write, even as the engraving featured various inclusions intended to mark Wheatley as unfree, including her being identified in the title as "A Negro Servant to Mr. J. Wheatley of Boston." Houston Baker describes Wheatley's portrait as "revolutionary" in that it upended conceptualizations of enslaved Black people who lived for "gross manual labor" by day or spent "their nights shuffling to the sound of exotic banjos."[68] An image of a Black poetess, captured by a Black artist, might not have been enough to prove that Wheatley authored her own work. Skepticism about Wheatley's ability to author required that she seek publication in England, and that she defend herself at trial before eighteen White men of esteem—including Massachusetts governor Thomas Hutchinson, as well as a number of slaveholders and clergy.[69] Whites doubted the authenticity of Wheatley's authorship, as well as the quality of her writings. Thomas Jefferson, one of Wheatley's most prominent detractors, expounded upon his distaste for her poetry, citing her work as "below the dignity of criticism"; he added that despite exposure to Western civilization via slavery, Blacks had yet "uttered a thought above the level of plain narration" or "an elementary trait of painting or sculpture."[70] Jefferson was unimpressed and unconvinced by Wheatley's poetry because he could not believe in a fecund Black visuality. The combination of words and images did not urge Jefferson toward a picture of freedom. Similarly, when the freeborn Black astronomer Benjamin Banneker sent Jefferson a written letter about the immorality of slavery to accompany his almanac for 1792, Jefferson again refused to acknowledge that neither conditions of slavery nor the "natural" characteristics of race predetermined Black peoples' intellectual abilities.[71] While slavery organized Black bodies as subject to authentication and circumspection, the combination of text and images could not accelerate the validation of Black intellect.

Graphic portrayals of individual free Black people did not evolve the cultural disposition toward Black freedom, overall. Unlike fine art, popular-culture depictions of freedom would have been supremely important. Ephemeral productions of free people could reach a larger swath of viewers in the early republic. Whether as lithograph prints, rented or sold in local shops, or as newspaper images that circulated across state boundaries, pictorial imagery that appeared in cheaply and readily available media became essential to campaigns about the question of slavery. Eventually, prominent Black abolitionists used imagery to describe fugitivity in "major slave narratives," spectacularly recasting "the iconography of slave escape," but these takes on the Black body perpetually avoided fixing the image of the free person to the permanence of the page.[72] Although news media offered the power of editorship and the cloak of pseudonymity, free African Americans and White abolitionist sympathizers avoided illustrating the likeness of the free Black subject who actively participated in the antislavery movement. Instead, popular depictions such as the image of the cross section of the slave ship along with images of slavery's shackles and neck clamps represented the human beings for whom the diverse antislavery movement imagined itself an advocate. While antislavery supporters intended for images of Black enslavement to work enthymematically, to inspire concern about the inhumanity of slavery, most antislavery pictures carried other, unintended consequences, instead perpetuating notions of the Black body as "insensate," inherently able to withstand slavery's abuses, as indicated in the association with cruel objects.[73] Items used for enslavement connected the Black body to other things, either by force or by habit. While abolitionist propaganda represented slavery's mistreatment of the Black body, these images utilized problematic visions of Blackness in order to criticize Whites. Rather than depicting Whiteness to critique White social practices, these items continued to rely on Blackness as representable, as a thing available for visual subjugation. Once again, antislavery media culture failed to propose visual arguments against slavery that presented viewers with the means to receive Black freedom.

Anti-Abolitionism

Illustrations that countered antislavery activism offered a much more robust narrative of Black freedom. These items described abolitionism as threatening, and situated antislavery activism within the domestic confines of the home to comment on the space of the nation. For example, Edward Clay's "Practical Amalgamation" series proposed national suspicion toward Black and White abolitionists, showing that the organized movement to end slavery and emancipate people of African descent also enabled Black people to fraternize with Whites and infringe on Whites' personal space. Clay's body of caricature was explicitly anti-Black. However, images in his "Practical Amalgamation" series also targeted abolitionism as an idea, as well as White abolitionists for their interracial socializing. Clay imagined all mixed-race, mixed-gender gatherings on behalf of abolition as opportunities for interracial sex. Clay's "Practical

Figure 4.7. Edward Williams Clay, *An Amalgamation Polka*, 1845, "Practical Amalgamation" series. (Courtesy of American Antiquarian Society)

Amalgamation" series represents a larger assault on interracial marriage in politics and popular culture of the early nineteenth century, discrediting antislavery projects with devout "anti-abolitionist" perspective on interracial sex as a chief motive of abolition.[74]

Clay issued the "Practical Amalgamation" series over time, starting in 1839, and made his case through scenes of mixed-race liaisons, often between Black men and White women at social gatherings with dance and music. In these settings, Black and White abolitionists are equally culpable in their sexual desire for physical contact with one another. Items like his 1845 *An Amalgamation Polka. Respectfully dedicated to Miss Abby Kelly* [*sic*] portrayed a host of prominent antislavery activists (figure 4.7). This scene of interracial pairings shows White men dancing with Black women, and White women collaborating with Black men. Abby Kelley Foster, the abolitionist and (White) women's-rights activist, is shown dancing with Frederick Douglass; similarly, Maria Weston Chapman and Garrison appear dancing with unidentified African Americans.[75] While this and many other of Clay's images featured actual abolitionists such as

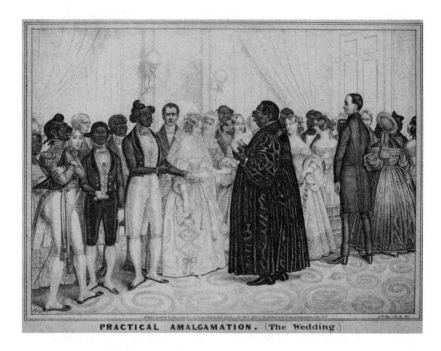

Figure 4.8. Edward Williams Clay, *Practical Amalgamation: The Wedding,* ca. 1839, "Practical Amalgamation" series. (Courtesy of American Antiquarian Society)

Garrison and John Quincy Adams, the absence of specificity around Black women functions to obscure real women as objects of White desire—perhaps Clay's own.

Sex was central to how Clay treated the U.S. abolitionist movement. The pornographic nature of some of his explicitly anti-abolitionist prints resulted in the indictment of print sellers who intended to distribute scenes of lewd interracial sex, especially one plate featuring sex with a Black woman.[76] Interracial sex is an escalating act in these prints, beginning at social gatherings but leading up to interracial marital unions, such as the one depicted in *Practical Amalgamation: The Wedding* (figure 4.8). In such prints, lustful Black men hover over White women amid parlor furnishings. Whereas the withdrawing room was imagined as a sanctuary to protect White women from the abuses of the street, in anti-abolitionist imagery the abolitionist parlor represents a setting for interracial trysts. Not only is the antislavery rendezvous an opportunity for intimate physical contact, but Black and White social mixture serves as a precursor for interracial procreation. In figure 4.8, a Black man marries a seemingly forlorn White woman with a Black reverend presiding over the cere-mony as a mixed-race audience watches over the abolitionist nuptials in a carpeted-parlor. Tavia Nyong'o argues that sex, as much as politics, was a central feature in the polar relationship between abolitionist and anti-abolitionist depictions of the Black body. The "Practical Amalgamation" series countered the U.S. abolitionist movement's "rhetoric of violated, feminized blackness" and Black abolitionists' promotion of respectable "appearances" with images of sexual aggressors driving the antislavery movement.[77]

Although Clay's specificity about particular abolitionists along with his collusion of sex and politics were important elements of his anti-aboli-tionist work, perhaps none of these alone were as significant as his ability to locate abolition and its consequences in specific settings. Scenes from Clay's "Practical Amalgamation" series place interracial fraternizing in specific locales such as the ballroom setting for the *Amalgamation Polka* or the waltz. Yet, the most disturbing scenes of antislavery's peculiar lust for racial hybridity happened in the domestic space of the parlor. Much of Clay's work imagined that abolition accelerated racial mixture in order to corrupt the private interiors of U.S. homes by enabling free Blacks to have sex with Whites and reproduce children of "mixed-race" ancestry. In scenes like his *Fruits of Amalgamation* (figure 4.9), the parlor setting is as important as any single character in the image, showing the upside-down world of the abolitionist interior as host to a number of inappro-priate interactions. While a White woman nurses her "Negro" child, her husband sits on their plush sofa, rests his feet in her lap, and reads the *Emancipator*, the abolitionist periodical that eventually became Benjamin Lundy's *Genius of Universal Emancipation*.[78] Such problematic liaisons fill the image page as Garrison enters the parlor with a Black woman on his arm while a Black and White dog huddle together over a copy of the *Age of Reason*—an indirect critique of abolitionism's suggestively irrational reliance on religious morality. These images reveal the material culture of the parlor and its architecture as complicit in the private encounters among abolitionists. In this well-appointed home, replete with carpets and footstools, a White man is the servant, entering the room with a tray of refreshments. Theater culture appears in the background as one of the couple's haughty enjoyments, depicted in a framed portrait of Othello and Desdemona hanging over the couch. The setting for race mixture is every bit as problematic as the abolitionist activists who occupy the space.

THE FRUITS OF AMALGAMATION.

Figure 4.9. Edward Williams Clay, *Fruits of Amalgamation*, ca. 1839, "Practical Amalgamation" series. (Courtesy of American Antiquarian Society)

Moreover, the room wherein such intimate encounters can occur represents a world of corrupted domesticity, where Black men trample over White women's bodies, and thus White women's virtue. Clay argues that the domestic interior, both personal and national, that entertains abolitionism is also willing to entertain interracial sex, Black middle-class aspiration, and White servitude.

Clay's commentary on domestic interiority, then, was also a comment on the nation and the larger transatlantic world as a kind of domestic interior. Abolition's impact on social relations, sexual desire, domestic decorum, White women's chastity, and Black men's political power, were all problems of the early republic and the organizing strictures of the transatlantic parlor as a cohesive space. Clay's anxieties about the impact of abolitionism extended beyond a focus on Blacks in the United States; he imagined a transatlantic Blackness by drawing upon the Diaspora to picture Black freedom implicated in a fiendish and international plot of sexual domination. In Clay's *Johnny Q., Introducing the Haytien Ambassador to the Ladies of Lynn, Mass* (figure 4.10), he depicts a swooning huddle of White women, enamored by a bowing gent who smiles and tips his hat to the ladies.[79] The

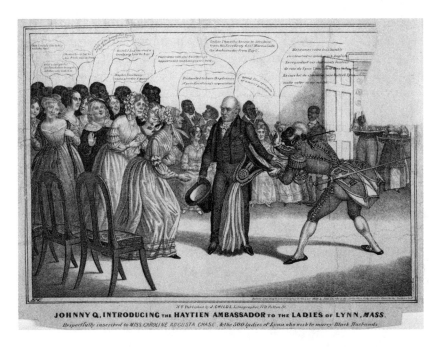

Figure 4.10. Edward Williams Clay, *Johnny Q., Introducing the Haytien Ambassador to the Ladies of Lynn, Mass.*, 1839. (Courtesy of American Antiquarian Society)

ambassador's large posterior and phallic sword signifies his sexual prowess, underscoring the lascivious nature of the amalgamation series. In a malapropic mangle of French and "Anglish," he refers to the "rose buds ob Lynn" who "make vater in [his] mouse." The ambassador lusts for these White women abolitionists, much as they yearn for him and any other Black man available. To this image, Clay added a dedication to "Miss Caroline Augusta Chase & the 500 ladies of Lynn who wish to marry Black Husbands." John Quincy Adams is all that stands between a cadre of eager White women and the Haitian ambassador, introduced to them as "Gen. Marmalade." A group of eager Black men waits in the background as the White women compliment Marmalade's "perfume" (his scent), and refer to him as his "Excellency!" From left to right, the image sandwiches unsuspecting White women and Adams between the robust sexual desire of Black men in the United States and this eager General Marmalade.

Clay's illustration reveals that Haiti's revolution and the stories of Black male revolutionaries such as Toussaint L'Ouverture loomed large in the White imaginary, not just in the minds of African Americans. Although

Clay did not name L'Ouverture in the illustration, many lithographic depictions of the Haitian leader appeared in transatlantic print culture. Images such figure 4.11, which pictures the triumphant leader on horseback wearing military regalia and wielding a sword, were readily available from print sellers as early as 1802. Clay's Marmalade does not clearly signify L'Ouverture or his successor, Jean-Jacques Dessalines, but rather an archetypal Black revolutionary working to abolish slavery from elsewhere in the Atlantic world. While in the United States, people of African descent were thinking of Haiti and its revolutionaries as important examples of resistance, Whites like Clay mobilized the idea of the transatlantic Black revolutionary to promote fears about racial impropriety.[80] Anti-abolitionist images caricatured Black types to underscore Black freedom as disastrous for the nation writ large, but also to attach such concepts to a larger Atlantic world that existed beyond the domestic confines of the national parlor.

Freedom Follies

Hostile pictures mixed disproportioned bodies with malapropic patois and broken English to delegitimize Black freedom. Racist caricatures that ridiculed free Black communities in New York, Boston, and Philadelphia shared many similar characteristics and worked in concert with one another to portray free Blacks as unfit for inclusion in concepts of U.S. national identity. With the expansion of print culture technologies, negative portrayals of free Blacks inundated major northern cities and portrayed free communities as visually overwhelming. The gradual growth of free Black communities remained remarkable in the early nineteenth century, but pictures of freedom exaggerated the impact of emancipation by increasing the appearance of free Black people in the cultural imaginary. These items ignited a disproportionate set of understandings about Black freedom as cartoonists fantasized that small cadres of free people were immensely large and powerful.

Spectacle as a "condition" resulted from the supposedly innate Black ways that free people engaged the public—loudly, flamboyantly, and without regard for White onlookers.[81] While many elite free people of African descent focused on verbal developments to represent a new Black visuality, their efforts reappeared entirely skewed in mainstream print cultures as hostile Whites portrayed the free community through satirical

TOUSSAINT LOUVERTURE

Figure 4.11. Toussaint Louverture, 1802. (Courtesy of Moorland-Spingarn Research Center, Howard University)

illustrations. These images purposefully misrepresented the simultaneous practices of publicity among the Black middle class. Accordingly, strategies of diminished visibility in African American public culture and the focus on textuality did not suppress the powerful impact of racist illustrations. Caricature succeeded by seizing portrayals of the free Black body and using these images to depict freedom as overwhelming the Northeast, and by implication, the United States. Caricatures used the fact of Black visibility as "a symbolic substitute for substantive" economic and political power; these items diminished opportunities to think about other material forms of empowerment by insinuating that Black progress was already out of hand.[82] With the popularity of racist caricature, free women of African descent appeared everywhere, were seen by everyone, but with no thorough attention given to the character of their individual appearances.

Caricature images of Black Bostonians offered them no distinction from Blacks in New York or Philadelphia. These images positioned free Blacks in the North as displaced southerners, or as "Black Rednecks," who moved north but retained an "aversion to work, proneness to violence, neglect of education, sexual promiscuity, improvidence, drunkenness," and a commitment to "reckless searches for excitement, lively music and dance."[83] Local caricatures of Black people in specific cities represented them as a collective body with a common penchant for visual display. These items promoted White anxiety about Black visibility, associating exhibitions of freedom with public consumption. Together these images portrayed a *northern posture* toward freedom and positioned free Black people as unfit for northern life, evidenced in the ways they failed to fit into northern public spaces and social customs. These types of portrayals of Black New Yorkers intended to present the free middle class as self-important, and expanded the anxiety about Black freedom to another locale. They likened Black New Yorkers to Blacks in Boston and Philadelphia by emphasizing their fixation on the trappings of middle-class identities, such as fine clothes and dance lessons. Collectively, these images provided a sense of what the ascertainment of leisure meant for people of African descent; they provoked anxieties about freedom and posed a number of unsettling questions about the possibilities latent within emancipation. Are middle-class African Americans *better* or *better-off* than Whites? If freedom also functioned as a conduit to middle-class status, should free Blacks also be candidates for national belonging? Plates in the "Life in New York" series attempted to avoid these new questions about free people as citizens by continuing to make salient any characteristics that connected Blackness to slavery. These images showed Black raciality as constituted in the absence of visual literacy to preempt further contemplation about emancipation.

Even in the North, however, the social implications of emancipation remained muddled by slavery's ocularity, obscuring the demographic and structural impact of Black freedom. The 1830 census documented some 2,328,642 "Blacks," of whom 2,009,043, or 86.3 percent, were enslaved. Census counts, despite some discrepancies, indicate that many Blacks living in the United States lived in slavery, outnumbered by the 10,532,060 Whites accounted for on the census for that year.[84] However, Whites who focused on the space around them or who conceptualized the North as a discrete entity might have held different conceptions of U.S. demographics by race. Although the 5,417,167 northern Whites outnumbered the 125,214 people counted as "Black" on the census in 1830, the census listed 122,434 of these African descents as "free."[85] By the numbers, free Blacks in the North outnumbered enslaved people, but they remained outnumbered by Whites as a group. Moreover, free Black people were the smallest population until the U.S. census added additional categories to count Native Americans, Asians, and Hispanics for the 1860 census. Although the enslaved population in the North declined each year, the number of enslaved Blacks tallied on the national census increased every census year, from 697,681 in 1790 to 3,953,760 in 1860. These numbers reveal that free Blacks were not exactly "taking over," demographically; free Black people remained far outnumbered by the number of Blacks still living in slavery, and free people comprised a smaller proportion of the entire U.S. population, moving toward the Civil War.

Picturing freedom remade the existence of free Black communities into opportunities for amusement. Illustrations that ridiculed free Black people described them, their behaviors, and their self-perceptions as problematic. Specifically, anti-Black caricatures framed Black speech and Black appearances as contrary to acceptable notions of polite decorum. Most specifically, in each northern city noted for a prominent Black abolitionist population, Whites acting against the expansion of free communities circulated negative portrayals of local Blacks. Regionally specific depictions of free Black people challenged local populations and undermined free people's attempts to organize free communities. While free Black people developed organizational structures to help their poor and promoted the abolition of slavery, Whites living in northern cities produced negative renditions of these same activities. For example, White Bostonians hostile to the idea of emancipation enjoyed some of the earliest instances of racial satire with the dissemination of "Bobalition" broadsides. These items, produced between 1816 and 1837, ventriloquized Black public discourse through written "mispronunciations and malapropisms" that mocked annual celebrations of freedom among Boston's free Black community and the July 14, 1808, legislation to legally end the transatlantic slave trade.[86] "Bobalition" broadsides, large printed sheets of text and images, used mocking pictures of Black people and images of speech to portray the notion of Black civic engagement and political equality as ridiculous and nonthreatening. Items announcing the "Splendid Celebration. of the 'bobalition; of Slavery, by the African Society" (figure 4.12) used pictures of free Blacks dressed in full military gear and a parody of Black speech to illustrate a parade celebration of abolition. With three columns of malapropic text, the broadside shared a narrative of failed formality among free African descendants, planning events to happen in "Bosson, Uly 14, 1823." The author of this material portrayed a satirical performance of free Black consciousness that was intended to undermine specific groups of free Black Bostonians. For example, the broadside included a complaint against "De Colonization Shocietee" for its unwillingness to let free Blacks live and die in the United States, then "go to de spense of bury um." Such finely detailed provocations directly targeted groups such as the African Society, a Boston group of free Black people who organized to provide funeral benefits and life insurance to other members of the free community.[87] Examples like this reveal the way in which artists and illustrators confronted specific Black Bostonians with negative imagery, much like cartoonists in Philadelphia, while also generalizing all free people of African descent. Black Bostonians held annual demonstrations of an emergent national identity as early as 1808 with festivals and parades to celebrate the close of the transatlantic slave trade.[88] Items like "Bobalition" broadsides took issue with these elaborate proclamations of national belonging, but also with the establishment of institutional organizations to help deal with the social inequalities of freedom in the aftermath of slavery.[89] The "Bobalition" broadside circulated to delay and deny Black people's claims to national identity. "Bobalition" broadsides responded to the festivals, parades, banquets, and church services celebrated among free Black Bostonians by suggesting that these events were superficial declarations of self-importance. Amid the pomp and circumstance illustrated on the page, the Black characters celebrating "bobalition" can hardly enunciate the specifics of their excitement as the image of phonetic (mis)pronunciation underscores their ridiculousness.

Splendid Celebration.

OF THE
"BOBALITION"
Of Slavery, by the African Society.

General Order.

BOSSON, Uly 14, 1823, and little }
more dan half, }
To de Sheef Marshal of de day de President of de Society send he most superbitous complement, GREETING:
SIR,

I hereby send you a copy of de constructions which are to gubern your conduck on dis more horsepicious annibersary. You will take ticakelar care to call at my office in Nightshade Row, sactly at seben o'clock, little fore or little arter, as de almanack maker say, where I tell you more bout um dan what you tink of now.

SAMBO SMASHPIPES, Pres't.
Per order, CESAR GRAFFO, Sec'ry.

P. S. I send you de following regular toste and boluntares, which will be drunk on dis blessed occashun.

TOASTS.

De day we keep as Jubumlee—May he not come too often, so we get too much on de bre d, and raise de debil like some uder folks wa know about.
70 cheer—Moosic, "Pau he civil."

Uncle Sam—'saw ne got twenty-four posts to he house, hope he no let " Alexander de Rusty" deliver his ole de stuy cattle on de common outside of he own big cowyard.
Moosic—" Who come dare ?"

De tate of Massachusetts—Like frog she jump from de Brooks, and t-ll de publicans, when he tink she for bait, and catch de fish, yours 'tis.
Moosic—" Governor's March!"

" De man of de people"—Why de debil de people so say so stead of de newspapers?
Song—" Governor's coach coming along.

De Mayor of Bosson—Ah! he debil of a hard horse for some folks to ride.
300 sober look—no grin—Song, " Clear de way."

Gubernur Brooks—Ah! bress he old soul!—may he neber want butter to spread on a Medford cracker.
700 cheer, grin all round demoud.

De Militia—Spose he put a pompoo on he leather hat—he keep he long feather for china duster to gib he wife.
Moosic—March away.

De memory of Misser Peter Guss—If he no lis fo see our selfishcalum, who know but what he good old soul fly ober our head, and grin like cheesy-cat to see how glad we be?
Na cheer—Solemn Dirge.

De reward of old boot-black, street-sweeper, and so fort—If he no catch um here, where de debil he go to catch um in tudder world, long side of " poor Yorick ?"
Moosic—" York you're wanted."

De fourteenth of Uly, 1876—Hope dat sellybrashun find our great big little grandchilleun happy as we be now, and de houses so want to be repaired.
Song—" Gross way off at sea."

De Fair Sec—Ah! when we tink of dem, bress our hearts, we forget ebery ting else.
Song—My tub is I be der see.

De king of France—Whas he send his army into Spain, guess he dident stop to reckon how many snow-balls it take to heat an oven.
Song—" Ore de mountains as we creep."

De king of England—He no more like Massa President Monroe dan trow your hat in one corner of de room and no pick um up again.—Wander if he great too got well of de gout yet ?
Moosic—" O what anguish."

De new mill-dam—Spose massa Emmons deliver oration dere once a week, how long he take fore mid-der man make well, and get fresh water in de middle of de ocean ?
De land of our forefaders, Africa—
Breathes dere de man mid soul so dead,
Who wouldn't break de rascal's head,
Who steal de nigger from he land ?
De day—it be de Sunday of African glorificashun—Let us fill de cup of New-England—toke up de moosic of de banjoe, sing good song to our faders, and den go to bed and rest.
7000 cheers and half

De liberty of de press—He like great fire, which sooner or fasser will burn up de liberty of mankind, and de Hartford Convention long wid um.
Song—" De street was a ruin."

De African School—Hope de sun of science still shine on um, but pot so hot as to scorch de head of de little scholar, and make um forget all he ought to member.

VOLUNTEERS.

WESS-BOSSON—May de tinte soon come which he no longer be disgrace to de City, and make de brack man brish for de white people's debility.
Moosic—Rogue's March.

De memory of Poor Pompey—Chah! let de dead ress.

De Colonization Shocietee—What de debil's de reason dey cant let poor nigger lib here as well as go to de spense of bury um five tousand mile tudder side beyond de water.
25 cheers grin and half a piece.

Massa Willbyforce—Spose he good feller—but dont hear much bout um lately, in de cause of mansipashum—Hope he no get mad and wont play. 300 guess and no grin.

De Fourt of Uly—Neber see folks in Bosson half so sober when dey two thirds drunk.
Moosic—Hail Liberty?

Massa Judge Strey—What de debil he brackguard Massa Pickering for good many year ago, and now cram sugar plumb in the mout to make up wid um?
Song—" Fear of Bray."

De Gas Light Company—Why de debil dey no light up deir lamp, so folks see what dey bout ? Guess when deir big oil jug get afire year ago dey got no money to buy more with.
Song—See de bright hair'd golden sun."

Massa Cuming and M'Daffoe—Wonder wheder dey mean to hab nudder sham fight dis year—guess one's afraid and tudder don't want to.
De former Police officer—Since he resign, he bring his hogs to a fine market—Hope he no sell bad pork as what de Mayor and Aldermen say Massa W—did.
Song—" What de poor would you be et."

De Poets of New-England—Poor fellows, dey no get half crown a line like Massa Walter Scott; so dey blige to get what dey can, and more kick dan copper into de bargin.
Moosic—" See the storm a rising."

De Mayor of Bosson—Guess when you see him no do he duty, you catch weazel asleep.

De Newspaper Editors—Dey jus like de lawyers—fight like de old harry one day, and shake hands de next.
Fourt of Uly Orators—Shouldent tink some folks puff he own oration, when dicashum teach um better, and he find nuff scribbler who glad to do it for um.

De Sea Serpent—Some say he come to Nahant once more ? guess he want to see what sort of fish Massa M—got at de new hotel; hope he wont scare all de visiters to Marblehead.
Moosic—" When de mona shines o'er de deep."

De two News Rooms—Wonder which tell de mose tuf story, him wat lift up de top of de box, or him what tell um in de barn-yard?
Song—" A Clerk in London gay."

De City of Bosson—Guess he dont want for notions, if all true what you read in de newspaper.

De Bosson Dog—where de debil dey go to get five dollar to pay for de freedom of de city? Guess some of um bark at de City Council when cold wedder come along.
Song—" Bow-wow-wow, &c."

Copy-Right secured.

Materials like the "Bobalition" broadside indicate the importance of language to demarcating free Blacks and free Whites from one another. In racist popular culture, language worked as a signifier when coupled with an image of Black impropriety. The appearance of "words" that are not actually words at all, but look and sound enough like what they mimic, accentuated the role of the verbal in the reception of the visual text. Pictures of speech show that "a rhetoric of the written word is visual" by imploring a combination of words and images to confront the eyes, thus operating "synergetically" to communicate information to the reader/ viewer.[90] True to the dictates of parody, these caricatures employed imitation in the form of "direct quotation, alternation of words, textual rearrangement, [and] substitution" to make their claims about Black inferiority.[91] These tropes attempted to make the very real, and very threatening, public circulation of Black protest rhetoric seem less threatening by showing Black speech as idiotic. They emphasized Black speech and circulated in concert with African American rhetorical acts. Together, these items revealed the significance of audibility to positioning Black freedom within the public imagination. Although caricatures exacerbated the problem of visibility, these items also underscored a verbal component to the ridicule of African Americans.

Racist caricature used the powerful combination of words and images to portray free Black people as strange. Images of Blacks' speech as flawed or malapropic attempted to create a *voice* of Black freedom that coincided with problematic images. Voice serves as a moniker for an entire set of meanings about an individual, and functions as "the acknowledgement of the obligations and anxieties of living in community with others." Voice not only represents the speaker but also creates responsibility for others in the community who hear that voice as well.[92] In context, the "black" voices of anti-Black caricature pictured free Black speakers as unworthy of social contracts with White people. Caricatured Black voices symbolize the incongruence between free people's new visibilities demonstrated at local parades and the essence of Black raciality, which warranted enslavement and marginalization.[93] Black voices appear incomprehensible according to racist caricature, and thus make no demands on Whites or on local governments. The sound of an infirm grasp of English required no response and thus reaffirmed the Black speaker as unfit for citizenship. The "I" of the malapropic subject struggles to articulate itself to others. When coupled with ridiculous scenes of impropriety, audible racial differences represented the flawed eye/I of a figure still too uncivilized to engage notions of citizenship within the early republic. Slavery's peculiarly ocular existence reappeared in visions of Black speech in this period. This powerful combination of the visual and verbal in anti-Black caricatures explained racial deficiency as performable, not just visible. Black speech as imaged in city-specific depictions of African Americans shows free people who chronically drop their vowels when discussing the politics of the "New York 'lection" (election), and pronounce their "v" sounds as "b" sounds when referring to one another as "Black debils." These flagrant malapropisms offered cues to White readers for the performance of Black racial difference. Caricature suggested that although free people could afford to pursue foreign languages and European pastimes, the mishandling of English betrayed their lofty ambitions. The pictured vernacular argued that despite the means to purchase goods and establish their own schools and churches, neither wealth nor freedom could mute the sound of racial difference among free Black people.

Racist illustrations were an essential element to projects meant to exclude free Blacks from early ideas of citizenship. The fact that free people of African descent were not equal to Whites in national politics remained much clearer than the actual definition of "citizen" or U.S. national belonging. Even as late as 1812, White lawmakers struggled to conceptualize the meaning of "citizen" for a young nation that embraced its diverse makeup as a state made up of other individual states.[94] While the Constitution did not offer clear terms for defining U.S. nationality until the Fourteenth Amendment in 1868, "it marked the boundaries of citizenship through exclusion"; able, White, property-owning men were citizens, while women, people of African descent, and the disabled were not.[95] The political practice of nationhood in the early republic remained unilaterally vague, pitting "national stability and active citizen participation" against one another, excluding non-White and nonmale persons from civic participation, which collectively complicated the manner in which a person might convey "citizen" status in social interaction.[96] The ideal of a White, masculine, and able polis, combined with bourgeois concepts for engaging the "public sphere," ultimately excluded particular bodies from the fullest privileges of civic participation. This slippery slope of race and citizenship in the early republic meant that Blacks organizing in the urban North contended with the fact that neither individual Whites, nor the emergent nation-state at large, regarded free Blacks as part of the citizenry. At the same time, Whites who cleaved to the vision of a "colorblind" citizenship after the American Revolution consistently needed to adjust the notion of national belonging to accommodate the burgeoning separate Black national identity flourishing within individual states.[97]

The slow erosion of slavery further complicated Black people's relationship to U.S. national identity. African descendants occupied a bizarre interstice before the Civil War, living outside of slavery and outside notions of citizenship. By the turn of the nineteenth century, many Blacks were born or emancipated into U.S. sovereignty with no direct linkage to locations in Africa. While various gradualist laws proposed emancipation for Black people born after a specified date, the status of free Blacks remained one of second-class citizenship. Laws that variously prohibited free people of African descent from interracial marriage, from testifying against Whites in court, from voting, and from holding public office circumscribed the manner in which people of African descent could participate in larger concepts of the nation.[98] By the 1820s, communities of free Blacks were identifiable, taking up specific locales in various northern cities. Whites who were hostile to the idea of Black freedom found it increasingly difficult to exclude people of African descent from the nation as Black communities became increasingly self-sufficient, and small but powerful cadres of middle-class Black abolitionists were promoting the end of slavery. White discomfort with free Blacks resulted from "the ways republican ideology implicitly and explicitly defined Blacks as unequal" as a result of the poverty constituted in slavery, while simultaneously promoting definitions of citizenship that emphasized "public, political virtue" as themes rooted in "economic independence."[99] Although race previously functioned as an adequate signifier of class, Black emancipation and the rise of a Black middle class complicated such readings. Once again, discursive approaches to the Black body and national belonging remained unhelpful, as juridical and dialogic confines could not keep out people of African descent.

Accordingly, anti-Black caricatures discredited Black freedom in order to forestall questions of citizenship. Although these items were often city-specific, hostile cartoons actually blanketed the northern states, creating an antagonistic climate for imagining Black people as citizens. These images created a larger atmosphere of visual hostility, targeting free African Americans throughout the Northeast. Imbert's "Life in New York" series contributed to this feeling. In the lithograph titled *A Five Points Exclusive Taking the First Steps towards the Last Polish* (figure 4.13), a group of New York women of varying complexions wear brightly colored gowns and ballet slippers as they await instruction from Mr. Bonenfant,

Figure 4.13. Edward William Clay, *A Five Points Exclusive taking the First Steps towards the Last Polish*, ca. 1833. (Courtesy of The Library Company of Philadelphia)

their French dance trainer. Similar to the other individuals in the image, race and ethnicity are written on Bonenfant's body through his dress (he wears a French flag pin on his lapel) and his accent. Directing with the bow of his violin, Bonenfant instructs his pupils: "allons mademoiselle raise ze' leg wis ze red ribbon so bring him to ze ozer leg wis de blue ribbon, hold up ze' head elevate ze' bosom, hold in ze' stomach and stick out behind! Tres bien ver well." The image shows four women and their teacher convened for the women's betterment. Although European identity appears as part of the visual commentary, Blackness and free Black women are clearly present for instruction. Mr. Bonenfant's saloon is a space used to instruct Black women patrons into becoming more demure and acceptable specimens, starting with their physical postures and their "behinds." A legible list of rules appears within the image, instructing these Black patrons against courting more than "ten partners at one time" and appearing in public without proper shoes and attire. These regulations posted to the saloon's (would-be) wall appear in the center of the image and guide the reader to understand Bonenfant's classroom as a place to improve upon Black women's inattention to detail and natural lack of refinement. In this image, four Black women share a single line of speech that manages to avow their lack of knowledge with the utterance of an inarticulate question: "now M' Boneyfong is dat 'ere step right?" Free Black women's struggle toward elegance is verbalized in a single mispronunciation.

In images such as the *Five Points Exclusive*, the intricate problems of space, race, and class come into sharper relief. Dancing was a common leisure activity among Black women in antebellum New York, both for poorer Blacks who visited dance halls and for wealthier Blacks who enjoyed dancing at formal or "fancy balls."[100] However, to locate the setting of a dance class among middle-class aspiring Black women at Five Points shows how caricature conflated disparate poles of the free community. By picturing women of means within a New York City neighborhood known for poor Blacks and unsavory carousing, such as drinking and sex, the cartoonist ignored the class distinctions among free Blacks that were already clearly demarcated by 1820—the distinctions that some Black elites struggled to make apparent.[101] The illustrator makes no distinction between Five Points Blacks who likely would have been too poor for fancy dresses or paid dance lessons, thereby ignoring the differences between classes of Blacks and the spaces that they occupied. In this rendition of Black women's leisure, the illustrator showed freedom and class as intertwined to suggest that whenever people of African descent were publicly portraying freedom, they were also in pursuit of middle-class belonging and social acceptance. Emancipation and freedom were not merely human desires but also affronts to White social and economic orders. These items were anti-Black because they imagined all Blacks as alike, and as collectively outside the notion of acceptable behavior. Such racial attitudes put Black social life on display as a primary site for racial transgressions.

Shades of Invisible

Cartoons like the "Life in New York" series did not promote acceptance of free Black populations, but neither did they promote free Black people leaving the country—a popular notion by 1816, when the infamous American Colonization Society openly promoted Blacks' "return" to Africa. Much of popular culture illustrated the burgeoning idea of a separate Black America, even if only for a cultural foil. Illustrations like the "Life in New York" image of two free Blacks encountering an Irishman marked Blacks in the United States off from those in other empires of the Atlantic (figure 4.14). Once again, this gaudily dressed Black couple appears on a New York street. In addition to her busy dress and large feathered hat, this woman peers through an eyeglass to examine a tattered and shoeless White man standing before them. The Black couple has just left "Patent Steam, Scouring Establishment [for] Clothes of all kinds." The White man wears a shirt with holes, and offers the couple his patched and worn jacket as he explains, "Blakey I say? Can't you by the powers of your stame engine shift me this coat for a new one? I trust by the looks of yours you're the very mon I have been looking for since I left Kilarney" [sic]. Although Imbert's illustrator used raggedy clothing and malapropic speech to label this man an Irish immigrant, none of this seems to register with the free couple. The Black man takes offense, responding, "What you mean sir! I'm a merchant, I larn you better? can't you rid dat dere sign, ply to the office," and his partner misidentifies White ethnicity: "Aint it too gusting for a lady of quality to be salted so in street by Russians." The positions, the texts, and the composition of the image reiterate many of the problems of other caricatures in the "Life in New York" and "Life in Philadelphia" series. The White man, though ragged, stands barefoot in the street while the Black couple stands on the sidewalk. There is a question of his literacy, as the Black man asks "can you read," but not of the White man's ability to perceive. He asks for an item of clothing from this overdressed couple,

Figure 4.14. Life in New York. (Courtesy of American Antiquarian Society)

while the Black woman cannot tell the difference between an Irishman and a Russian, even with the help of the monocle. The lowliness of the Irishman marks him as distinct from the impropriety of free Blacks. While this figure still "belongs" to Ireland, naming Killarney as a home and signaling his lack of assimilation through speech and dress, the still maladjusted free Blacks belong to the U.S., specifically.

The contrasts between White and Black impropriety are part of the cultural work of nationalism taking shape in racist caricatures. In the overaspiring malapropic Black speaker, the U.S. consumer could continually protect the middle-class parlor from formerly enslaved Black people with lofty goals. Caricatured speech reassured consumers that race was behavioral, performed unconsciously by people of African descent and thus sure to reveal itself in social interactions—no matter how much freedom reorganized social encounters. In these joint efforts to constitute a national home space in notions of discourse and articulation, both White and Black media purveyors pictured freedom beyond the confines of the individual to a larger problem of acculturation. In a national public culture, competing pictures of freedom collectively excluded African descendants from definitions of U.S. national belonging. Print media both for and against the abolition of slavery variously used language in the process of picturing freedom to create a voice for Black people. The malapropic sound of racist caricatures asserted that people of African descent—unworthy of the privacy and sacredness associated with private sphere women of the parlor—were not ever supposed to be seen or heard as members of the critical public.

Racial popular cultures illustrate difference in a way that discourse alone could not resolve. African Americans attempted to eradicate disparities in education as a way to address how Blacks "were strategically and rigorously prevented from acquiring literacy" through slavery.[102] However, while supporters of abolition fixated on representing Black people as upstanding and worthy of national belonging, hostile Whites produced media that represented Black freedom as antithetical to U.S. citizenship. Whereas still-fragile notions of nationhood continued to emphasize political discourse and self-sufficiency as paramount, depictions of inarticulate Black spendthrifts portrayed free people of African descent as still too close to slavery to fit into yet larger notions of the young nation. Image makers in the North made productive use of the gap in pictures of Black freedom left by purveyors of the antislavery movement. Caricatures appearing throughout the Northeast showed people of African descent in different cities as one single ignorant mob with a number of undesirable habits. These images acknowledged the efforts of free Black people to make good on fantasies of the bourgeois public sphere, turning free people's hard work in education and literacy into caricatured portrayals of a problematic Black visibility. These pictures emphasized the body with illustrations of the overdressed, awkwardly posed free man and woman seeking admission to the nation as a home.

It is in this context that Black women offered U.S. visual culture comforts about the erosion of slavery. While free Black women were questioning their relationships to the nation in print, political caricature also ruminated on Black national belonging with a voice that made inclusion unnecessary—even impossible. While Blackness as depicted in satirical cartoons sounded un-American and inaudible, antislavery materials did little to improve Black people's visibility or to produce an image of freedom that could rival anti-abolitionist pictures. Abolitionist media also manufactured and manipulated Black women's visibility to suit the needs of the cause, narrating the image of the supplicant enslaved woman with the honed literacy skills of Black women in the middle class. While nineteenth-century print culture examined parts of the body, Black female bodies hardly ever appeared in ways that connected to the voices of Black abolitionist women. While caricaturists like Clay deployed Black female bodies for explicitly damaging means, "progressive" politics advanced in the name of the antislavery movement also utilized Black female bodies in problematic ways. Antislavery iconography diminished the visibility of Black abolitionists who actively worked to create socially acceptable public appearances. When considered together, both abolitionist and anti-abolitionist materials worked to advance negative perceptions of the free Black body in public.

Read collectively, picturing freedom at the national level failed to consider the postslavery future of free Black people, even as a diverse body of print culture in the early republic slowly began to coalesce around shared notions of Black visibility. Neither pro- nor anti-abolitionist illustrations positioned people of African descent in ways that connected freedom to civic ideals. Instead, they each began to embed Black visibility into a national visual narrative of *objecthood* and White political privilege—where Blackness either expanded or contracted White power. Racist caricaturists insisted upon positioning people of African descent outside notions of proper behavior befitting U.S. citizens, but their images also began to mark Black people within the United States as part of the spatial terrain of the developing nation. Although Black people might not yet, or ever, be U.S. citizens in the judicial sense, their self-perceptions and social appetites were beginning to mark them off from Blacks in other countries in the Atlantic world. Free Blacks were becoming the free "property" of the United States, not self-possessed citizens.

5

Racing the Transatlantic Parlor: Blackness at Home and Abroad

Transatlantic slavery produced a more comfortable home environment for its benefactors. The transatlantic parlor provides a metaphor for thinking through the Atlantic world as a home wherein a diverse cadre of viewers in the United States, England, and France attempted to reconsider Blackness and free Black people as permanent constituents in the wake of a dissolving slave trade. The transatlantic parlor, though diverse within itself, represents interlocked empires, joined together through collective unease about how to make sense of national identity and Blackness shorn from captivity. The Atlantic world—organized by slavery and maintained through transatlantic abolitionist movements—cohered "around a geographic claim, regarding the spatial scope of key historical processes" from the sixteenth century to the present.[1] The transatlantic parlor is a home for diverse peoples with various relationships to slavery and abolition. I theorize this space as central to the task of domesticating Black freedom, or for bringing free Black people under control through display, through their re-presentations on the printed page and the location of these prints within the home. Through an analysis of various depictions of Black freedom, I explore the ways in which material representations of free people transformed to show Black people as subject to parlor ideologies of decorum. The transatlantic parlor becomes a place that includes Black freedom within its periphery, rather than Black slavery, making Black freedom acceptable within its confines.

Transatlantic Traffic

Clay depicted the Philadelphia life of Minta and Cato as replete with other fashionable free people at a Blacks-only social gathering (figure 5.1).[2] Minta

Figure 5.1. Edward Williams Clay, *"Shall I hab de honour to dance de next quadrille . . . ?,"* "Life in Philadelphia" series, 1828. (Courtesy of The Library Company of Philadelphia)

and Cato are decidedly somewhere in this print in the "Life in Philadelphia" series, perhaps at a "fancy ball." Ms. Minta's bright-pink ball gown with lace detail and pink floral headdress only add to her communal belonging, as a band of elaborately decorated Black women appear similarly adorned in the backdrop. The equally dapper Mr. Cato—dressed in a blue tailcoat, white pantaloons, and ruffled shirt—bows to address his companion. Minta and Cato stand out among their comrades—even as they fit in—because these title characters are the only two people shown in conversation. Depicted with their words shown below the encounter, the voices of Minta and Cato speak for the whole group of free Black people in the image. Although Cato politely removed his hat to illustrate his gentlemanly status, he failed with Minta when he asked: "Shall I hab de honour to dance de next quadrille wid you Miss Minta?" To Cato's chagrin, the feverish pursuit of Minta's other suitors forced her to decline his request. Minta explained: "Tank you, Mr. Cato—wid much pleasure, only I'm engaged for de next nine set!" Although Minta can lay no claim to beauty, she remained popular among Black men, with nine other beaus waiting for a dance. Unlike the demure White women of *Godey's Lady's Book*, Black women were brash in the "Life in Philadelphia" cartoons. Characters such as Minta represented the inverse of true womanhood with comic attempts at middle-class derivations of "lady" that went awry with the articulation of Black speech and audacious public appearances. That she had nine admirers did not imply that Minta was attractive but instead suggested her promiscuity. This picture of freedom suggested that Black women like Minta garnered unwarranted favor as objects of desire among Black men while also suffering from an innate lack of self-awareness about racial character flaws.

Clay's body of work belonged to a transatlantic world of caricature and lithography. One Washington, D.C., paper advertised the availability of "ENGRAVINGS, CARICATURES, &c.," such as "Cruikshank's Illustrations of Phrenology" for three dollars, as well as "Life in Philadelphia, exhibited in a Series of plates" along with "French Lithographic Prints" and "Jones' Views in London."[3] The English caricaturist George Cruikshank came from a famous family of illustrators and had already garnered international fame before moving on to book illustrations by 1828; his works on phrenology were often pirated.[4] That this advertisement for Clay's prints appeared alongside the work of Cruikshank insinuates his significant popularity in a transatlantic marketplace. Clay likely encountered English pictorial satire in Philadelphia since British printmakers had disseminated works by important artists like William Hogarth since the early seventeenth century.[5] Alternately, Clay might have learned more about English caricature during his very influential trip to Europe at the end of the 1820s. Martha Jones credits Clay's 1826 voyage to Paris for inspiring his satirical prints. He began sketching character types while onboard ship, before encountering British caricatures and French satirical cartoons about difference. Indeed, Clay's illustrations about Black life in Philadelphia were constituted in the artist's exposure to European ways of seeing race and representing social pretensions.[6] Moreover, just as U.S. audiences could purchase English prints, European audiences likely had access to Clay's work. Thus, Clay, too, circulated in the Atlantic, taking his inspiration from the travel routes that connected one slaving nation to another.

Reproductions of Minta's attempt to entice Black men through jewelry and revealing attire, similar to depictions of other free Black women in the series, traveled throughout other slaving empires of the Atlantic world. English and French reproductions of this particular scene from "Life in Philadelphia" reveal the transatlantic popularity of the series and portray the popularity of anti-Black images across the ocean. Moreover, the international circulation of "Life in Philadelphia" turned free Blacks into unofficial representatives of the early American republic and of U.S. race relations, even as they were subjected to pictorial ridicule. Hostile depictions of Black social mobility marked the beginnings of a racial progress narrative and signified the burgeoning project of American empire. In the United States, such racial satire addressed local interactions with free Black people, but for European viewers across the ocean, these same materials spoke to questions of national and international identities. Through the intercontinental sharing of racist popular culture, media consumers of the Atlantic world simultaneously shared common ways of racial seeing. Just as antislavery activism and abolitionist legislation spanned the sea, so too did hostile portrayals of free Black people.

In this chapter, I refer to the transatlantic parlor as a place wherein viewers of slaving empires considered pictures of Black freedom, turning to visual culture, explicitly, as a tool for the domestication of free Black people. I argue that Black freedom comes into the jurisdiction of the Atlantic world through images of a flawed Black domesticity. Hostile illustrations like this depiction of Minta and Cato predicated the possibility of Black freedom and national belonging on Black women's domesticity, which served as the pivot upon which people of African descent could properly fit, and therefore remain, within the transatlantic parlor. Illustrators depicted free Black bodies as at home, insofar as free Black people remained marginalized via an inherent defect of race. Such concepts were crucial to imagining the continuity of an Atlantic world built upon slavery. I explore the transatlantic circulation of Black freedom by continually referring back to variations on this "Life in Philadelphia" image for how different versions of this image represented common practices of domestication—housebreaking—among viewers in the United States, England, and France.

I begin with a discussion of transatlantic printmaking. The English reproduction of "Life in Philadelphia" reveals British technological advancements in printing as important as English illustrators produced caricatures with finer detail and more explicit hostility than U.S. artists. I follow this with an analysis of the transatlantic parlor as a historically contextualized metaphor for visual culture in the Atlantic world, which functioned as the glue among diverse empires and extended the homeland of the empire throughout the Atlantic via colonization. Although ways of seeing Blackness varied within and across empires, distinguishing practices in the metropole from practices within the colony, it is in the shared need for differentiation that I argue for the existence of a transatlantic disposition toward Blackness. This context is important to understanding the robust milieu of cultural production to which Clay contributed "Life in Philadelphia," as well as for understanding how visual culture held together the transatlantic parlor by reconciling Black freedom. In the third section, I reveal Black women's domesticity as essential to imagining Black freedom, and imagining people of African descent as at home when outside of Africa. Popular representations of Black womanhood—and especially Black motherhood—determined many of these conceptualizations. Finally, in the last section, I offer a reading of the most elaborate and expensive reproduction of this "Life in Philadelphia" image to argue that through manipulations of materiality and image detail, cultural producers revised pictures of freedom to become comfortable with Blackness as a permanent inscription in the parlor.

Transatlantic Paper Trails: Printmaking in the Atlantic

Printmaking connected a diverse Atlantic world, collapsing the space between disparate places through printed materials. For example, Black women's friendship albums arrived in Philadelphia after English manufacture, and much of the U.S. and British antislavery propaganda zigzagged across the ocean as well. The transatlantic world of printmaking assembled a heterogeneous audience that became an interdependent group of viewers. "Printed images," including illustrations, caricatures, and physiognomy sketches "hung on the walls of taverns and coffee houses, and displayed in the windows of urban print shops," were available to a diverse viewing public.[7] Communication traveled the same trade routes used for sugar and human cargo, with the transmission of news setting trends for the flow of all information dispelled through the Atlantic world.[8] The emergence of new goods in a given locale, such as rice in the Carolinas, made trade ports into points of contact for the transference of information. The circulation of print could take anywhere from three to eight weeks, or the time it took for a ship to voyage between England and the British America colonies, depending on point of origin and travel conditions.[9] In short, print media induced an "Atlantic world that was shrinking as communication improved."[10] Although it is difficult to quantify the number of prints in circulation by 1830, by the turn of the nineteenth century, a number of different processes already existed for the mass reproduction of imagery, including lithography and aquatint. To be sure, "the essence of prints is in their multiplicity," and while social upheavals, like war, briefly interrupted their availability on city streets, artists who created print images intended to circulate these items among a great number of viewers, both locally and internationally.[11]

English reproductions of the "Life in Philadelphia" series provide a robust example of the "circuit of culture," as they appeared across the Atlantic almost simultaneous to the U.S. series.[12] The artist William Summers, with the help of Charles Hunt, engraver, reprinted ten of Clay's original fourteen prints in aquatint, publishing them with Harrison Isaacs in London during the early 1830s. Either of these men may have acquired a set of the U.S. originals from a sale of lithographs. Isaacs reissued the prints of "Life in Philadelphia" with new scenes about Blacks in the United States, specifically, and removed the caricatures that parodied Whites and Quakers. Shown as large and smiling (figure 5.2), the English reproduction of Minta traveled the ocean on lithographed sheets of "Life in Philadelphia" and appeared with finer detail for English viewers.[13] This version of the caricature sharply contrasts with the original, even as it depicts the same scene. Free Blacks of Philadelphia interact in a furnished room with wood flooring in the Summers and Hunt illustration. Unlike the U.S. prints of this scene that locate Minta and Cato in a somewhat blank background, surrounded by shadowy compatriots, the English edition situates Black freedom in a carefully delineated setting. Later, I describe the specificity of place in transatlantic caricature, but here I mean to stress the extent to which English print producers improved upon the composition of U.S. illustrations.

The specificity of English reproductions resulted, in part, from advances in British printing technologies. English caricatures were already "played out" by 1837, when they had been popular for more than fifty years from their public introduction during the 1770s.[14] British artists entered into popular caricature with images of the Macaroni—a satirical illustration

Figure 5.2. William Summers and Charles Hunt, *"Shall I hab de honour to dance de next quadrille . . .?,"* 1831, "Life in Philadelphia" London series. (Courtesy of The Library Company of Philadelphia)

of an overdressed sophisticate, decked out in powdered wig and exquisite haberdashery. The "macaroni type," recognizable by "fine sprigged fabric, tight clothes, oversized sword, tasseled walking stick, delicate shoes, and an enormous wig," popularized caricature for English audiences by reveling in both a "suspicion of luxury" and a love of refinement."[15] In addition to the consumption of early caricatures, English audiences were already entertaining their own cartoon serials by 1821, when George and Robert Cruikshank printed the "Life in London" series.[16] The learned Cruikshanks enjoyed artistic pastimes, including drama and literature, using these experiences as fodder for their cartoons about English life.[17] "Life in

London" offered an illustrated narrative on three young men about town whose wealth and privilege distinguished them from other classes of Londoners. George Cruikshank went on to depict popular Black figures with his commissioned piece on Harriet Beecher Stowe's *Uncle Tom's Cabin* and other works for Charles Dickens.

English representations of free Black people reiterated many of these fixations on self-aggrandizement and preparation for city life. However, English reproductions of U.S. caricatures also helped British viewers contend with Black freedom as a "rhetorical problem."[18] Although the day-to-day enactments of British slavery happened in the distant colonies, English audiences considered British antislavery discourse on a national and international level with the Abolition of Slavery Act of 1833—banning slavery in the British colonies, effective 1834. English audiences viewed caricatures of U.S. Blacks simultaneous to entertaining questions about Blackness and freedom in the British colonies. Cheap prints depicting exaggerated features and bad manners, outlandish clothes and malapropic patois among free Black people were relevant to English audiences contemplating the implications of Black emancipation. This local significance appears in an array of hostile illustrations produced by British caricaturists. For example, many of the English, both White and Black, believed that under the law, people of African descent who converted to Anglican Protestantism in eighteenth-century England summarily gained their freedom. However, this notion also turned up as folly in caricatures that depicted free people trying to wash away Blackness "within" infants.[19] These items reveal that British printers had their own needs for picturing freedom as evidenced by illustrations of gross Black etiquette as incongruent to uniquely English amusements.

The English engraver and print seller Gabriel Shire Tregear created an entirely separate series, "Tregear's Black Jokes: Being a Series of Laughable Caricatures in the March of Manners amongst Blacks," based on a number of plates from "Life in Philadelphia."[20] Tregear printed more of his own unique stories about fancy people of African descent, getting rid of stock characters depicted in the original U.S. series, like Minta, but replacing them with other notorious characters such as "La Belle de Philadelphia" (figure 2.11). Tregear parodied Black freedom for British audiences in scenes that illustrated public life on cobblestone streets and performance arts staged in theater-like settings. Tregear printed caricatured renditions of a "Cinderella and the Black Prince," and "Othello" with a Black "Desdemona" to illustrate free Black people explicitly engaged in White performances. Again, prints coincided with the emergence of Blacks in transatlantic theater culture, but they incorporated malapropic "English" to show self-important social outcasts vying for national belonging with bastardized social customs. Ridicule about a Black actor performing Shakespeare seems to directly target Ira Aldridge, the Black actor who played a number of Shakespearean characters, both in the United States at the African Grove Theater in New York, as well as in various venues in England, including the Royalty Theatre in East London.[21] A constant in these scenes of grandeur was that Tregear featured Black women being complimented for White feminine virtues unrealized on the page. These women betrayed lovers who admired their "snow White" and "alabaster skin." Black men loved them for their "aquiline" noses and snow-white complexions, inserting the joke in the visual, as these features did not appear within the image. Such pictures located humor in the obvious lack of these attributes on Black characters, and in Black women's inability to recognize their distance from White Western notions of beauty. Although these people referred to one another as "Ms. White" or "B. White," the scenes in racist caricature showed them as anything but, as their dark complexions contrasted against their brightly colored clothes. These illustrations evidence the way in which racialized standards of beauty were explicitly hierarchical and directly imposed upon Black women almost instantaneously with emancipation. The combination of White beauty as a standard and the joke of Black thespianism functioned to emphasize a contrast between Black self-concepts and the inevitable failure of freedom to help them achieve White social standing.

Tregear constructed comedy in these distinctions of perception, showing Blacks' blind views of one another as counter to how they actually appeared to White viewers. With these examples, illustrators offered audiences the chance to read a caricature and realize their vision as distinct from the perceptions of free Black characters on the page. If the reader properly understood the picture of Black impropriety, then she realized that the problematic spectatorship practice existed within the Black object. That is to say, the problem of perception remained essential to Black raciality. In this way, some English cartoons appeared nastier and more grotesque than the U.S. versions because they were much less ambivalent about their claims. In these stories, Blackness determined deficiency, evidenced in speech, dress, and manners that proved free people were moronic. "Tregear's Black Jokes" explicitly confronted the idea that people of African descent were not English subjects just because they were free.

Even after emancipation, Blacks in England, like their U.S. counterparts, appeared woefully unfit for national belonging. In the British imagination, freedom allowed Blacks and Whites to fraternize with disastrous consequences because Black people were also "obsessed with the destructive pursuit of everything that is White: White ceremonies, White sexual partners, White dress codes, White employment."[22] With Whiteness at the root of all of their desires, Black people's freedom inherently constituted an assault on Whiteness itself in the English imagination. Emancipation not only meant the end of bondage, but according to print culture, it also meant the opportunity to infringe on all things that had once been restricted to White citizens.

Blackness and Belonging

Shared pictures connected a diverse Atlantic world through interrelated ways of seeing Black freedom. The transatlantic parlor, as a "contact zone," a place for shared meanings, contained within it common methods for understanding peoples of the Atlantic world, as well as for defining those entities beyond its oceanic boundaries.[23] Picturing freedom for transatlantic circulation framed emancipation through an "imperialist gaze," where cultural producers employed a skewed power dynamic to maintain colonizer-colonized, subject-object binaries.[24] The imperialist gaze is represented in depictions of African descendants, but also in other types of visual accounts intended to maintain a *historically* organized imbalance of power via the visual. Accordingly, the colonial United States as scoped from the viewpoint of the British Crown replicates the dynamics of an imperialist gaze. Various forms of British ephemera labeled U.S. Americans as disloyal, especially after the Revolutionary War. In what Lester Olson describes as a "rhetorical iconography" of imperial community, English popular ephemera depicted the U.S. as a traitorous colony trying to overturn British rule, "moralizing" early America's transition from proud colonial subject to a competing colonizing power.[25] In the evolution of the United States within its Atlantic identity, British popular culture imagined its former colony as a severed snake broken into pieces that depicted the disjointed colonies as venomous. Although these illustrations addressed different needs in different Atlantic world locales, it is in their transatlantic circulation that such items introduced viewers to a shared set of perceptions—that of the changing relationship between colonizer and the colonized.

This is not to say, however, that all slaving empires viewed race or Black visibility in the exact same ways. Blackness and people of color throughout the Atlantic world were subject to different approaches to colorism and hypervisibility, according to the practices in a given location. In fact, definitions of "Black" or "colored" could vary within a single slaving empire. For example, English laws of race and property that governed the British Isles did not necessarily correspond to the colonies. Lawmakers ensnarled a complicated web of color and freedom for people in preemancipation Jamaica to prohibit White men from bequeathing large amounts of property to "Negros" or "mulattos."[26] Although "status and skin colour were connected" when making these determinations, lawmakers went one step further and required free people to carry certificates and wear badges of freedom to make their social status undeniably visible.[27] Race, and subsequently, color, resulted in different experiences for "African women" and their "daughters" born throughout the Americas, with issues such as proximity to White owners for sexual liaison and the rigidity of racial determinants in the "civic sphere" resulting in vastly different experiences by locale.[28] In some instances, a bondsperson's proximity to Whiteness, constituted in racial "mixture," enhanced one's entitlement to freedom. In Antigua and Jamaica, for example, the "disproportionately large percentage of women among free coloureds" suggests that "sexual favours" were a means of lobbying for manumission.[29] Concepts of Blackness and non-Whiteness varied by location, but the extent to which such categories mattered further evidences the fact that slavery required a visual understanding of racial difference, which empires would continue to struggle with, even in distinct processes of abolition.

Across differences, there remained a common need for continuity among empires in transition. Just as slavery organized the Atlantic world, abolition and antislavery maintained this cohesion through visual cultures. Ways of seeing and theories of visuality were but one realm through which peoples of a changing Atlantic world could evolve their ways of life. Transatlantic efforts to abolish slavery summarily ignited other kinds of social movements that were necessary to other constituencies; thus transatlantic White women's rights and early feminist movements were also a part of this connective framework. Activists who toured for lectures and authored protest literatures addressed interconnected audiences spread across the Atlantic Ocean.[30]

French audiences needed to resolve their own problems with enslavement and the nation space, much like the United States and England.

French courts recognized the "Freedom Principle" from the sixteenth century, honoring the idea that "breathing" French air or standing on French soil should be a declaration of freedom.[31] Similar to Mansfield's ruling on *Somerset* in England, France upheld the metropole as sacred and thus unable to contain within it the brutal practice of slavery. However, with a disproportionately small population of Black people, in comparison to England, legal decisions about Blacks in France were not decided by the lack of positive law or the inability to find legal measures to define treatment of Black people. Instead, growth of the small population of Black people in Paris during the eighteenth century was curtailed by 1777 with passage of Declaration pour la police des Noirs, which prohibited the entry of African descendants into France.[32] This law required slave owners to dock chattel persons at French ports, where they could await return to the colonies, rather than admit Black people to move freely about the nation. Black bodies were problematic within the empire proper, thus the absence of slavery in France actually resulted from trenchant anti-Blackness that coincided with the proliferation of slavery in the Francophone colonies. Notions about what France should look like, as compared to the racial demographics of the colonies, helped influence such legal processes.

Ideas about Black freedom within France also corresponded to the violent emergence of emancipation in Saint-Domingue. While the British Empire waged a revolutionary war with the United States, it simultaneously defended itself from the threat of a rising French dominion—trading ownership of West Indian colonies with France during the American Revolution.[33] Competition between the French and British Crowns for territory helped secure the British loss of parts of Canada and the United States. However, France paid dearly for its support of U.S. independence with the French Revolution in 1789 and the loss of Saint-Domingue, its highest-grossing colony.[34] When people of African descent rebelled in 1791 with a revolutionary war to overturn slavery, giving way to the emergence of independent Haiti in 1804, their protests sent fear throughout the Atlantic world. In the United States, for example, the federal government issued the Fugitive Slave Act of 1793, offering legal support to owners who sought to pursue Black runaways. News about these processes inspired people of African descent in other locations, but also informed the shape of French abolition. Stories about the massacring of White planters in what became Haiti quickly arrived in France, diminishing favor for Blacks already within and hastening the active suppression of French abolitionism.[35] Consequently, picturing freedom was not limited to the humorous and the noble; the Haitian Revolution also inspired visual imagery that proposed violence as a constituent element of Black freedom. Many writers and illustrators imagined African-born and African-descended people emancipating themselves from slavery by force, taking clubs and machetes to White people's heads or conducting hedonistic blood sacrifices as a part of asserting their freedom.[36]

English printmakers also had localized needs for illustration, in addition to the advanced means of production. Caricatures of Black Londoners satisfied anxiety about the effect of freedom on everyday life as England's Black population drastically increased moving into the nineteenth century. Gretchen Gerzina points to a noticeable Black presence in England through populations of foreign students who studied abroad, the expatriates who fought on the Loyalist side in the American Revolution, and the reintroduction of planters returning from the West Indies with their Black servants.[37] Whereas the style and grandeur of Black servants in England once underscored the wealth of a White owner, emancipation transformed attitudes about Blacks' dress and public appearances. Emancipation ignited annoyance and distaste as Whites imagined free Blacks as part of the pompous nouveau riche.[38] Popular culture represented Black freedom as threatening, bringing about the end of "variety and luxury" that slavery brought to "ordinary lives"; popular imagery recast the "visual contrast and drama" of "the Black page" from English portraiture into a signal of the end of English comforts in ephemeral prints.[39] Once people of African descent took to theft of material goods in the process of stealing themselves, fine haberdashery connected English Blacks to a larger sense of belligerence. Representative appreciation for finely dressed Blacks in art declined, as Black conspicuousness could no longer be attributed to a wealthy White owner. Londoners continually signified Blackness as a "metonym of a colorful and jolly time," imagining people of color happily enslaved by Whites, until the emergence of emancipation when illustrators repositioned picturesque Blacks as wild.[40] Black freedom connoted a loss of imperial control.

When images of Minta and other free Black women portrayed in U.S. caricatures arrived at European ports in the early 1830s, they proved that the U.S. example of emancipation was particularly popular among audiences in other countries. English reprints of the "Life in Philadelphia" series hailed viewers still contemplating the meaning of Black freedom. British adaptations of Clay's vision continued to lampoon free people of African descent for their class aspirations but also to reflect concerns about race and national identity. Artists who issued English reproductions of "Life in Philadelphia" were sure to characterize Black figures as "American" as an added means of othering. Antagonism toward free Blacks in the United States simultaneously offered the opportunity to disparage the United States as a former British colony. In this strange way, people of African descent in the United States became African *Americans* through the transatlantic circulation of racist imagery, rather than within the domestic exchange of images within the national home. Whereas popular depiction was essential to the fantasy of "unified" culture in the context of the "early United States" as itself a "colonial project," derogatory pictures of free Blacks that traveled across the Atlantic did the important work of transforming the persona of the United States from former colony to potential imperial power.[41] People of African descent were vibrant participants in U.S. public life by the nineteenth century and "clearly understood" the ways in which "American domestic politics were driven" by events taking place in the "larger Atlantic world"; Blacks, like their White counterparts, recognized that "Americans were emphatically 'Atlanticist.'"[42] However, depictions of Black people began to transform the character of U.S. identity in the Atlantic world, igniting a trajectory of the transatlantic export of Black representation and cultural production as an "exceptionally" U.S. commodity.

Domesticity and Domestication

Viewers reigned in free Black bodies through picturing freedom. The earliest conceptualizations of Black freedom would have seemed incompatible with the Atlantic world as a home. However, the intimate spaces of discrete homes provided settings in which viewers experimented with the place of Blackness in the transatlantic as home. Anne McClintock draws the important connection: that "as domestic space became racialized, colonial space became domesticated" through compensatory displays of "imperial spectacle" and the exhibition of Victorian domesticity in the British colonies, especially in Africa.[43] The trinkets of imperialism in the Victorian parlor coincide with the underscoring of domesticity in the colonies, working in tandem to indicate the completion of the colonial endeavor. However, I want to suggest that Victorian space was always already racialized. Increased emphasis on objects of conquest helped to expand the boundaries of the domestic interior but also to maintain rigid differentiation among those entities within its borders.

Representations of Black women, in particular, were especially important to grasping Black freedom as an element of the Atlantic world, rather than a contaminant. Viewers who contemplated the permanence of Black freedom in the context of the transatlantic parlor engaged in a larger cultural project, to which Black women's domesticity was essential. Ironically, it was in the problematizing of Black domesticity that transatlantic viewers began to take up ideas of free Black people belonging to the Atlantic world. Many caricaturists emphasized Black women's incapacity to mother or nurture, emblematic traits of the cult of domesticity, in order to posit the inferiority of free Black people and of black home interiors. This perception bridged the gap between Black freedom as the betrayal of a natural, servile role for African peoples, and the undeniable fact of a forcefully emergent Black freedom. Cultural producers with anxiety about inter/national home space and the permanence of free Black populations produced illustrations that emphasized Black women as unable to behave as true women—unable to create homes and nurture Black families. Illustrators depicted the failures of a wild Black femininity in caricatures, making Black women's freedom the scapegoat for White discomfort with emancipation and the question of Black citizenship. After more than one hundred years of utilizing the Black female body as a site of labor production, viewers in Atlantic empires reimagined free Black women as useless to the state and unsuitable for inter/national inclusion.

Racist caricatures targeted Black women, specifically, in two ways that supported modes of picturing freedom. First, hostile illustrations questioned Black women's domesticity, often showing them as laughable mothers or as wanton sexual objects. Suspicious maternal skills and sexual promiscuity are key aspects of Black womanhood in hostile depictions. Such notions became essential to the dissolution of slavery, only to accelerate over time and long after abolition. In the absence of forced labor, Whites who fretted about the emergence of emancipation considered Black women's domesticity as a joke, viewing Black women who remained in the home or tethered to the "private" sphere as lazy.[44] Hazel Carby argues that "ideologies of black female domesticity and motherhood" emphasize their roles as domestics and as "surrogate mothers to white families," thus problematizing the possibility of a Black woman's domesticity when set in the context of her own family.[45] Underscoring this point, illustrations that attempted to imagine Black homes often showed free women of African descent as unable to organize proper private dwellings for Black families. Women who were considered wild and in need of

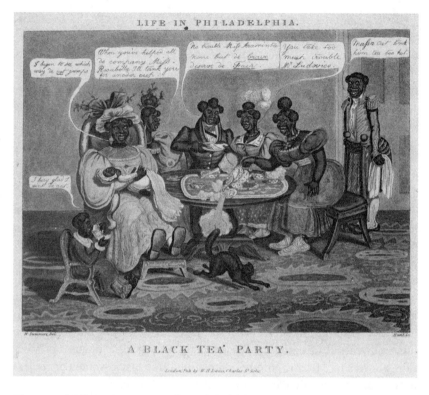

Figure 5.3. William Summers, *Life in Philadelphia: A Black Tea Party*, 1833, "Tregear's Black Jokes" series. (Courtesy of The Library Company of Philadelphia)

control were incapable of providing the order and stability associated with Victorian notions of domesticity.

Scenes like *Life in Philadelphia: A Black Tea Party* (figure 5.3) portrayed chaos in the Black home space, showing several Black women seated for tea and remiss in their duties to the household.[46] Again, under the title of "Life in Philadelphia," free Black people gather at a table in a carpeted room, elaborately dressed in colorful clothing and lots of jewelry. Viewers might notice the disorder in this scene without reading the conversation captions. In the center of the page, a cat flees from the gathering to escape being scalded by hot tea that one Black woman haphazardly spills on the floor. A closer look reveals the child seated at the far left explaining, "I bery glad I not de cat"; these inclusions initiate the narrative by pointing to "Miss Rosabella," lady of the house, as a dangerous free woman. The Black woman, seated next in order, beside the child, rests her feet and holds a baby, whom she seems to ignore. Instead, this mother focuses her attention on the interaction surrounding the one Black man at the table: "I begin to see which way de cat jumps." Her comment refers to "Mr. Ludovico," as he flirts with another guest at the event, presumably distracting "Miss Rosabella." The Black servant, a man who watches from the door, offers a final explanation at the end of the image: "Massa cat tink him tea too hot." At best, this depiction accentuates the Black lady of the house presiding over a chaotic tea; at worst, she castrates a flirtatious partner with hot water, scaring his "cat" away from a potential love interest.

This image targeted free Black women who eluded productive relationships to the empire and failed to replenish a bonded labor force. Women in this scene focus on the opportunity for sexual trysts, neglecting children and the domestic house pet. This portrayal, and others like it, represented women of African descent as licentious but unappealing, available but unattractive. More, these Black women presumably birthed babies but lacked "maternal instincts" or motherly sympathy steeped in ideologies of womanhood. Free Black women in hostile illustrations live outside the bounds of sentiment. They favor overt sexuality instead of chastity. Pictures of freedom focused upon Black women retained tropes of the "Jezebel-Mammy" dichotomy, constructing free women as simultaneous perpetrators of miscegenation and as wild figures manageable only by enslavement.[47] Jezebel never really is an object of affection; she is merely emblematic of Black women's sexual availability and is used to justify White desire. Likewise, though she might produce offspring from this union, Jezebel is no mother because her children do not belong to her in the context of slavery. Only Mammy can actually mother, and this expression of caring is only when she is in utilitarian relationships with Whites, not with her own children. Mammy has no presumption of bloodline with the people she "mothers"; only a labor relationship can evidence her domesticity. Without the benefit of capitalistic reproduction, Black gender and sexuality lacked a frame for value in the transatlantic parlor. Hortense Spillers elaborates how slavery structured "mothers" of African descent out of motherhood and rendered Black women's sexual reproduction as a thing not equated with mothering or matrilineal privilege.[48] Thus, the work of picturing freedom in the context of slavery was to suture this peculiar logic to a negligent Black womanhood. Sexual liaisons with free Black women were unfruitful for Whites because they produced no capital gain for a slave owner and no kinship ties for the production of family. Accordingly, Black women are not mothers to their children, in slavery or in freedom, because, although the Black female body can birth a child, a Black woman may not keep it or develop a parental relationship. If "the stamp of the commodity haunts the maternal line," making the branding wounds of the slavery market the only transference between Black mothers and their children, then freedom—the discontinuation of branding at the marketplace—needed to mean the dissolution of any connection whatsoever.[49]

This commentary on the embodied space of Black women's domesticity coincides with concerns about the geographic and architectural space of the Atlantic world as home. The English enjoyment of tea provides some distinctiveness for British audiences, but it also shows Blackness as a debilitating signifier, with Black women's domesticity—emblematized in children and the home interior—appearing overrepresented. This treatment of Black womanhood was essential to the recuperative work of Victorian popular imaginary, as Jennifer Brody points out, where Black women functioned to construct the Whiteness of Englishness.[50] Accordingly, the stability of White domesticity, as in domestic determinations of nationhood, depended upon the inclusion of Black women *within* the boundaries of the home. Moreover, in keeping with McClintock's point, the untamed and yet domesticated space of the colony represents another kind of home that is apart from the metropole. Free Black women that portray a flawed domesticity in hostile illustrations are in between homes, and it is in their domestication for display in the parlor that they become properly controlled. The western coast of Africa, once a vital node in the formation of the transatlantic parlor, similarly demands domestication via abolitionist colonization.[51] Caricature helped readers grope through new concepts of the Black libido, as a method for coping with White anxieties about a changing transatlantic parlor. Imagining a problematic woman at the helm of Black domesticity helped viewers slowly prepare for abolition and incorporation.

Race in the Transatlantic Parlor

Space is the unseen character in transatlantic efforts to picture freedom. Transatlantic space happened everyday as "practiced place," produced through the occurrences that happened within.[52] The transatlantic world cohered around practices of slavery, with popular culture helping viewers develop meanings for its dissolution. Fraught with contested significations, the transatlantic parlor, then, hosted various narratives of forced dispersal and pleasurable explorations—playing host to Somerset's fugitivity, the transport of Black women's friendship albums, and Clay's inspirational voyage across the ocean. The Atlantic world lacked stability as it evolved through changed trade relations among empires and resistance to slavery in various colonies. The transatlantic space occurred through daily practice, and given its fluidity, it occurred in contradistinction to the rigid *place* of the parlor. "Place," ordered by elements "distributed in relations of coexistence," happens through the "instantaneous configuration of positions."[53] Created by things that cannot be in the same area at the same time, "place" means to be here but not over there. In its rigidity, the place of the parlor provided stability, while the changing space of the Atlantic moved in constant evolution. While the parlor's inert objects occupied definite "places" in relation to other things, the corresponding historical actors bound up together through the impulses of empire moved through the Atlantic world.

Cultural producers who issued pictures of Black freedom in lithographs and other mediums slowly began to resituate Blackness within the *place* of the transatlantic parlor, as a means of coping with the transformations of *space* in the Atlantic world. Texts such as England's *New Comic Annual for 1831* (figure 5.4) offered viewers the opportunity to work through anxieties about freedom that were relevant to the British Empire, but also provided a chance to think through a new place for free Blackness within the home.[54] Offered in cloth and leather bindings, the *Annual* re-presented "Life in Philadelphia" as what the authors called an "unconnected tale" about Blacks from England. This concocted story described English persons of African descent as they changed through transatlantic interactions. The authors mapped an original narrative onto preexisting illustrations of free Blacks taken from both the "Life in Philadelphia" and "Life in New York" series. The *Annual* provided readers with the same images of elaborately dressed, socially awkward Black men and women, but in the form of colorless etchings for an illustrated tale about Black impropriety. In this story, an unnamed master sends fourteen formerly enslaved Blacks from England to the United States for an experiment in manumission. "Bacchus" and "Mr. Tomson," two White male narrators, explain how Black people are fundamentally unable to appreciate freedom. In a detailed story of emancipation's exploits, Bacchus scoffs at the idea of Black freedom because "negroes knows nothing about liberty" [*sic*] and "for a glass of real Jamaica they would sell themselves." Similarly, a third

"Pride," said I, "is the canker-worm which eats up half the virtues; it is the mill-dew, the dry-rot of the heart; it converts the noblest actions into selfishness; it is a painted sepulchre which encloses all the vices. Pride and Freedom are distant as the poles." This produced a dissertation on the blessings attendant upon humility, when I observed a group of old friends in the persons of Plato, Cæsar, and Doll, three of my freed blacks. On my approaching them, Plato, an itinerant vender of boots, was addressing Cæsar and Doll as follows:

"Lord a' marcy, why Cæsar, is dis you; why, when you 'rive from New York?"

When Cæsar, who had many times escaped a severe flogging for malversation in the field, by Plato taking the

Figure 5.4. New Comic Annual for 1831. (Reprinted from the original)

unnamed gentleman argues that independence "dwells only in the mind" and likens slavery to the class bondage that threatens people across race.[55] The idea of Black freedom is immediately a question of economics, both in how people of African descent cheapen themselves and for the ways in which the class imperatives of bondage, and therefore liberty, supersede questions of race. Together the storytellers deduce that "slavery may enchain the body, but cannot control the mind," that freedom "may be as generally found with the Negroes in the plantations of our West India colonies" as among free people in England. The *Annual* proposed that slavery was not antithetical to freedom and that bondage was not so much a hindrance to people of African descent as their unscrupulous internal drives—an inherent knack for classlessness. Blackness was plagued by a class problem and not by race or racism. The narrators argued that if a "man" acquires "a few thousand pound; he will instantly load himself with the fetters of carriage, horses, and servants."[56] The wasteful inclinations of free Black people proved their inability to benefit from emancipation.

The *Annual* perpetuated themes of Blacks as highfalutin, but situated the English experiment with emancipation in a larger spatial story. In a narrative written *onto* the images of "Life in Philadelphia," formerly enslaved people from England appear ruined through their U.S. encounters. Manumitted Blacks arrive in New York with only enough money for one outfit, but end up flashy and self-important, much like Black people in the United States. The *Annual* described Blacks in England as perfectly free in bondage under the British Empire, only to wind up corrupted by emancipation and by transatlantic mobility. Black people who moved to the United States caroused with other newly free Black populations. The narrative suggested that enslaved persons under the British Crown were "reared" differently from people of African descent elsewhere in the Atlantic world. Meant to suit readers in British parlors, the *Annual* claimed that English "negroes" originated from better "stock" than Blacks across the ocean. Once emancipated, however, these more humble people became crass and amoral as they navigated the Atlantic outside the constraints of slavery.

The *Annual*'s approach to picturing freedom aimed to appease English audiences dealing with emancipation, despite its reliance on images of Black people in the United States. It offered ways to think through the sight of free Blacks as at home in England and as part of the British Empire. One of the self-important characters, "Sancho," is a clear reference to Ignatius Sancho, a Black English man of letters. The "real-life" Sancho was renowned in eighteenth-century England as a formerly enslaved man who bartered for his own freedom and went on to craft important works in British literature and music. The *Annual* made certain reference to Sancho by caricaturing him as a freed domestic who went on to "ape his master" by developing a love for the "Bell Letters"—a play on Sancho's published letters distributed in London during the 1780s.[57] Sancho's caricatured representation as a pompous and overly indulgent free person depicted a fixation on the intersections of race and class among English readers, similar to other humorous illustrations produced in London. The *Annual* showed English readers representations of freedom that coincided with U.S. visions, picturing freedom as the lack of taste among free Black people. By including reference to both U.S. life and Sancho as a significant figure in Black English history, producers of the *Annual* accentuated the role of the Atlantic as an important figure in the story of Black racial difference.

The presence of the Atlantic as a transformative entity appeared in both English and U.S. depictions, proving *transatlantic* circulations were significant to audiences on either side of the ocean. Printers created many duplications of a "Life in New York" image, with and without color, changing the title, to issue a *Cut Direct, Or, Getting up in the World* (figure 5.5) in various forms. The version appearing in the *Annual* portrayed classism among free Blacks and suggested that this prejudice only heightened through travel across the ocean. In the original black-and-white print, a "boot Black" once befriended in slavery accosts a free Black couple. Though the well-off pair feigns ignorance of this scruffy man who shines shoes, he recognizes them with a proclamation: "Lord'a marcy why Caesar is dis you, why when you 'rive from New York?" According to the lithograph, if Caesar does know Plato, he no longer identifies with a shabbily dressed person whose mouth is open to reveal all of his jagged teeth. Caesar denies Plato's embrace and responds, "You must be mistaking in de person Black man!" More, Caesar's Partner, Doll, is primarily ornamental in presence but shows her indignation: "What does the imperdent nigger mean my love?"[58] In the *Annual*'s retelling of the story with additional lines of text, Plato the boot Black is thrilled to meet his old friend Caesar, although the latter pretends not to know him. Readers of the *Annual*'s version know that these two were in fact previously involved because the narrator explains that Plato suffered many a "flogging" when covering for Caesar's "malverstation." Once Caesar and Doll gain their freedom, however, they trade old friendships and egotistically deny any recollection of their former lives in bondage. Pictured in direct contrast to Plato, who

Figure 5.5. Life in Philadelphia: The Cut Direct, Or, Getting up in the World.
(Courtesy of The Library Company of Philadelphia)

is dressed in tattered clothes and a broken hat, Caesar and Doll represent Black freedom as self-indulgent, steeped in the refusal of other Black people and of slavery. This kind of detail is important because it shows that just as lawmakers began the juridical processes to suppress the transatlantic transport of human chattel, popular culture producers began to imagine that Black mobility in the Atlantic world was highly problematic. Caricaturists problematized transatlantic movement among free Blacks.

British printers issued books to offer fuller narratives than those contained within a single sheet lithograph. These materials explained the same issues of hypervisibility and racial seeing, but with more detail. While the cheap plate must tell a complete story through a single image and a few lines of words, the *Annual* bound the same tale in book form, with added details that suited English nationalistic purposes. Moreover, with the addition of White intermediaries like Bacchus and Tomson, readers could enjoy racial imagery with a well-defined distance between Black characters and White narrators. Black voices are delineated from

White voices within the text, distinguishing mimesis and the "actual" performance of Black racial difference. White readers could alternate between the performance of White voice and the performance of Black voice within the story.

Finally, printers created a lasting material, protecting the illustrations of "Life in Philadelphia" inside book covers and bindings, resituating caricature materials on the parlor shelf. While the new scenes on the page morphed the image of Black freedom in the space of transatlantic travel, the more permanent location on the parlor shelf simultaneously altered the place of Blackness in the home. Symbolically, Black freedom traveled the Atlantic, but cultural producers also changed its materiality by moving caricature within the parlor, from lithographs on poor-quality paper to pricey books. In these new forms, readers could enjoy illustrations of freedom but also put them away or close them, placing such pictures elsewhere within the home. No longer were the lithographs scattered on a side table, peripherally visible as people moved about the parlor; picturing freedom in new mediums began to shift the place of Blackness within the domestic interior of the Atlantic world.

French cultural producers similarly offered a way for free Blackness to recede into the background of the transatlantic imaginary. The French reproduction of the Minta and Cato image from "Life in Philadelphia" resulted in the most important iteration of the caricature after the original, changing the image to an enduring format that outlived the context of transatlantic abolitionism. In the form of scenic panoramic wallpaper, the French artist Jean-Julien Deltil extrapolated the original image from the series to set the characters among larger scenes of colorful free Black people (figure 5.6). Deltil designed the painting, which producers re-created in thirty-two different panels, using 223 colors, for what would become the scenic wallpaper "Vues d'Amerique du Nord" (Views of North America), manufactured by Zuber et Cie in Rixheim (approximately sixty-five miles south of Strasbourg). The panel colors were applied with 1,690 hand-carved woodcut blocks to transcribe this panorama, painted in the style of the landscape paintings that were so popular during the period.[59] In the third iteration of the imagistic life of Minta and Cato, their travels from lithographic prints in Philadelphia to hand-painted landscape prepared for mass-produced wallpaper in France, the couple represented free Blackness in the larger Atlantic world. "Vues" intended to "highlight the remarkable spectacle of prosperity among former enslaved Blacks and the novelty of racial integration," with Clay's sixth plate reimagined for a

Figure 5.6. "Vues d'Amerique du Nord." (Courtesy of John Nicholas Brown Center for Public Humanities and Cultural Heritage, Brown University)

message about U.S. democracy in Jacksonian America.[60] The effort and expense to produce this wallpaper allowed it to maintain the pretensions of "art" even as it was mass-produced, with the finished item covering walls at dimensions of 14 feet in length, 6 feet, 8 inches high. "Scenic wallpapers," like "Vues," gained popularity for their comparison to landscape paintings, even as companies issued them to satisfy "an essentially bourgeois clientele."[61] "Vues" offered audiences the sense of a "high culture" depiction of Black racial difference, refining the tone of racial consumption to a more "civilized" and less overtly ideological format, as compared to caricature. Interpreted through the medium of hand-paint—perhaps less acute than ink on stone—many of the faces shown in the wallpaper are somewhat obscure, offering fewer of the stylistic elements and "phenotypical" characteristics of caricature that pervaded lithographs.

Unlike the original series of "Life in Philadelphia" featuring Minta and Cato as one of many free couples at a gathering, or the etched version appearing in the *New Comic Annual*, Black figures shown hand-painted in scenic wallpaper illustrated North America in sum. Shown in absence of the accentuated features that represented Black inhumanity in parody, illustrations of free Blacks in "Vues" used these figures as colorful attributes to add depth to a larger scene of exotic and industrious North

America. Moreover, without the inclusion of voice as shown in printed captions, the collection of free Black people in "Vues" represented a less critical perception of freedom. Comparatively, the French production focused less on reproducing the satirical aspect of cartoons, even as it implied that people of African descent were not entirely incorporated into the larger social fabric. The irony that "Vues" relied on reinterpretations of racist caricature to produce an admiring picture of U.S. race relations is in part attributed to the fact that Deltil likely never left France to experience his own view of North America. Instead, he consumed other narrative materials to produce the panorama, perhaps relying on items like the *Picturesque Itinerary,* a nearly six-hundred-page document describing scenes of free Blacks in U.S. life.[62]

While "Vues" excluded uniquely French disdain toward the sight of free Black people, the artist invoked many imagistic tropes to other people of African descent. Compared to Whites in the scene, Blacks pictured in "Vues" lack action altogether. Without further contextualization or speech to propel the story forward, the sum of their deeds is simply to appear in a landscape of U.S. ingenuity. On wallpaper, Black people are free but not integrated in the scene. Black exhibitions of freedom juxtapose Whites who are extremely active, riding horses, walking through the park, and gesturing. Alternately, the artist illustrates Black people as focused on the act of display, even among one another. Free Black people appear in the public setting of the park to cause frenzy. These people are vibrant, yet closed off from everyone else in face-to-face scenes of engagement. Other Black women stand around Minta and Cato as if to observe the exchange, sealing this group interaction off from the rest of the park dwellers. This French organization of Black life in the United States suggested that free people represented their own contingency within the Atlantic world through common habits of seeing and similar inclinations toward hypervisibility. Vues depicted free Black people huddling together, self-segregated from White onlookers, who are both captivated and offended by the presence of Black freedom. Of the six White park dwellers also shown in the frame, four look directly at the cadre of African Americans, while one White woman appears so enthralled that she turns her head to look behind as she walks away. Although Black people appearing in this panorama are styled similarly to Whites who also accessorized with hats, coats, and parasols, the combination of colors used to illustrate free Blacks invokes greater contrast. "Vues" argues that Blackness in itself is more noticeable. Zuber's image of Black life in the United

States obscured the real-time racist context from which these images sprang; "Vues" suppressed the caricatured origins of picturing freedom, along with the racial animus that produced hostile illustrations.

"Vues d'Amerique du Nord" represented Black freedom in an everlasting format. First, as wallpaper, the French contribution to transatlantic visual culture resulted in a material that could permanently appear in the parlor. The likely cost as well as the quality associated with the production of "Vues" suggests that producers intended for this item to outlive books and cheap lithographs. Second, in the style of the depiction, "Vues" pictured freedom in a manner that could live within the transatlantic parlor in perpetuity. With no malapropic speech and no overt anxiety about the question of race mixing, Minta and Cato reference a "colorful" couple of African descent sharing public space with Whites. Zuber's scenic wallpaper tells a story of Black freedom in "North America" that emphasized community and publicity, showing Black people creating spectacles that Whites could neither duplicate nor ignore.

Views of North America

The transatlantic trade of illustrations helped to domesticate Black freedom for viewers of slaving empires. The combination of print, material, and visual cultures provided transatlantic audiences with multiple opportunities to handle the free Black body. The transatlantic parlor provided a place wherein viewers could contemplate impact of Black emancipation. The transatlantic parlor cohered around various political, economic, and cultural currents, where hostile images that limited the Black female body to breeding and servitude also helped viewers reconceptualize Black freedom within the nation state. Images of Minta, and other free Black women who could not properly see how they appeared to others, but whose robust sexuality infected social relations, were key to imagining Black freedom in the context of slavery.

Picturing freedom helped audiences of slaving empires contemplate the permanence of Black populations. Racial caricatures played on the anxieties of race and nationhood, but refashioned the idea of Black emancipation into controllable formats. Blackness enters the transatlantic parlor in permanent capture, as wallpaper for the home, as the cultural counterpart to the political and economic transformations of abolition. Constituent viewers who reimagined citizenship on the terrain of the Black body developed new narratives of space and belonging through illustrations. In these opportunities to handle the free Black body on the page, viewers simultaneously experimented with national and international identities. A quickly evolving transatlantic world understood Black freedom as curious and distinct from citizenship. Through picturing freedom, the transatlantic parlor congealed together as an international community. Blackness comes to be home in the slaving empire via the complex and critical conceptualizations that are the earliest pictures of freedom.

Epilogue: The Specter
of Black Freedom

The 2009 inauguration of Barack Obama as the first Black president, and forty-fourth elected president of the United States, updated the image of Black national identity. At the national introduction of Obama's presidential potential during the 2004 Democratic National Convention, viewers witnessed the galvanizing possibilities of a viable Black candidate. Obama represented a fitting conclusion to the story of Black visibility in the United States, from slavery through civil rights. A Black president suggested that civic protections against racism could foster great success among people of African descent, and that when such a candidate emerged, U.S. Americans, across race, were willing to elect *him*. Many commentators eagerly promoted Obama, the man, as a sign of postracism, problematically using his racial identity as proof of the irrelevance of race.[1] Similarly, the election of a Black president has meant the election of a Black First Family to the White House. The "hagiographic" media frenzy extends to the entire family—two daughters; wife, Michelle Obama; and her mother—and the Obama presidency functions as a sign like no other.[2] Obama represents a twenty-first-century sign of Black freedom for transatlantic circulation, and it is this sheer *representability* that is, at once, the source of his ability to inspire and disillusion.

The vision of freedom realized in a Black president harkens a visual history that has instantiated U.S. identity in a transatlantic context since the earliest ruminations on the abolition of slavery. The view of the Black president in the context of the White House brings this peculiar trajectory into sharp relief. When President Obama greets the world from the Diplomatic Reception Room of the White House, the colorful cast of characters that appear in "Vues d'Amerique du Nord" support his presentation. First Lady Jacqueline Kennedy installed the panoramic wallpaper in the Diplomatic

Figure E.1. "Obama Delivers Remarks on Iran," 2009. (Pool/Getty Images News/ Getty Images)

Reception Room in 1961 as part of her highly publicized restoration of the John F. Kennedy White House, and it remains there today.[3] At press events on foreign affairs, like Obama's remarks on Iran (figure E.1), it is not just the flags and the presidential seal as emblems of nationhood or the watchful eyes of George Washington that sanction Obama's belonging in the White House.[4] It is also the shadowing presence of Minta, Cato, and their complicated representation of Black freedom pictured on the wall behind him that serves to validate his presence. While the video cameras shown in the image hone in on Obama, the colorful fantasy of Black freedom represented in Minta and Cato make the cut of the photograph margins. The figures of this image do not represent the legions of actual people of African descent who navigated the Atlantic world, built the nation, resisted enslavement, pursued abolition, suffered Reconstruction, and organized movements for civil rights. Representations of Black freedom offer room for interpretation that can morph over time, without changing composition.

The Diplomatic Reception Room is suggestive of a parlor, with its plush carpet, lamps, and end tables. It is where the president and the First Lady receive guests of the White House, as well as news media. In this space, both Obama and the Black people on the wall serve to make meaning about the United States as a home for racial diversity. Although Obama's presence there is politically significant, much like any other president, there remains an ornamental quality to his belonging in the White House that is unique unto him. Images such as this press photo show that the racial contrast between the first president and the forty-fourth is just as significant as the chronology. The ability of the Diplomatic Reception Room, and therefore the White House and the U.S. presidency, to *contain* a Black president reveals the nation as able to harbor Black freedom to an *exceptional* degree. Whereas the value of free Black people in "Vues" is that they alone can speak to the liberal underpinnings of U.S. democracy, so too does the representation of a Black president serve as a moniker of the neoliberal democratic nation-state.

However, *picturing freedom* is a restricted kind of progress because the state can so easily co-opt pictures and redeploy them for state power. While these visions of Black freedom serve narratives about the United States, they each offer limited representational value for people of African descent. Hostile caricatures that ridiculed Black freedom in the United States were already available in wallpaper format, rearticulated as positive portrayals, when the U.S. Congress passed the 1850 Fugitive Slave Act, and the U.S. Supreme Court determined *Dred Scott* in 1857. Likewise, Obama provides an undeniably important vision of Black progress in the United States, even as he "affirms the violent operations of American empire" and manages a number of racially inflected crises of capital.[5] However, "Vues" remains available for purchase today. Each of these appearances is important to the representation of U.S. race relations as both Obama and the Black people on the wall are called upon to emblematize racial progress. Each of these forms of visibility contribute to a homegrown idea of the United States as an advanced arbiter of multiculturalism, without regard for how Black visibility corresponds to the lives of Black people, both historically and contemporaneously.

Still today, the infectious visual culture of slavery produces the most legible representations of freedom. The wide circulation of freedom images depends on continually repealing slavery, thereby engaging it as well. Such visions portray people of African descent achieving middle-class stability with no explicit connection to the atrocities of Atlantic world slavery. For sure, it is Michelle Obama, the "black American" wife "who carries within her the blood of slaves and slave owners," according to the president, that offers the opaque history of transatlantic slavery to the margins of a twenty-first-century picture of freedom.[6] Such details reveal Obama's proximity to the legacy of transatlantic bondage, without centering or politicizing its relevance to his Kenyan father.

Although Black people are colorful muses for *picturing freedom*, often the most popular pictures are not their own. Picturing freedom does not close "the space between black subjectivity and the black imago—the imagined mental image of blacks."[7] Instead, these items reveal that Black freedom is not Black citizenship. The most widely circulated representations of Black freedom work in service of the empire and the reconstitution of the Atlantic world, built upon slavery, which is to be quickly forgotten.

Notes

NOTES TO THE INTRODUCTION

1. The images are part of the Dickerson family cased portrait collection. Although the names of these individuals remain unknown, the Library Company of Philadelphia (hereafter cited as LCP) identifies this set of approximately sixteen images with the Dickerson family of Philadelphia. The archive includes two friendship albums belonging to daughters of the Dickerson family, all gifted together (Phillip Lapsansky, "Afro-Americana: Meet the Dickersons," *1993 Annual Report* [Philadelphia: LCP, 1994]).

2. The artist Robert Douglass Jr. was born free in Philadelphia in 1809. He created a number of important illustrations, including works on behalf of U.S. abolitionists. Douglass earned a Quaker education, which included the study of art and languages. Despite his skill and privilege, racial prejudice limited Douglass's notoriety. In response, Douglass sought emigration to England, although his noncitizen status barred him access to a U.S. passport. Eventually, Douglass succeeded in finding a way to leave the United States for England and then the West Indies (Samella S. Lewis, *African American Art and Artists* [Berkeley: University of California Press, 2003], 17–19).

3. Beaumont Newhall, *Daguerreotype in America* (New York: Courier Dover, 1976), 39; Richard Rudisill, *Mirror Image: The Influence of the Daguerreotype on American Society* (Albuquerque: University of New Mexico Press, 1971); Sarah Weatherwax, "Catching a Shadow: Daguerreotypes in Philadelphia, 1839–1860," LCP, www.librarycompany.org/catchingashadow/section1/index.htm.

4. Deborah Willis and Barbara Krauthamer, *Envisioning Emancipation: Black Americans and the End of Slavery* (Philadelphia: Temple University Press, 2013), 24; Deborah Willis, *Reflections in Black: A History of Black Photographers, 1840 to the Present* (New York: Norton, 2000); Deborah Willis, ed., *J. P. Ball, Daguerrean and Studio Photographer* (New York: Garland, 1993).

5. Leigh Raiford, "Photography and the Practices of Critical Black Memory," *History and Theory* 48 (December 2009): 119.

6. Sharon F. Patton, *African-American Art* (New York: Oxford University Press, 1998), 72.

7. John L. Jackson Jr., "A Little Black Magic," *South Atlantic Quarterly* 104 (Summer 2005): 397.

8. Scholarship on visual representations of Black people in the nineteenth century overwhelmingly focuses upon depictions of enslavement (Marcus Wood, *Blind Memory: Visual Representations of Slavery in England and America, 1780–1865* [Manchester: Manchester University Press, 2000]; Maurie D. McInnis, *Slaves Waiting for Sale: Abolitionist Art and the American Slave Trade* [Chicago: University of Chicago Press, 2011]; Molly Rogers, *Delia's Tears: Race, Science, and Photography in Nineteenth-Century America* [New Haven, CT: Yale University Press, 2010]).

9. W. J. Thomas Mitchell, *Picture Theory: Essays on Verbal and Visual Representation* (Chicago: University of Chicago Press, 1994), 9; W. J. T. Mitchell, *What Do Pictures Want? The Lives and Loves of Images* (Chicago: University of Chicago Press, 2005); John Berger, *Ways of Seeing* (London: British Broadcasting Corporation; Harmondsworth, Penguin, 1972).

10. While the Atlantic world also cohered around other kinds of relationships than those of the transatlantic slave trade, and as early as the fifteenth century, the colonial relationships forged in service of slavery are the exigency against which early exhibitions of Black freedom were judged (Peggy K. Liss, *Atlantic Empires: The Network of Trade and Revolution, 1713–1826* [Baltimore: Johns Hopkins University Press, 1983]; John Thornton, *Africa and Africans in the Making of the Atlantic World, 1400–1800* [Cambridge: Cambridge University Press, 1998]).

11. Legal dictates on human property and reproduction were such that children followed the "condition of the mother." Sexual relationships between White masters and Black women produced unfree children, a determination that was calculated for slavery in the British Americas, whereas English property law continued to follow patrilineal bloodlines (Martha Hodes, *White Women, Black Men: Illicit Sex in the Nineteenth-Century South* [New Haven, CT: Yale University Press, 1997], 28–31; Felipe Smith, "The Condition of the Mother: The Legacy of Slavery in African American Literature of the Jim Crow Era," in *Women and Slavery: The Modern Atlantic*, ed. Gwyn Campbell, Suzanne Miers, and Joseph Calder Miller [Columbus: Ohio University Press, 2007]: 231–32).

12. Jennifer Lyle Morgan, "Women in Slavery and the Transatlantic Slave Trade," in *Transatlantic Slavery: Against Human Dignity*, ed. Anthony Tibbles (London: National Museums & Galleries on Merseyside, 1994), 62–65.

13. Deborah Willis and Carla Williams, *Black Female Body: A Photographic History* (Philadelphia: Temple University Press, 2002).

14. Brian Wallis, "Black Bodies, White Science: Louis Agassiz's Slave Daguerreotypes," *American Art* 9 (Summer 1995): 40.

15. Bibi Bakare-Yusuf, "Economy of Violence: Black Bodies and the Unspeakable Terror," in *Feminist Theory and the Body: A Reader*, ed. Janet Price and Margrit Shildrick (New York: Routledge, 1999), 321.

16. Erica Armstrong Dunbar, *Fragile Freedom: African American Women and Emancipation in the Antebellum City* (New Haven, CT: Yale University Press, 2008).

17. Paula Giddings, *When and Where I Enter: The Impact of Black Women on Race and Sex in America* (New York: William, Morrow, 1984), 59.

18. Patterson characterizes different experiences of freedom. Personal freedom, or the sense that one is not being coerced by others, is distinct from sovereignal freedom, or the right to act as one wishes, even if that means infringing upon others. Each of these is separate from the civic capacity to participate in governance of one's community (Orlando Patterson, *Freedom: Freedom in the Making of Western Culture* [New York: Basic, 1991], 1–9).

19. Orlando Patterson, *Slavery and Social Death: A Comparative Study* (Cambridge: Harvard University Press, 1982), 98.

20. Judith Wilson, "One Way or Another: Black Feminist Visual Theory," in *Feminism and Visual Culture Reader*, ed. Amelia Jones (New York: Routledge, 2003), 22.

21. Nicholas Mirzoeff, "On Visuality," *Journal of Visual Culture* 5 (April 2006): 67. Mirzoeff offers an extended examination of visuality and "countervisuality" as the "claim to the right to look." While I agree that the right to look is a moment of contestation, this project proposes a specifically Black "visualization of history" that is extratextual, extralegal, and, while seemingly ignited by resistance as a motive, is not inherently "counter" (Nicholas Mirzoeff, *Right to Look: A Counterhistory of Visuality* [Durham, NC: Duke University Press, 2011], 24).

22. Hal Foster, preface to *Vision and Visuality*, ed. Foster (Seattle: Bay Press, 1988), ix.

23. Michele Wallace, *Invisibility Blues: From Pop to Theory* (London: Verso, 2008). For more, see Kimberly Lamm, "Visuality and Black Masculinity in Ralph Ellison's *Invisible Man* and Romare Bearden's Photomontages," *Callaloo* 26 (Summer 2003): 813–35.

24. Nicole R. Fleetwood, *Troubling Vision: Performance, Visuality and Blackness* (Chicago: University of Chicago Press, 2011).

25. Stuart Hall, "What Is This 'Black' in Black Popular Culture?," in *Black Popular Culture*, ed. Gina Dent (Seattle: Bay Press, 1992), 21–36.

26. W. T. Lhamon, *Jump Jim Crow: Lost Plays, Lyrics, and Street Prose of the First Atlantic Popular Culture* (Cambridge: Harvard University Press, 2003), 2.

27. David Bindman and Henry Louis Gates Jr., eds., *The Image of the Black in Western Art: From The Age of Discovery to the Age of Abolition: Artists of the Renaissance and Baroque* (Cambridge: Harvard University Press, 2010), vii–xix; Langston Hughes, Milton Meltzer, and C. Eric Lincoln, *A Pictorial History of Blackamericans*, 5th rev. ed. (New York: Crown, 1983).

28. Raiford, "Critical Black Memory," 118.

29. David Armitage distinguishes three approaches to the Atlantic, Circum-Atlantic (transnational), Trans-Atlantic (international), and Cis-Atlantic (national within an Atlantic context) histories, which "are not exclusive but rather reinforcing" (David Armitage, "Three Concepts of Atlantic History," in *The British Atlantic World, 1500–1800*, ed. Armitage and Michael J. Braddick [New York: Palgrave Macmillan, 2009], 28). The "transatlantic" is about links between places scattered around the Atlantic Ocean, and the articles that foster their engagement with one another (Heidi Slettedahl Macpherson and Will Kaufman, eds., *New Perspectives in Transatlantic Studies* [Lanham, MD: University Press of America, 2002]; David Armitage and Michel J. Braddick,

eds., *The British Atlantic World, 1500–1800,* 2nd ed. [New York: Palgrave Macmillan, 2009], 20–28).

30. Scholars debate motives for the decline of British slavery, citing profitability and changes in public moral sentiment. For more, see Eric Williams, *Capitalism and Slavery* (Chapel Hill: University of North Carolina Press, 1944); and Seymour Drescher, *Econocide: British Slavery in the Era of Abolition* (Chapel Hill: University of North Carolina Press, 2010).

31. Mary Louis Clifford, *From Slavery to Freetown: Black Loyalists after the American Revolution* (Jefferson, NC: McFarland, 1999); Alan Gilbert, *Black Patriots and Loyalists: Fighting for Emancipation in the War for Independence* (Chicago: University of Chicago Press, 2012).

32. Eliga H. Gould and Peter S. Onuf, *Empire and Nation: The American Revolution in the Atlantic World* (Baltimore: Johns Hopkins University Press, 2005); Jonathan R. Dull, *A Diplomatic History of the American Revolution* (New Haven, CT: Yale University Press, 1987).

33. Sue Peabody, *"There Are No Slaves in France": The Political Culture of Race and Slavery in the Ancien Regime* (New York: Oxford University Press, 1996); C. L. R. James, *Black Jacobins* (New York: Vintage, 1989); Wim Klooster, *Revolutions in the Atlantic World: A Comparative History* (New York: New York University Press, 2010).

34. Mary Louis Pratt, "Arts in the Contact Zone," in *Mass Culture and Everyday Life* (New York: Routledge, 1997), 63.

35. Fritz Hirschfeld, *George Washington and Slavery: A Documentary Portrayal* (Columbia: University of Missouri Press, 1997), 53.

36. Sue Peabody, "Free upon Higher Ground: Saint-Domingue Slaves' Suits for Freedom in the U.S. Courts, 1792–1830," in *World of the Haitian Revolution,* ed. David Patrick Geggus and Norman Fiering (Bloomington: Indiana University Press, 2009), 264.

37. Joanne Pope Melish, *Disowning Slavery: Gradual Emancipation and "Race" in New England, 1780–1860* (Ithaca, NY: Cornell University Press, 1998); Gary B. Nash, *The Forgotten Fifth: African Americans in the Age of Revolution* (Cambridge: Harvard University Press, 2006).

38. Thomas Childs Cochran, *Pennsylvania: A Bicentennial History* (New York: Norton, 1978), 51–58; Gary Nash, *First City: Philadelphia and the Forging of Historical Memory* (Philadelphia: University of Pennsylvania Press, 2006).

39. Robert E. Wright, *First Wall Street: Chestnut Street, Philadelphia, and the Birth of American Finance* (Chicago: University of Chicago Press, 2010), 3.

40. Philadelphia's Black community numbered approximately 14,500 across classes by 1830, with elite household incomes ranging broadly (Joseph Willson, *Elite of Our People: Joseph Willson's Sketches of Black Upper-Class Life in Antebellum Philadelphia,* ed. Julie Winch [State College: Pennsylvania State University Press, 2000], 167; Julie Winch, *Philadelphia's Black Elite: Activism, Accommodation, and the Struggle for Autonomy, 1787–1848* [Philadelphia: Temple University Press, 1988]).

41. Emma Jones Lapsansky, "'Since They Got Those Separate Churches': Afro-Americans and Racism in Jacksonian Philadelphia," *American Quarterly* 32, no. 1 (1980): 54–78.

42. Mona Domosh and Joni Seager, *Putting Women in Place: Feminist Geographers Make Sense of the World* (New York: Guilford, 2001), 8.

43. Kenneth L. Ames, *Death in the Dining Room & Other Tales of Victorian Culture* (Philadelphia: Temple University Press, 1992).

44. Saly McMurry, "City Parlor, Country Sitting Room: Rural Vernacular Design and the American Parlor, 1840–1900," *Winterthur Portfolio* 20, no. 4 (1985): 261–80.

45. Stephen Prickett, *Victorian Fantasy* (Waco, TX: Baylor University Press, 2005); Marc Hewitt, ed., *Victorian World* (New York: Routledge, 2012), 1–55.

46. Catherine Karusseit, "Victorian Domestic Interiors as Subliminal Space" *SAJAH* 22, no. 3 (2007): 171.

47. Ella Rodman Church, "Household Furnishing Department, City Interiors, the Parlor," *Godey's Lady's Book*, May 1884 (Philadelphia).

48. Ibid.

49. Thad Logan, *Victorian Parlour* (Cambridge: Cambridge University Press, 2001), 7–16.

50. Ibid.

51. Katherine C. Grier, *Culture & Comfort: Parlor Making and Middle-Class Identity, 1850–1930* (Washington, DC: Smithsonian Books, 1988), 3–6.

52. Lyn H. Lofland, *Public Realm: Exploring the City's Quintessential Social Territory* (Hawthorne, NY: Aldine de Gruyter, 1998), 10.

53. Karen Halttunen, *Confidence Men and Painted Women: A Study of Middle-Class Culture in America, 1830–1870* (New Haven, CT: Yale University Press, 1982), xiv; Barbara Welter, "Cult of True Womanhood: 1820–1860," *American Quarterly* 18 (Summer 1966): 151–74.

54. Evelyn Brooks Higginbotham, "African-American Women's History and the Metalanguage of Race," *Signs* 17, no. 2 (1992): 261.

55. Gillian Brown, *Domestic Individualism: Imagining Self in Nineteenth-Century America* (Berkeley: University of California Press, 1990), 15.

56. Patricia Hill Collins, *Black Feminist Thought: Knowledge, Consciousness, and the Politics of Empowerment*, 2nd ed. (New York: Routledge, 2000), 47.

57. Emma Jones Lapsansky, "Friends, Wives, and Strivings: Networks and Community Values among Nineteenth-Century Philadelphia Afroamerican Elites," *Pennsylvania Magazine of History and Biography* 108 (January 1984): 5.

58. Ibid.

59. Simon Gikandi, *Slavery and the Culture of Taste* (Princeton, NJ: Princeton University Press, 2011), 111.

60. Paul Gilroy, *Black Atlantic: Modernity and Double Consciousness* (Cambridge: Harvard University Press, 1993), 40.

61. Ibid.

62. Amy Kaplan, "Manifest Domesticity," *American Literature* 7 (September 1998): 582.

63. Deborah Poole, "An Excess of Description: Ethnography, Race, and Visual Technologies," *Annual Review of Anthropology* 34 (2005): 163.

64. Stephen Best, "Neither Lost nor Found: Slavery and the Visual Archive," *Representation* 113 (Winter 2011): 151.

65. Ivy G. Wilson, *Specters of Democracy: Blackness and the Aesthetics of Politics in the Antebellum U.S.* (New York: Oxford University Press, 2011); Michael A. Chaney, *Fugitive Vision: Slave Image and Black Identity in Antebellum Slave Narrative* (Bloomington: Indiana University Press, 2008).

66. Kali N Gross, "Examining the Politics of Respectability in African American Studies," *University of Pennsylvania Almanac* 43 (April 1997): 15–16.

67. Gwendolyn DuBois Shaw, *Portraits of a People: Picturing African Americans in the Nineteenth Century* (Seattle: University of Washington Press, 2006), 13.

68. Kirk Savage, *Standing Soldiers, Kneeling Slaves: Race, War, and Monument in Nineteenth-Century America* (Princeton, NJ: Princeton University Press, 1997).

69. Amy Matilda Cassey Album, 1833–1856, LCP. Cassey was part of Philadelphia's "Black elite," active in local antislavery and literacy organizations. For more on Cassey's personal album, see Erica Armstrong Dunbar, "Writing for True Womanhood: African-American Women's Writings and the Antislavery Struggle," in *Women's Rights and Transatlantic Antislavery in the Era of Emancipation*, ed. Kathryn Kish Sklar and James Brewer Stewart (New Haven, CT: Yale University Press, 2007).

70. Lauren Gail Berlant, *Female Complaint: The Unfinished Business of Sentimentality in American Culture* (Durham, NC: Duke University Press, 2008), 5.

71. Stuart Hall, "Encoding/Decoding" in *Cultural Studies Reader,* ed. Simon During, 2nd ed. (New York: Routledge, 1993): 507–17.

72. Dunbar, *Fragile Freedom*; Julie Winch, *A Gentleman of Color: The Life of James Forten* (New York: Oxford University Press, 2002); Gary B. Nash, *First City: Philadelphia and the Forging of Historical Memory* (Philadelphia: University of Pennsylvania Press, 2002); Winch, *Philadelphia's Black Elite.*

73. Monica Miller, *Slaves to Fashion: Black Dandyism and the Styling of Black Diasporic Identity* (Durham, NC: Duke University Press, 2009); Daphne A. Brooks, *Bodies in Dissent: Spectacular Performances of Race and Freedom, 1850–1910* (Durham, NC: Duke University Press, 2006).

74. Jean-Paul Sartre, *Being and Nothingness: An Essay on Phenomenological Ontology* (New York: Philosophical Library, 1956); Frantz Fanon, *Black Skin, White Masks* (New York: Grove, 1982).

75. Leon F. Litwack, *North of Slavery: The Negro in the Free States, 1790–1860* (Chicago: University of Chicago Press, 1961); Benjamin Quarles, *Black Abolitionists* (New York: De Capo, 1969); Shirley J. Yee, *Black Abolitionist Women: A Study in Activism, 1828–1860* (Knoxville: University of Tennessee Press, 1992).

76. Sarah Mapps Douglass, "A token of love from me, to thee," Amy Matilda Cassey Album, 1833, LCP, 5.

77. Edward Williams Clay, "Back to Back," 1829, LCP; Richard J. Powell, *Cutting a Figure: Fashioning Black Portraiture* (Chicago: University of Chicago, 2008).

NOTES TO CHAPTER 1

1. Barbara L. Solow, ed., *Slavery and the Rise of the Atlantic System* (Cambridge: Cambridge University Press, 1993), 2.

2. Martha Jones, "Time, Space, and Jurisdiction in Atlantic World Slavery: The Volunbrun Household in Gradual Emancipation New York," *Law and History Review* 29, no. 4 (2011): 1034.

3. Susan Anne Livingston Ridley Sedgwick, portrait of Elizabeth Mumbet Freeman, 1811, Massachusetts Historical Society, Boston.

4. Catharine Maria Sedgwick, "Mumbett" manuscript draft, 1853, Catharine Maria Sedgwick Papers, Massachusetts Historical Society, Boston. For more on Sedgwick, see Mary Kelley, *Private Women, Public Stage: Literary Domesticity in America* (New York: Oxford University Press, 1984).

5. The family patriarch Theodore Sedgwick represented Freeman in court, before hiring her to work as a paid servant of the Sedgwick family.

6. My discussion is based upon the marked-up draft of Sedgwick's biography on Freemen. For the published version, see Miss Sedgwick, "Slavery in New England," *Bentley's Miscellany* 34 (1853): 417.

7. The term "peculiar institution" was first used in the "Speech on the Reception of Abolition Petitions" by South Carolina legislator and seventh vice president of the United States John C. Calhoun (John C. Calhoun, "Speech on the Reception of Abolition Petitions," http://web.utk.edu/mfitzge1/doc/374.RAP1837.pdf).

8. Charmaine Nelson, *Representing the Black Female Subject in Western Art* (New York: Routledge, 2010), 124.

9. Chaney, *Fugitive Vision*, 11,

10. *Brom & Bett v. J. Ashley Esq.*, 4A (Berkshire County Courthouse, Great Barrington, Massachusetts, Inferior Court of Common Pleas 28 May 1781).

11. Sedgwick, "Mumbet," 20.

12. *Pennsylvania Gazette* advertisements for Black fugitives from the Mid-Atlantic region, Virginia, and South Carolina report that most runaways were overwhelmingly male, were ages twenty to twenty-nine, and were born on the "American Continent" (Billy G. Smith and Richard Wojtowicz, *Blacks Who Stole Themselves: Advertisements for Runaways in the Pennsylvania Gazette, 1728–1790* [Philadelphia: University of Pennsylvania Press, 1989]).

13. C. Riley Snorton, *Nobody Is Supposed to Know: Black Sexuality on the Down Low* (Minneapolis: University of Minnesota Press, 2014).

14. Claude H. Nolen, *African American Southerners in Slavery, Civil War, and Reconstruction* (Jefferson, NC: McFarland, 2001), 82; Eugene Genovese, *Roll, Jordan, Roll: The World the Slaves Made* (New York: Vintage, 1976), 366.

15. Lawmakers enacted "slave codes" throughout the North and the South to dictate the management of unfree Black people, reinforcing and protecting slavery through specifications about rules and punishments (Graham Russell Hodges, *Slavery and Freedom in*

the Rural North: African Americans in Monmouth County, New Jersey, 1665–1865 [Madison: University of Wisconsin, 1997], 24–26; Patience Essah, *A House Divided: Slavery and Emancipation in Delaware, 1638–1865* [Charlottesville: University Press of Virginia, 1996], 33–35; Winthrop D. Jordan, *White over Black: American Attitudes toward the Negro 1550–1812* [Chapel Hill: University of North Carolina Press, 1968], 82–83). "Black codes" followed this logic, associating "Negros" with chaos and disorder (Leon Higginbotham, *In the Matter of Color: Race and the American Legal Process, the Colonial Period* [New York: Oxford University Press, 1980], 80–82; Barbara Young Welke, "Law, Personhood, and Citizenship in the Long Nineteenth Century: The Borders of Belonging," in *Cambridge History of Law in America*, vol. 1, ed. Michael Grossberg and Christopher Tomlins [Cambridge: Cambridge University Press, 2008], 353–55).

16. Saidiya V. Hartman, *Scenes of Subjection: Terror, Slavery and Self-Making in Nineteenth-Century America* (New York: Oxford University Press, 1997), 40.

17. Elaine Scarry, *Body in Pain: The Making and Unmaking of the World* (New York: Oxford University Press, 1985), 27.

18. Walter Johnson, *River of Dark Dreams: Slavery and Empire in the Cotton Kingdom* (Cambridge: Harvard University Press, 2013), 42; see also Michael Tadman, *Speculators and Slaves: Masters, Traders, and Slaves in the Old South* (Madison: University of Wisconsin Press, 1989).

19. Simone Browne, "Everybody's Got a Little Light under the Sun: Black Luminosity and the Visual Culture of Surveillance," *Cultural Studies* 25 (January 2012): 551–53.

20. Patricia J. Williams, *Alchemy of Race: Diary of a Law Professor* (Cambridge: Harvard University Press, 1991): 218–20.

21. Black women who labored in intimate proximity to Whites, and especially White women, often obtained information via eavesdropping on private conversation and through their care for White children (Marli Frances Weiner, *Mistresses and Slaves: Plantation Women in South Carolina, 1830–80* [Urbana: University of Illinois Press, 1997], 120).

22. Kenneth M. Stampp, *Peculiar Institution: Slavery in the Ante-bellum South* (New York: Knopf, 1956), 206.

23. Jonathan Prude, "To Look upon the 'Lower Sort': Runaway Ads and the Appearance of Unfree Laborers in America, 1750–1800," *Journal of American History* 78 (June 1991): 128.

24. Martin Jay, "Sartre, Merleau-Ponty, and the Search for a New Ontology of Sight," in *Modernity and the Hegemony of Vision*, ed. David Michael Levin (Berkeley: University of California Press, 1993), 156.

25. Walter Johnson, *Soul by Soul: Life inside the Antebellum Slave Market* (Cambridge: Harvard University Press, 2001), 137.

26. Ibid., 119.

27. Nicolas Mirzoeff, *An Introduction to Visual Culture*, 2nd ed. (New York: Routledge, 2009), 68.

28. Matthew Frye Jacobson, *Whiteness of a Different Color: European Immigrants and the Alchemy of Race* (Cambridge: Harvard University Press, 1998), 9.

29. George Lipsitz, *Possessive Investment in Whiteness: How White People Profit from Identity Politics*, rev. ed. (Philadelphia: Temple University Press, 2009), 2–6.

30. James O. Horton, *In Hope of Liberty: Culture, Community, and Protest among Northern Free Blacks, 1700–1860* (New York: Oxford University Press, 1997), 41.

31. William H. Williams, *Slavery and Freedom in Delaware, 1639–1865* (Wilmington, DE: SR Books, 1996), 39.

32. "BOSTON, MAY 6.Yesterday the Freeholders and other Inhabitants," *South Carolina Gazette; And Country Journal*, July 6, 1773.

33. David Waldstreicher, *Runaway America: Benjamin Franklin, Slavery, and the American Revolution* (New York: Hill and Wang, 2004), 3.

34. Ibid.

35. Richard Dyer, *White* (New York: Routledge, 1997), 45.

36. Eric Lott, *Love and Theft: Blackface Minstrelsy and the American Working Class* (New York: Oxford University Press, 1993), 161.

37. David Roediger, *Wages of Whiteness: Race and the Making of the American Working Class*, rev. ed. (New York: Verso, 1999), 117.

38. Clint C Wilson, Félix Gutiérrez, and Lena M Chao, eds., *Racism, Sexism, and the Media: The Rise of Class Communication in Multicultural America* (Thousand Oaks, CA: Sage, 2003), 116.

39. Marita Sturken and List Cartwright, *Practices of Looking: An Introduction to Visual Culture* (New York: Oxford University Press, 2009), 50.

40. Rachel Hall, "Missing Dolly, Mourning Slavery: The Slave Notice as Keepsake," *Camera Obscura* 61 (May 2006): 80.

41. David Waldstreicher, "Reading the Runaways: Self-Fashioning, Print Culture and Confidence in Slavery in the Eighteenth-Century Mid-Atlantic," *William and Mary Quarterly* 56 (April 1999): 243–72.

42. bell hooks, *Black Looks: Race and Representation* (Boston: South End Press, 1992), 127.

43. John Hope Franklin and Loren Schweninger, *Runaway Slaves: Rebels on the Plantation* (New York: Oxford University Press, 1999), 170.

44. Wood, *Blind Memory*, 80.

45. Smith and Wojtowicz, *Blacks Who Stole Themselves*, 3.

46. Ronald Zboray, *A Fictive People: Antebellum Economic Development and the American Reading Public* (New York: Oxford University Press, 1993), 196–201.

47. David D. Hall, *Cultures of Print: Essays in the History of the Book*, (Amherst: University of Massachusetts Press 1996), 57; Scott Casper et al., eds., *A History of the Book in America*, vol. 3, *The Industrial Book, 1840–1880* (Chapel Hill: University of North Carolina Press, 2007), 179; William J. Gilmore, "Elementary Literacy on the Eve of the Industrial Revolution: Trends in Rural New England, 1760–1830," *Proceedings of the American Antiquarian Society* 92, no.1 (1982): 87–171.

48. "RUNAWAY, From the Subscriber's Plantation in St. Stephen's Parish," *South Carolina Gazette*, September 26, 1771.

49. Franklin and Schweninger, *Runaway Slaves,* 64.

50. "FORTY DOLLARS Reward. RAN Away, on the 29th August, a Mulatto," *Pennsylvania Gazette,* October 3, 1792.

51. Harriet Jacobs, "Incidents in the Life of a Slave Girl," in *Classic African American Women's Narratives,* ed. William L. Andrews (New York: Oxford University Press, 2003), 289.

52. Lauren Berlant, *Queen of America Goes to Washington City: Essays on Sex and Citizenship* (Durham, NC: Duke University Press, 1997), 230.

53. W. Jeffrey Bolster, *Black Jacks: African American Seamen in the Age of Sail* (Cambridge: Harvard University Press, 1997).

54. www/pbs.org/wgbh/aia/part4/4h1541.html. Copy from the American Beacon, July 4, 1835, courtesy of the North Carolina Division of Archives and History.

55. "TO BE SOLD at Private Sale, and delivered Immediately; TWENTY," *South Carolina and American General Gazette,* December 12, 1766.

56. "TO BE SOLD, at Public Venue, At the Usual Place in Charles-Town" *South Carolina Gazette,* January 12, 1769.

57. "To Be Sold," *Virginia Gazette,* February 17, 1738. The *Virginia Gazette* featured a number of these advertisements that detail ready-made plantations, furnished with homes, outhouses, animals and human chattel; often associated with the death of a former owner.

58. *South Carolina Gazette; And Country Journal,* June 30, 1772.

59. "Brought to the WORK-HOUSE," *South Carolina Gazette; And Country Journal,* December 7, 1773.

60. U.S. runaway notices often referred to "country marks," or ethnic markings on the bodies of kidnapped Africans, distinguishing these fugitives from those who were "this country-born." Many advertisements indicate "that not only Africans recognized their differences, but others did as well" (Michael Gomez, *Exchanging Our Country Marks: The Transformation of African Identities in the Colonial and Antebellum South* [Chapel Hill: University of North Carolina Press, 1998], 39).

61. Hartman, *Scenes of Subjection,* 57. Hartman uses these terms interchangeably.

62. Ibid., 69.

63. Amani Marshall, "'They Will Endeavor to Pass for Free': Enslaved Runaways' Performances of Freedom in Antebellum South Carolina," *Slavery & Abolition* 31 (June 2010): 167.

64. "Performativity," as Michelle Wallace points out, "is visual" in that the gestures and acts that coalesce into an identity are acted out with reception in mind. The performance calls on the viewers, and where power and domination help cue that presentation, the sense of observation might be even stronger (Michelle Wallace, *Dark Designs and Visual Culture* [Durham, NC: Duke University Press, 2004], 122).

65. "Marcus Hook, Chester County, August 23, 1763," *Pennsylvania Gazette,* September 1, 1763.

66. "RUN Away from the Subscriber, Living at Middletown, in East," *Pennsylvania Gazette,* April 15, 1756. Stillwell took out a second, and slightly altered ad almost a year

later, this time reporting that Cato left twelve months ago, that he has made many name changes and possibly had forged a free pass ("Middletown, Monmouth County, East New Jersey, Aug. 1, 1757," *Pennsylvania Gazette*, August 11, 1757).

67. Samira Kawash, *Dislocating the Color Line: Identity, Hybridity, and Singularity in African-American Literature* (Stanford: Stanford University Press, 1997), 50–52.

68. Brooks, *Bodies in Dissent*, 8.

69. Fred Moten, *In the Break: The Aesthetics of the Black Radical Tradition* (Minneapolis: University of Minnesota Press, 2003), 16.

70. Charles Henry Rowell and Fred Moten, "'Words Don't Go There': An Interview with Fred Moten," *Callaloo* 27 (2004): 955–66.

71. John L. Jackson Jr., *Real Black: Adventures in Racial Sincerity* (Chicago: University of Chicago Press, 2005), 18.

72. Stefano Harney and Fred Moten, *Undercommons: Fugitive Planning and Black Study* (Brooklyn: Minor Compositions, 2013), 11.

73. Steven M. Wise, *Though the Heavens May Fall: The Landmark Trial that Led to the End of Human Slavery* (Cambridge, MA: Da Capo, 2005), 1–12.

74. Jennifer Lyle Morgan, *Laboring Women: Gender and Reproduction in New World Slavery* (Philadelphia: University of Pennsylvania Press, 2004), 145.

75. "RAN away from the Subscriber, living in Norfolk," *Virginia Gazette*, January 24, 1752.

76. Graham Russell Hodges and Alan Edward Brown, eds., *"Pretends to Be Free:" Runaway Slave Advertisements from Colonial and Revolutionary New York and New Jersey* (New York: Garland, 1994), xiv.

77. Simon Schama, *Rough Crossings: Britain, the Slaves and the American Revolution* (London: BBC Books, 2005).

78. F. O Shyllon, *Black Slaves in Britain* (New York: Oxford University Press, 1974).

79. Frances Hargrave, *An Argument in the case of James Sommersett a negro. Wherein it is attempted to demonstrate the present unlawfulness of domestic slavery in England. To which is prefixed a state of the case. By Mr. Hargrave, One of the Counsel for the Negro*, 2nd ed. (London: Printed for the Author: and Sold by W. Otridge, opposite the New Church, in the Strand; 1775), 11.

80. Candidus, *A Letter to Philo Africanus, upon slavery; in answer to his of the 22d of November, in the General Evening Post; together with the opinions of Sir John Strange, and other eminent lawyers upon this subject, with the sentence of Lord Mansfield, in the case of Somerset and Knowles, 1772, With His Lordship's Explanation of that Opinion in 1786* (London: Printed for W. Brown, Bookseller, Corner of Essex-Street, Strand, 1788), 11.

81. William M. Wiecek, "Lord Mansfield and the Legitimacy of Slavery in the Anglo-American World," *University of Chicago Law Review* 42 (Autumn 1974): 87.

82. David Brion Davis, *The Problem of Slavery in the Age of Revolution, 1770–1823* (New York: Oxford University Press, 1999), 231–32.

83. William R. Cotter, "The Somerset Case and the Abolition of Slavery in England," *History* 79 (February 1994): 32.

84. David Brion Davis, *Challenging the Boundaries of Slavery* (Cambridge: Harvard University Press, 2003), 64.

85. Howard Jones, *Mutiny on the Amistad: The Saga of a Slave Revolt and Its Impact on American Abolition, Law, and Diplomacy* (New York: Oxford University Press, 1987).

86. David Brion Davis, *Inhuman Bondage: The Rise and Fall of Slavery in the New World* (New York: Oxford University Press, 2006), 13.

87. Ibid., 15.

88. Iyunolu Folayan Osagie, *Amistad Revolt: Memory, Slavery and the Politics of Identity in the United States and Sierra Leone* (Athens: University of Georgia Press, 2010).

89. "Ladinos," or Spanish-speaking Africans, were distinct from "bozales," enslaved Blacks who were kidnapped and taken to Spain or the Americas from Africa, in that ladinos were acculturated into Spanish life, especially language and customs. For more, see Junius P. Rodriguez, ed., *Historical Encyclopedia of World Slavery*, vol. 1 (Santa Barbara: ABC-CLIO, 1997), 97.

90. Osagie, *Amistad Revolt*, 17.

91. J. E. Twitchell, *Amistad Captives, and the Origin and Growth of the American Missionary Association* (New York: American Missionary Association, 1898), Beinecke Rare Books and Manuscript Library, Yale University.

92. Donald Jacobs, *Courage and Conscience: Black and White Abolitionists in Boston* (Bloomington: University of Indiana Press, 1993), 60.

93. Huey Copeland, "Glen Ligon and Other Runaway Subjects," *Representations* 113, no. 1 (2011): 79–80.

94. "From the Boston Courier," *Liberator*, September 13, 1839.

95. Ibid.

96. Michel Foucault, *Discipline and Punish: Birth of the Prison*, trans. Alan Sheridan (New York: Vintage, 1995), 216.

97. Marcus Rediker, *Amistad Rebellion: An Atlantic Odyssey of Slavery and Freedom* (New York: Penguin, 2012); Richard J. Powell, "Cinqué: Antislavery Portraiture and Patronage in Jacksonian America," *American Art* 11 (Fall 1997): 49–73.

98. "We Last Week Visited the Amistad Captives; Not the Great Originals," *Colored American*, June 27, 1840.

99. "Items," *Liberator*, May 22, 1840.

100. "We Last Week Visited the Amistad Captives; Not the Great Originals," *Colored American*, June 27, 1840.

101. William H. Townsend, *Sketches of the Amistad Captives* (1839–1840), Beinecke Rare Books and Manuscript Library, Yale University.

102. Racial paranoia, or "distrustful conjecture about purposeful race-based maliciousness and the 'benign neglect' of racial indifference" (John L. Jackson, Jr. *Racial Paranoia: Unintended Consequences of Political Correctness* [New York: Basic Civitas, 2008], 3).

103. Richard Delgado and Jean Stefancic, eds., *Critical White Studies: Looking behind the Mirror* (Philadelphia: Temple University Press, 1997), 589.

NOTES TO CHAPTER 2

1. "Fashionable Expensive Poor," *Colored American,* November 23, 1839.

2. The *Christian Recorder,* an African American newspaper published by the African Methodist Episcopal Church in Philadelphia, circulated from 1861 to 1902. It frequently advertised the sale of parlor furnishings and also printed a number of opinion columns on how to best decorate a polite and tasteful drawing room.

3. These items are dissimilar from the postbellum items that consumers filled with newspaper clippings, but they may also be considered together. "*Scrapbook* has been a flexible term, used alongside *album* and *portfolio* and *commonplace book*" (Ellen Gruber Garvey, *Writing with Scissors: American Scrapbooks from the Civil War to the Harlem Renaissance* [New York: Oxford University Press, 2012], 15).

4. Stephen Loring Jones, "A Keen Sense of the Artistic: African American Material Culture in 19th Century Philadelphia," *International Review of African American Art* 12, no. 2 (1995): 4–29; James Andrews, *Lessons in Flower Painting: A Series of Easy and Progressive Studies* (London: Charles Tilt, 1836).

5. The "language of flowers" circulated as a popular literary discourse throughout Britain, France, and the United States beginning at the turn of the nineteenth century. Although floral manuals offered inconsistent definitions for flower meanings, both from one country to another, as well as from one manual to another, the "language of flowers" retained its transatlantic significance as a discourse of femininity (Beverly Seaton, *Language of Flowers: A History* [Charlottesville: University of Virginia Press, 1995]).

6. Sarah Mapps Douglass, "Fuchsia," Mary Anne Dickerson Album, 1848, LCP.

7. Charles L. Blockson, *Underground Railroad* (New York: Prentice-Hall, 1987).

8. Winch, *Philadelphia's Black Elite,* 240; Evelyn Brooks Higginbotham, *Righteous Discontent: The Women's Movement in the Black Baptist Church, 1880–1920* (Cambridge: Harvard University Press, 1993), 306.

9. Berlant, *Female Complaint,* viii.

10. Beverly Guy-Sheftall, *Words of Fire: An Anthology of African-American Feminist Thought* (New York: New Press, 1995), 4.

11. Rebecca Primus and Farah Jasmine Griffin, *Beloved Sisters and Loving Friends: Letters from Rebecca Primus of Royal Oak, Maryland, and Addie Brown of Hartford, Connecticut, 1854–1868* (Chino Valley: One World, 2001), 6.

12. White men hypersexualized Black women in slavery to justify rape with mythologies of sexual availability. Cultural producers fetishized free Black women by distorting their bodies for ridicule and sexual fantasy (bell hooks, *Black Looks,* 62; Charmaine A. Nelson, *Representing the Black Female Subject in Western Art* [New York: Routledge, 2010], 120; Leslie W. Lewis, *Telling Narratives: Secrets in African American Literature* [Urbana: University of Illinois Press, 2007], 137).

13. Elizabeth Barnes, "Affecting Relations: Pedagogy, Patriarchy, and the Politics of Sympathy," *American Literary History* 8 (Winter 1996): 597–614; Shirley Samuels, *Romances of the Republic: Women, the Family and Violence in the Literature of the Early*

American Nation (New York: Oxford University Press, 1996); Jane Tompkins, *Sensational Designs: The Cultural Work of American Fiction, 1790–1860* (Durham, NC: Duke University Press, 1986).

14. Hazel V. Carby, *Reconstructing Womanhood: The Emergence of the Afro-American Woman Novelist* (New York: Oxford University Press, 1987), 49.

15. Martin Summers, *Manliness and Its Discontents: The Black Middle Class and the Transformation of Masculinity, 1900–1930* (Chapel Hill: University of North Carolina Press, 2004), 42.

16. Higginbotham, "Metalanguage of Race," 272.

17. Farah Griffin, *If You Can't Be Free, Be A Mystery: In Search of Billie Holiday* (New York: Free Press, 2001), 72.

18. E. Frances White, *Dark Continent of Our Bodies: Black Feminism and the Politics of Respectability* (Philadelphia: Temple University Press, 2001), 36.

19. Victoria Wolcott offers a historiography of "respectability," citing the "values of hard work, thrift, piety, and sexual restraint" defining one pole, versus determinations of "class status and privilege through dress, deportment, and organizational affiliation" as another (*Remaking Respectability: African American Women in Interwar Detroit* [Chapel Hill: University of North Carolina Press, 2001], 5).

20. *Oxford American Dictionary*, s.v. "optics."

21. Fatimah Tobing Rony, *The Third Eye: Race, Cinema, and Ethnographic Spectacle* (Durham, NC: Duke University Press, 1996), 4.

22. D. Soyini Madison, "Pretty Woman through the Triple Lens of Black Feminist Spectatorship," in *From Mouse to Mermaid: The Politics of Film, Gender, and Culture*, ed. Elizabeth Bell, Lynda Haas, and Laura Sells (Bloomington: Indiana University Press, 1995), 234.

23. W. E. B. Du Bois, *Souls of Black Folk* (New York: Library of America, 1986), 364; Shawn Michelle Smith, *Photography on the Color Line: W. E. B. Du Bois, Race and Visual Culture* (Durham, NC: Duke University Press, 2004).

24. Mary Wood Forten, mother of Charlotte Forten, also maintained her own personal album (Moorland-Spingarn Library at Howard University; hereafter cited as MRS).

25. Mary Forten, "Good Wives," Amy Matilda Cassey Album, LCP, 22. "Good Wives" also appeared in a naughty book of poems that joked about premarital sex and marriage as a tedious undertaking. For more, see Thomas Tegg, *The Common-place Book of Humorous Poetry: Consisting of a Choice Collection of Entertaining Original and Selected Pieces* (London: Cheapside, 1826).

26. Dunbar, *Fragile Freedom*, 196.

27. Middle-class identity for the free Black community sometimes marked personal qualities, but frequently included persons who labored for pay. Many Black women of the "middle class" did a number of jobs, combining "motherhood, income-producing labor" as well as "public service" and lecturing (Emma Jones Lapsansky, "Friends, Wives, and Strivings: Networks and Community Values among Nineteenth-Century Philadelphia Afroamerican Elites," *Pennsylvania Magazine of History and Biography* 108 [January 1984]: 8).

28. Deborah Gray White, "The Cost of Club Work, the Price of Black Feminism," in *Visible Women: New Essays on American Activism*, ed. Nancy A. Hewitt and Suzanne Lebsock (Urbana: University of Illinois Press, 1993), 257.

29. Frederick Douglass, Amy Matilda Cassey Album, 1850, LCP, 34.

30. Patricia Hill Collins, "What's in a Name?: Womanism, Black Feminism, and Beyond," *Black Scholar* 26, no. 1 (Winter/Spring 1996): 9–17.

31. Pier Gabrielle Foreman, *Activist Sentiments: Reading Black Women in the Nineteenth Century* (Urbana: University of Illinois Press, 2009), 7.

32. William L. Andrews, ed., *Sisters of the Spirit: Three Black Women's Autobiographies of the 19th Century* (Bloomington: Indiana University Press, 1986), 23.

33. Jocelyn Moody, *Sentimental Confessions: Spiritual Narratives of Nineteenth-Century African American Women* (Athens: University of Georgia, 2001), 20.

34. Robin Bernstein, "Dances with Things: Material Culture and the Performance of Race," *Social Text* 27, no. 4 (2009): 11.

35. Shirley Samuels, introduction to *Culture of Sentiment: Race, Gender and Sentimentality in Nineteenth Century*, ed. Samuels (New York: Oxford University Press, 1992), 4.

36. Karen Halttunen, *Confidence Men and Painted Women: A Study of Middle-Class Culture in America, 1830–1870* (New Haven, CT: Yale University Press, 1982), xiv.

37. Lori D. Ginzberg, *Women in Antebellum Reform* (Illinois: Harlan-Davidson, 2000); Jean Fagan Yellin, *Women & Sisters: The Antislavery Feminists in American Culture* (New Haven, CT: Yale University Press, 1989).

38. Chief among these thinkers is David Hume, who produced both philosophies of sentiment as well as racist conceptualizations of knowledge (David Hume et al., *A Treatise of Human Nature: A Critical Edition* [New York: Clarendon, 2007], 1173). For the consequences of Hume's philosophy of sentiment, see Jacqueline Taylor, "Hume on the Standard of Virtue," *Journal of Ethics* 6, no. 1 (2002): 43–62. Similarly, Adam Smith also wrote "A Theory of Moral Sentiments" in addition to his work on capitalism.

39. Kimberly Wallace Sanders, *Skin Deep, Spirit Strong: The Black Female Body in American Culture* (Ann Arbor: University of Michigan Press, 2002); Jayna Brown, *Babylon Girls: Black Women Performers and the Shaping of the Modern* (Durham, NC: Duke University Press, 2008), 72.

40. Willis and Williams, *Black Female Body*, 2.

41. Lapsansky, "Meet the Dickersons"; Erica R. Armstrong, "A Mental and Moral Feast: Reading, Writing, and Sentimentality in Black Philadelphia," *Journal of Women's History* 16, no. 1 (2004): 78–102.

42. Eliza Ann Howell, daughter of free Black migrants, married Frederick Hinton when she was sixteen. She attended St. Thomas church with her husband before her death (Willson, *Elite of Our People*, 147–50).

43. Ann Howell Hinton, Martina Dickerson Album, 1840, LCP, 73.

44. Sarah Mapps Douglass, Martina Dickerson Album, 1843, LCP, 83.

45. Margaretta Forten, Amy Matilda Cassey Album, 1834, LCP, 14.

46. Catherine Kelly, *In the New England Fashion: Reshaping Women's Lives in the Nineteenth Century* (Ithaca, NY: Cornell University Press, 1999), 79.

47. Amy Ann Abbott Album, 1832, LCP.

48. Mary Wood Forten Album, MSR Center, Howard University.

49. Douglass signed, dated, and cited his contribution at the bottom to acknowledge it as a "copied" contribution, which originally appeared in *Token*, a nineteenth-century giftbook that also featured short stories from writers like Nathanial Hawthorne (Robert Douglass, "First Steamboat on the Missouri," Friendship Album of Martina Dickerson Album, September 25, 1841, LCP).

50. Robert Douglass, Friendship Album of Mary Anne Dickerson, LCP, 3. The eighteenth-century poet William Shenstone offered this abolitionist poem along with others in his *Poems of William Shenstone*, vol. 1, (n.p.: Press of Whittingham, 1822). The original image was so popular during its time that Douglass and many others republished the poem and the image. For more, see Lydia Maria Child, *An Appeal in Favor of That Class of Americans called Africans* (Boston: Allen and Ticknor, 1833); Jasmine Nichole Cobb, "'Forget Me Not': Free Black Women and Sentimentality," *MELUS: Multi-Ethnic Literature of the United States* 40 (forthcoming).

51. Amy Cassey, Amy Matilda Cassey Album, November 1838, LCP.

52. Alison Piepmeier, *Out in Public: Configurations of Women's Bodies in Nineteenth-Century America* (Chapel Hill: University of North Carolina Press, 2004), 175.

53. Mary Wood Forten Album, 1834, MRS.

54. Sarah Mapps Douglass, Friendship Album of Amy Cassey, LCP, 6.

55. Melvin Dixon, *Ride Out the Wilderness: Geography and Identity in Afro-American Literature* (Urbana: University of Illinois Press, 1987), 18.

56. Stacy Alaimo, *Undomesticated Ground: Recasting Nature as Feminist Space* (Ithaca, NY: Cornell University Press, 2000), 137.

57. Maureen Honey, *Shadowed Dreams: Women's Poetry of the Harlem Renaissance* (New Brunswick, NJ: Rutgers University Press, 2006), xxxix.

58. Prominent examples include Alice Walker, *In Search of Our Mothers' Gardens* (Orlando: Harcourt, 1983); Marita Bonner, "Purple Flower," in *Black Female Playwrights: An Anthology of Plays before 1950*, ed. Kathy A. Perkins (Bloomington: Indiana University Press, 1990): 191–200.

59. Beverly Seaton, *Language of Flowers: A History* (Charlottesville: University Press of Virginia, 1995).

60. E. E. Perkins, *Elements of Drawing and Flower Painting: In Opaque and Transparent Water-Colour* (London: T. Hurst, 1835).

61. Henriette Dumont, *Language of Flowers: The Floral Offering* (Philadelphia: H. C. Peck & Theo Bliss, 1852)

62. Maurice O. Wallace, *Constructing the Black Masculine: Identity and Ideality in African American Men's Literature and Culture, 1775–1995* (Durham, NC: Duke University Press, 2002).

63. Robert Reid-Pharr, *Conjugal Union: The Body, the House, and the Black American* (New York: Oxford University Press on Demand: 1999), 7.

64. Kali Gross, *Colored Amazons: Crime, Violence, and Black Women in the City of Brotherly Love, 1880–1910* (Durham, NC: Duke University Press, 2006), 35.

65. Deborah Gray White, "Jezebel and Mammy: The Mythology of Female Slavery," in *Race, Ethnicity and Gender: Selected Readings*, ed. Joseph F. Healey and Eileen O'Brien (Thousand Oaks: Pine Forge Press, 2004), 127.

66. Lapsansky, "Separate Churches," 59.

67. Lapsansky, "Meet the Dickersons," *1993 Annual Report*, 17.

68. Henry Mayer, *All on Fire: William Lloyd Garrison and the Abolition of Slavery* (New York: St. Martin's, 1998), 174.

69. William Lloyd Garrison, "Abolition Cause," Amy Matilda Cassey Album, 1833, LCP.

70. Edwin Wolf 2nd, *From Gothic Windows to Peacocks: American Embossed Leather Bindings, 1825– 1855* (Philadelphia: LCP, 1990), 3.

71. Fred B. Adelson, "Art under Cover: American Gift-Book Illustrations," *Magazine Antiques* 126, no. 3 (1984): 646.

72. Wolf, *Gothic Windows to Peacocks*, 3.

73. Paul R. Mullins, "Racializing the Parlor: Race and Victorian Bric-a-Brac Consumption," *Race and the Archeology of Identity*, ed. Charles E. Orser Jr. (Salt Lake City: University of Utah Press, 2001), 163.

74. Marilyn Maness Mehaffy, "Advertising Race/Raceing Advertising: The Feminine Consumer(-Nation), 1876–1900," *Signs: Journal of Women in Culture and Society* 23, no. 1 (1997): 131–74.

75. Mullins, "Racializing the Parlor," 161.

76. The embedded picture offers instruction on how to understand the overall image. Not only were these caricatures read as humorous, but in mitigating "first- and second-order representation," they also helped readers distinguish between their own sight and the misperceptions prevalent among free African American women (Mitchell, *What Do Pictures Want?* 210; Mitchell, *Picture Theory*, 445).

77. Emma Jones Lapsansky, "Friends, Wives, and Strivings: Networks and Community Values among Nineteenth-Century Philadelphia Afroamerican Elites," *Pennsylvania Magazine of History and Biography* 108, no. 1 (January 1984): 3–24.

78. Willson, *Elite of Our People*, 167.

79. For more on Remond, see William Edward Ward, *Charles Lenox Remond: A Black Abolitionist, 1838–1873* (Worcester, MA: Clark University Press, 1977).

80. Sarah Forten, "Original," Amy Matilda Cassey Album, 10 May 1833, LCP.

81. Herbert G. Gutman, *The Black Family in Slavery and Freedom, 1750–1925* (New York: Vintage, 1976); Francis Smith, *'Til Death or Distance Do Us Part: Love and Marriage in African America* (New York: Oxford University Press, 2009); Tess Chakkalakal, *Novel Bondage: Slavery, Marriage, and Freedom in Nineteenth-Century America* (Urbana: University of Illinois Press, 2011).

82. Amy Matilda Williams was born to clergyman Peter Williams Jr. and his wife, Sarah, of New York City, in 1809. She married Cassey in 1826, and once widowed in 1848, she married Remond in 1850 (Willson, *Elite of Our People* 165–67).

83. Janie Sumler-Lewis, "Forten-Purvis Women of Philadelphia and the American Anti-Slavery Crusade," *Journal of Negro History* 66 (Winter 1981–82): 282.

84. Darlene Clark Hine, *Hine Sight: Black Women and the Re-construction of American History* (Brooklyn: Carlson, 1994), 37.

85. Winch bases her claim on the timing of Forten's marriage and the birth of her first child ("Sarah Forten's Anti-slavery Networks," in *Women's Rights and Transatlantic Antislavery in the Era of Emancipation*, ed. Kathryn Kish Sklar and James Brewer Stewart [New Haven, CT: Yale University Press, 2007], 152–54).

86. Ibid., 153.

87. Dorothy Sterling, *We Are Your Sisters: Black Women in the Nineteenth Century* (New York: Norton, 1984), 130–31.

88. Marie J. Lindhorst, "Sarah Mapps Douglass: The Emergence of an African American Educator/Activist in Nineteenth Century Philadelphia" (PhD diss., Pennsylvania State University, 1995).

89. Marie Lindhorst, "Politics in a Box: Sarah Mapps Douglass and the Female Literary Association, 1831–1833," *Pennsylvania History* 65 (Summer 1998): 264.

90. Lapsansky, "Afro-Americana: Meet the Dickersons," 18; *An African American Miscellany Selections from a Quarter Century of Collecting, 1970–1995: An Exhibition February 5 through September 27, 1996* (Philadelphia: LCP, 1996).

91. Margaret Dikovitskaya, *Visual Culture: The Study of the Visual after the Cultural Turn* (Cambridge: MIT Press, 2005), 244.

NOTES TO CHAPTER 3

1. Nilgun Anadolu Okur, "Underground Railroad in Philadelphia, 1830–1860," *Journal of Black Studies* 25, no. 5 (1995): 540.

2. White Pennsylvanians petitioned against the immigration of people termed "colored" and "mulatto" into the state, even making requests for fines against Whites who promoted immigration (*Journal of the Forty-Second House of Representatives of the Commonwealth of Pennsylvania*, vol. 1 [Philadelphia: John Dunlap, 1782], 48; Edward Raymond Turner, *Negro in Pennsylvania: Slavery—Servitude—Freedom, 1639–1861* [Washington, DC: American Historical Association, 1911]). See also *Journals of the Senate of the Commonwealth of Pennsylvania, 1831–32*.

3. Okur, "Underground Railroad in Philadelphia, 1830–1860," 540.

4. Edward Williams Clay, "Life in Philadelphia," 1827–37, LCP.

5. College Art Association of America, *Salon of American Humorists* (New York: College Art Association, 1933), 18; William Murrell and Whitney Museum of American Art, *A History of American Graphic Humor* (New York: Whitney Museum of American Art, 1938), 17.

6. Alois Senefelder created the artistic process of lithography, producing a mechanical reproduction of print by first chemically treating the surface of stone or metal before applying printer's ink, which he then transferred to the final print surface, such as paper

(Alois Senefelder, *Invention of Lithography*, trans. J. W. Muller [New York: Fuchs & Lang, 1911]; Joseph Pennell, *Lithography* [F. Keppel, 1912]; Elizabeth Robins Pennell, *Lithography and Lithographers: Some Chapters in the History of Art* [New York: Macmillan, 1915]).

7. College Art Association of America, *Salon of American Humorists* 17.

8. Erika Piola, *Philadelphia on Stone: Commercial Lithography in Philadelphia, 1828–1878* (State College: Pennsylvania State University Press, 2012): 4; Edward Clay, *Philadelphia on Stone Biographical Dictionary*, LCP, www.lcpdigital.org.

9. Philip Lapsansky, "Graphic Discord: Abolitionist and Antiabolitionist Images," in *The Abolitionist Sisterhood: Women's Political Culture in Antebellum America*, ed. Jean Fagan Yellin and John C. Van Horne (Ithaca, NY: Cornell University Press, 1994), 201–30.

10. Winch, *A Gentleman of Color;* Darlene Clark Hine and Kathleen Thompson, *A Shining Thread of Hope: The History of Black Women in America* (New York: Random House, 2009). See also Eric Foner, *Forever Free: The Story of Emancipation and Reconstruction* (New York: Random House, 2005); Jacqueline Bacon, *Freedom's Journal: The First African-American Newspaper* (Lanham, MD: Lexington Books, 2007); Samuel Otter, *Philadelphia Stories: America's Literature of Race and Freedom* (New York: Oxford University Press, 2013).

11. Guy Debord, *Society of the Spectacle* (Detroit: Black and Red, 1970).

12. Nancy Reynolds Davison, "E. W. Clay: American Political Caricaturist of the Jacksonian Era" (PhD diss., University of Michigan, 1980), 5.

13. Gary Nash and Jean Soderlund, *Freedom by Degrees: Emancipation in Pennsylvania and Its Aftermath* (New York: Oxford University Press, 1991).

14. Pennsylvania's unfree Black population dropped from 6,000 in 1765, to 3,760 in 1790, to 795 by 1810 (Gary B. Nash, *Race and Revolution* [Madison: Madison House, 1990]).

15. Joe William Trotter and Eric Ledell Smith, *African Americans in Pennsylvania: Shifting Historical Perspectives* (State College: Pennsylvania State University Press, 1997); Joe Trotter, *Great Migration in Historical Perspective: New Dimensions of Race, Class, and Gender* (Bloomington: Indiana University Press, 1991); Jacqueline Jones, *American Work: Four Centuries of Black and White Labor* (New York: Norton, 1998).

16. Wilma King, *Essence of Liberty: Free Black Women during the Slave Era* (Columbia: University of Missouri Press, 2006), 68.

17. Tera W. Hunter, "'The "Brotherly Love" for Which This City Is Proverbial Should Extend to All': The Everyday Lives of Working-Class Women in Philadelphia and Atlanta in the 1890s," in *African American Urban Experience*, ed. Joe Trotter, Earl Lewis, and Hunter (New York: Palgrave, 2004), 76.

18. Deborah G. White, *Ar'n't I a Woman? Female Slaves in the Plantation South* (New York: Norton, 1999), 32.

19. Monica L. Miller, *Slaves to Fashion: Black Dandyism and the Styling of Black Diasporic Identity* (Durham, NC: Duke University Press, 2009), 81.

20. Carol Mattingly, *Appropriate[ing] Dress: Women's Rhetorical Style in Nineteenth-Century America* (Carbondale: Southern Illinois University Press, 2002), 123–25; emphasis in original.

21. Pamela E. Klassen, "The Robes of Womanhood: Dress and Authenticity among African American Methodist Women in the Nineteenth Century," *Religion and American Culture: A Journal of Interpretation* 14 (Winter 2004): 39–82; Richard L Bushman, *Refinement of America: Persons, Houses, Cities* (New York: Vintage, 1993), 439.

22. Klassen, "Robes of Womanhood," 50.

23. Lapsansky, "Since They Got Those Separate Churches."

24. William L Breton, "Bethel African Methodist Episcopal Church," 1829, LCP.

25. W. E. B. DuBois, *Philadelphia Negro: A Social Study* (Philadelphia: University of Pennsylvania, 1899), 204.

26. Dunbar, *Fragile Freedom*, 64.

27. John F. Watson, *Annals of Philadelphia and Pennsylvania in the Olden Time* (Philadelphia: Lippincott, 1870), 479.

28. Ibid., 483.

29. Ira V. Brown, "Racism and Sexism: The Case of Pennsylvania Hall," *Phylon* 37, no. 2 (1976): 128.

30. Despite the visibility of the city's Black elite, "the antebellum black community was extremely poor," as "the poorest half of the population owned only one-twentieth of the total wealth" in 1838 and 1847 (Theodore Hershberg, "Free Blacks in Antebellum Philadelphia," in *Peoples of Philadelphia: A History of Ethnic Groups and Lower-class Life, 1790–1940*, ed. Allen F. Davis and Mark H. Haller [Philadelphia: University of Pennsylvania, 1973], 112–14).

31. Mia Bay, *White Image in the Black Mind: African-American Ideas about White People, 1830–1925* (New York: Oxford University Press, 2000).

32. Thomas Jefferson, *Notes on the State of Virginia* (Boston: Wells and Lilly, 1829).

33. Fanon, *Black Skin, White Masks* (New York: Grove, 1967), 109.

34. Fleetwood, *Troubling Vision*, 21–24.

35. George Yancy, *Look! A White: Philosophical Essays on Whiteness* (Philadelphia: Temple University Press, 2012), 5.

36. Robert Bernasconi, "Sartre's Gaze Returned: The Transformation of the Phenomenology of Racism," *Graduate Faculty Philosophy Journal* 18, no. 2 (1995): 201–21.

37. Jean-Paul Sartre, *Being and Nothingness: An Essay on Phenomenological Ontology* (New York: Philosophical Library, 1956), 343.

38. Bernasconi, "Gaze Returned," 343.

39. Sartre, *Being and Nothingness*, 231–33.

40. Ibid.

41. Ibid., 234.

42. Ibid., 258.

43. Ibid.

44. Ibid.

45. Jonathan Judaken, *Race after Sartre: Antiracism, Africana Existentialism, Postcolonialism* (Albany: State University of New York Press, 2008), 137.

46. For more, see Kathryn T. Gines, "Fanon and Sartre 50 Years Later: To Retain or Reject the Concept of Race," *Sartre Studies International* 9, no. 2 (2003): 55–68.

47. Shane White and Graham J. White, *Stylin': African American Expressive Culture from Its Beginnings to the Zoot Suit* (Ithaca, NY: Comstock, 1998), 90–91.

48. Emily Willson, Amy Matilda Cassey Album, LCP.

49. "The Hintons Were Married by Rev. Wm. Douglass." *Liberator*, January 21, 1837.

50. Gross, *Colored Amazons*, 61.

51. Ibid., 62.

52. Dale Cockrell, *Demons of Disorder: Early Blackface Minstrels and Their World* (Cambridge: Cambridge University Press, 1997), 16.

53. Stephen Johnson, ed., *Burnt Cork: Traditions and Legacies of Blackface Minstrelsy* (Amherst: University of Massachusetts Press, 2012); Cedric J. Robinson, *Forgeries of Memory and Meaning* (Chapel Hill: University of North Carolina Press, 2012); Lhamon, *Jump Jim Crow*; Lott, *Love and Theft*.

54. Clay produced a popular illustration of "Jim Crow," while Blackface stage performers also adapted lines of speech from such caricatures for stage performances. (Edward Williams Clay, "Mr. T. Rice as the Original Jim Crow," Lester S. Levy Collection of Sheet Music, Sheridan Libraries, Johns Hopkins University; Lhamon, *Jump Jim Crow*, 56).

55. Marvin Edward McAllister, *White People Do Not Know How to Behave at Entertainments Designed for Ladies & Gentlemen of Colour: William Brown's African & American Theater* (Chapel Hill: University of North Carolina Press, 2003), 15.

56. Marvin Edward McAllister, *Whiting Up: Whiteface Minstrels & Stage Europeans in African American Performance* (Chapel Hill: University of North Carolina Press, 2011), 19.

57. Michael De Nie, *Eternal Paddy: Irish Identity and the British Press, 1798–1882* (Madison: University of Wisconsin Press, 2004), 5.

58. L. Perry Curtis, *Apes and Angels: The Irishman in Victorian Caricature* (Washington, DC: Smithsonian Institution Press, 1997).

59. Kevin Kinny, "Race, Violence, and Anti-Irish Sentiment in the Nineteenth Century," in *Making the Irish American: History and Heritage of the Irish in the United States*, ed. Joseph Lee and Marion R. Casey (New York: New York University Press, 2006): 369.

60. Alexander Saxton, *Rise and Fall of the White Republic: Class, Politics and Mass Culture in Nineteenth-Century America* (New York: Verso, 1990), 77–84.

61. Ibid., 109.

62. Gary L. Bunker, "Antebellum Caricature and Woman's Sphere," *Journal of Women's History* 3 (Winter 1992): 6.

63. *Godey's Lady's Book*, January 1833 (Philadelphia).

64. Isabelle Lehuu, "Sentimental Figures: Reading *Godey's Lady's Book* in Antebellum America," in *Culture of Sentiment: Race, Gender and Sentimentality in Nineteenth-Century America*, ed. Shirley Samuels (New York: Oxford University Press, 1992), 79.

65. Isabelle Lehuu, *Carnival on the Page: Popular Print Media in Antebellum America* (Chapel Hill: University of North Carolina Press, 2000), 102–8.

66. Alison Piepmeier, *Out in Public* (Chapel Hill: University of North Carolina Press, 2004), 175. Sarah Josepha Hale was born in New Hampshire, but she edited *Godey's* from Boston between 1837 and 1877. For more on Hale, see Patricia Okker, *Our Sister Editors: Sarah J. Hale and the Tradition of Nineteenth-Century American Women Editors* (Athens: University of Georgia Press, 1995).

67. Martin J. Medhurst and Michael A. DeSousa, "Political Cartoons as Rhetorical Form: A Taxonomy of Graphic Discourse," *Communication Monographs* 48 (1981): 201.

68. The Jewish shopkeeper Sarah Stock Hart immigrated to the United States in 1807 and, along with her son, published lithographs and satiric cartoons in Philadelphia from 1830 to 1843 from her stationery store (Sarah Hart, *Philadelphia on Stone Biographical Dictionary*, LCP, www.lcpdigital.org; cf. Nancy Goldstein, *Jackie Ormes: The First African American Woman Cartoonist* [Ann Arbor: University of Michigan Press, 2008]).

69. Rollin Kirby, *Political Cartoons* (n.p.: 1930), 62.

70. Ann Ducille, "Colour of Class: Classifying Race in the Popular Imagination," *Social Identities* 7, no. 3 (2001): 409.

NOTES TO CHAPTER 4

1. Anthony Imbert arrived in the United States in 1824 or 1825 and opened a lithographic firm to become the premier lithographer in New York City. Under the name "Imbert's Lithography," he printed lithographs of city architecture, landscapes like Niagara Falls, as well as cartoons and caricatures (Anthony Imbert Print Collection [PR-225], Department of Prints, Photographs, and Architectural Collections, The New-York Historical Society).

2. Anthony Imbert, "Life in New York" graphic series, 1829–35, American Antiquarian Society (hereafter cited as AAS).

3. Plate number 4, *Inconveniency of Tight Lacing, St. John's Park Sept. 28, 1829*, in the "Life in New York" series, depicts three White dandies at the park, mocking the difficulties associated with fussy clothing. All other known images in the series depict African Americans.

4. Joanna Brooks, "The Early American Public Sphere and the Emergence of a Black Print Counterpublic," *William and Mary Quarterly* 62, no. 1 (2005): 86.

5. Guy Debord, "The Society of the Spectacle," in *The Visual Culture Reader*, ed. Nicholas Mirzoeff (New York: Routledge, 2002), 142–44.

6. Michael Warner, *Publics and Counterpublics* (New York: Zone, 2005).

7. Jürgen Habermas, *The Structural Transformation of the Public Sphere: An Inquiry into a Category of Bourgeois Society* (Cambridge: MIT Press, 1991), 27.

8. Martha S. Jones, *All Bound Up Together: The Woman Question in African American Public Culture, 1830–1900* (Chapel Hill: University of North Carolina Press, 2007), 26.

9. Houston A. Baker Jr., "Critical Memory and the Black Public Sphere," *Public Culture* 7, no. 1 (1994): 7.

10. Lapsansky, "Graphic Discord: Abolitionist and Antiabolitionist Images," 216.

11. Shane White, *Stories of Freedom in Black New York* (Cambridge: Harvard University Press, 2002).

12. David Nathaniel Gellman, *Emancipating New York: The Politics of Slavery and Freedom, 1777–1827* (Baton Rouge: Louisiana State University Press, 2006).

13. Carla Peterson, *Black Gotham: A Family History of African Americans in Nineteenth-Century New York City* (New Haven, CT: Yale University Press, 2011), 29.

14. Richard S. Newman, *Transformation of American Abolitionism: Fighting Slavery in the Early Republic* (Chapel Hill: University of North Carolina Press, 2002).

15. By visual arguments, I mean images specifically. The absence of pictures is distinct from the mobilization of "verbal images" and "visual imagery" in prose (Henry Louis Gates, *Figures in Black: Words, Signs, and the "Racial" Self* [New York: Oxford University Press, 1987], 175).

16. Teresa Zackodnik, *Press, Platform, Pulpit: Black Feminist Publics in the Era of Reform* (Knoxville: University of Tennessee Press, 2011); Nell Irvin Painter, *Sojourner Truth: A Life, A Symbol* (New York: Norton, 1996).

17. Henry Bibb, *Narrative of the Life and Adventures of Henry Bibb: An American Slave* (Madison: University of Wisconsin Press, 2001).

18. Kirt H. Wilson, "African American Rhetoric: Abolitionist Rhetoric," in *Encyclopedia of Rhetoric*, ed. Thomas O. Sloane (New York: Oxford University Press, 2001), 4.

19. Jacqueline Bacon and Glen McClish, "Reinventing the Master's Tools: Nineteenth-Century African-American Literary Societies of Philadelphia and Rhetorical Education," *Rhetoric Society Quarterly* 30, no. 4 (2000): 19–47.

20. Elizabeth McHenry, *Forgotten Readers: Recovering the Lost History of African-American Literary Societies* (Durham, NC: Duke University Press, 2002).

21. Leslie M. Alexander, *African or American? Black Identity and Political Activism in New York City, 1784–1861* (Urbana: University of Illinois Press, 2009), 55.

22. Chris Dixon, *African America and Haiti: Emigration and Black Nationalism in the Nineteenth Century*, (Westport, CT: Greenwood, 2000), 249.

23. Eric Burin, *Slavery and the Peculiar Solution: A History of the American Colonization Society* (Gainesville: University Press of Florida, 2005).

24. John Russwurm of the *Freedom's Journal* was a key casualty in this ideological dispute among African Americans. For more, see Mary Sagarin, *John Brown Russwurm: The Story of Freedom's Journal, Freedom's Journey* (New York: Lothrop, Lee and Shepard, 1970).

25. Richard S. Newman, *Black Founders: The Free Black Community in the Early Republic* (Philadelphia: LCP), 17.

26. David Walker, *David Walker's Appeal to the Coloured Citizens of the World* (State College: Pennsylvania State University Press, 2000), 137.

27. McHenry, *Forgotten Readers*, 42.

28. Richard Newman, Patrick Rael, and Phillip Lapsansky, eds., *Pamphlets of Protest: An Anthology of Early African American Protest Literature, 1790–1860* (New York: Routledge, 2001), 1.

29. James Forten, *Letters from a Man of Colour on a Late Bill before the Senate of Pennsylvania*, www.gilderlehrman.org/teachers/scholars/HSP03.EAA11.Osborne.pdf.

30. John W. Blassingame and Mae Henderson, *Antislavery Newspapers and Periodicals* (Boston: G. K. Hall, 1980), 1.

31. Jane Rhodes, "The Visibility of Race in Media History," *Critical Studies in Mass Communication* 10, no. 2 (1993): 184–90.

32. "Poetry," *Freedom's Journal*, February 22, 1828.

33. The *Aliened American* was published in Cleveland, Ohio, for only one year, with its first issue dated April 9, 1853 (James P. Danky, ed., *African-American Newspapers and Periodicals: A National Bibliography* [Cambridge: Harvard University Press, 1998]).

34. Michael Winship, *A History of the Book in America*, vol. 3, *The Industrial Book, 1840–1880*, ed. Scott E. Casper et al. (Chapel Hill: University of North Carolina Press, 2007), 68.

35. Books of specimens circulated widely (Fry and Steel, *A Specimen of Printing Types* [London: T. Rickaby, 1795]).

36. "Britannia Giving Freedom to Her Slaves," *Colored American*, May 9, 1840.

37. Under "apprenticeship" in the Anglophone Caribbean, formerly unfree Blacks were required to work for their former masters, uncompensated, for a designated period after the 1834 enforcement of the British Slavery Abolition Act. Governmental officials and planters touted apprenticeship as the opportunity to educate and prepare formerly enslaved people for freedom (Gad Heuman, "Riots and Resistance in the Caribbean at the Moment of Freedom," in *After Slavery: Emancipation and Its Discontents*, ed. Howard Temperley [London: Frank Cass, 2000], 135).

38. Laura Wexler, "'A More Perfect Likeness': Frederick Douglass and the Image of the Nation," in *Pictures and Progress: Early Photography and the Making of African American Identity*, ed. Maurice O. Wallace and Shawn Michelle Smith (Durham, NC: Duke University Press, 2012), 28.

39. Sarah Blackwood, "Fugitive Obscura," 105.

40. A number of African American newspapers, including the *Colored American* and the *North Star*, printed stories on, or related to, "female influence" from the late 1830s, until well after the Civil War. For more, see Martha Jones, *All Bound Up*.

41. Marilyn Richardson, *Maria W. Stewart, America's First Black Woman Political Writer: Essays and Speeches* (Bloomington: Indiana University Press, 1987).

42. Carla L. Peterson, *"Doers of the Word": African American Women Speakers & Writers in the North, 1830–1880* (New Brunswick, NJ: Rutgers University Press, 1995), 66.

43. Kathleen Hall Jamieson, *Double Bind: Women and Leadership* (New York: Oxford University Press, 1995), 14.

44. Yee, *Black Women Abolitionists*, 4–5.

45. McHenry, *Forgotten Readers*, 56–69.

46. Jane Rhodes, *Mary Ann Shadd Cary: The Black Press and Protest in the Nineteenth Century* (Bloomington: Indiana University Press, 1998), 17.

47. Sarah Douglass and other free Black women throughout the Northeast contributed pseudonymous poems and letters to the *Liberator*, promoting the immediate abolition of slavery as early as 1831 and two years before the establishment of AAS.

48. Katherine Clay Bassard, *Spiritual Interrogations: Culture, Gender, and Community in Early African American Women's Writing* (Princeton, NJ: Princeton University Press, 1999), 90; William L. Andrews, ed., *Sisters of the Spirit: Three Black Women's Autobiographies of the 19th Century* (Bloomington: Indiana University Press, 1986), 23.

49. Frankie Hutton, *Early Black Press in America, 1827 to 1860* (Westport, CT: Greenwood, 1993): 58.

50. Winch, *Philadelphia's Black Elite*, 84.

51. Black Public Sphere Collective, *The Black Public Sphere: A Public Culture Book* (Chicago: University of Chicago Press, 1995), 326.

52. The terms "antislavery" and "abolitionist" circulate interchangeably, both historically and in the scholarship. In the United States, "abolitionists" were usually militant reformers interested in immediate emancipation beginning in 1831, and distinct from British abolitionists who worked to abolish the slave trade by 1808. Many of the most radical abolitionists in the United States did this work within organizations that identified as "antislavery," a term that is often associated with a theoretical opposition to slavery, rather than the movement for "slave" emancipation in England, which began in 1823 (Davis, *The Problem of Slavery in the Age of Revolution, 1770–1823*, 21).

53. Radiclani Clytus, "'Keep It before the People': The Pictorialization of American Abolitionism," in *Early African American Print Culture*, ed. Lara Langer Cohen and Jordan Alexander Stein (Philadelphia: University of Pennsylvania Press, 2012), 292.

54. "An Emancipated Family," *American Antislavery Almanac for 1836* (Boston: Webster and Southard, 1835).

55. Lapsansky, "Graphic Discord: Abolitionist and Antiabolitionist Images," 203.

56. Mary Guyatt, "The Wedgwood Slave Medallion Values in Eighteenth-Century Design," *Journal of Design History* 13, no. 2 (2000): 93–105.

57. Jean Fagan Yellin, *Women and Sisters: The Antislavery Feminist in American Culture* (New Haven, CT: Yale University Press, 1992).

58. Inga Bryden and Janet Floyd, *Domestic Space: Reading the Nineteenth Century Interior* (New York: Manchester University Press, 1999), 66.

59. Louise Michele Newman, *White Women's Rights: The Racial Origins of Feminism in the United States* (New York: Oxford University Press, 1999), 62.

60. Angelina Grimké married Theodore Weld despite concerns among radical abolitionists who feared marriage would take her away from the antislavery movement (Chris Dixon, *Perfecting the Family: Antislavery Marriages in Nineteenth Century America* [Amherst: University of Massachusetts Press, 1997], 82–94).

61. Julie Roy Jeffrey, "Permeable Boundaries: Abolitionist Women and Separate Spheres," *Journal of the Early Republic* 21 (Spring 2001): 79–93.

62. Karen Sanchez-Eppler, "Bodily Bonds: The Intersecting Rhetoric of Feminism and Abolition," *Representations* 24 (Fall 1988): 30.

63. Their skillful participation within public discourse represented Black abolitionist women to a nationwide group of 2,500 readers of the *Liberator*. Educational associations simultaneously promoted intellectual advancement within free Black communities

and publicized this progression to others outside of these segregated networks (Jacqueline Bacon, "The *Liberator*'s Ladies' Department: 1832–37: Freedom or Fetters?," in *Sexual Rhetoric: Media Perspectives on Sexuality, Gender, and Identity,* ed. Meta G. Carstarphen and Susan C. Zavoina [Westport, CT: Greenwood, 1999], 3–19).

64. Marcus Wood, "Emancipation Art, Fanon and 'the Butchery of Freedom,'" in *Slavery and the Cultures of Abolition: Essays Marking the Bicentennial of the British Abolition Act of 1807,* ed. Brycchan Carey and Peter J. Kitson (Cambridge: D. S. Brewer, 2007), 14.

65. Lois A. Brown, "William Lloyd Garrison and Emancipatory Feminism in Nineteenth-Century America," in *William Lloyd Garrison at Two Hundred,* ed. James Brewer Stewart (New Haven, CT: Yale University Press, 2008), 56; Debra Gold Hansen, "The Boston Female Anti-Slavery Society and the Limits of Gender Politics," in *Abolitionist Sisterhood: Women's Political Culture in Antebellum America,* ed. Jean Fagan Yellin and John C. Van Horne (Ithaca, NY: Cornell University Press, 1994), 47.

66. Lynn Casmier-Paz, "Slave Narratives and the Rhetoric of Author Portraiture," *New Literary History* 34, no. 1 (2003): 91–116.

67. Although this portrait is often attributed to Moorhead, Gwendolyn Shaw argues that the evidence for this assertion is unclear (Gwendolyn Shaw, *Portraits of a People: Picturing African Americans in the Nineteenth Century* [Andover, MA: Addison Gallery of American Art, 2006], 58–61).

68. Houston A. Baker, *Journey Back* (Chicago: University of Chicago Press, 1983), 6; Anthony Appiah and Henry Louis Gates, *Africana: Arts and Letters: An A-to-Z Reference of Writers, Musicians, and Artists of the African American Experience* (Philadelphia: Running Press, 2004), 388.

69. Henry Louis Gates, *Trials of Phillis Wheatley: America's First Black Poet and Her Encounters with the Founding Fathers* (New York: Basic, 2010).

70. Jefferson, *Notes on the State of Virginia,* 146.

71. Angela G. Ray, "'In My Own Hand Writing': Benjamin Banneker Addresses the Slaveholder of Monticello," *Rhetoric & Public Affairs* 1, no. 3 (1998): 387–405.

72. Wood, *Blind Memory,* 79.

73. Robin Bernstein, *Racial Innocence: Performing American Childhood from Slavery to Civil Rights* (New York: New York University Press, 2011).

74. Elise Virginia Lemire, *"Miscegenation": Making Race in America* (Philadelphia: University of Pennsylvania Press, 2002).

75. Both Kelly and Chapman participated in radical factions of U.S. abolition in New England. For more, see Julie Roy Jeffrey, *Great Silent Army of Abolitionism: Ordinary Women in the Antislavery Movement* (Chapel Hill: University of North Carolina Press, 1998).

76. Helen Lefkowitz Horowitz, *Rereading Sex: Battles over Sexual Knowledge and Suppression in Nineteenth-Century America* (New York: Knopf, 2002), 214.

77. Tavia Nyong'o, *The Amalgamation Waltz: Race, Performance, and the Ruses of Memory* (Minneapolis: University of Minnesota Press, 2009), 101.

78. Lundy purchased the *Emancipator* in 1820 from Elihu Embree, who previously titled the paper the *Manumission Intelligencer* (1819). Lundy retitled the paper and migrated north, promoting "universal emancipation" before settling in a Baltimore, Maryland, office in 1830 (Stephen L. Vaugh, ed., *Encyclopedia of American Journalism* [New York: Routledge, 2008], 4).

79. Clay likely responded to a petition filed by 736 White women of Lynn, Massachusetts, who requested the "privilege" to marry Black men ("Amalgamation," *Liberator*, February 8, 1839).

80. Leon Denius Pamphile, *Haitians and African Americans: A Heritage of Tragedy and Hope* (Gainesville: University of Florida Press, 2001); Maurice Jackson and Jacqueline Bacon, *African Americans and the Haitian Revolution: Selected Essays and Historical Documents* (New York: Routledge, 2009).

81. Eric King Watts and Mark Orbe, "The Spectacular Consumption of 'True' African American Culture: 'Whassup' with the Budweiser Guys?," *Critical Studies in Media Communication* 19 (March 2002): 4.

82. Michele Wallace, *Invisibility Blues: From Pop to Theory* (London: Verso, 2008), 215.

83. Thomas Sowell, *Black Rednecks and White Liberals* (San Francisco: Encounter, 2005), 6.

84. I offer these numbers to give some sense of proportions. Scholars recognize that population statistics of unfree Black people entail a number of errors motivated by politics and efforts to avoid taxation. Additionally, census takers excluded "fugitives" or "runaways" from census rolls in the South (Franklin and Scheninger, *Runaway Slaves*, 279; Paul Finkelman, *Slavery and the Founders: Race and Liberty in the Age of Jefferson*, 2nd ed. [Armonk, NY: M. E. Sharpe, 2001], 11–18).

85. Campbell Gibson and Kay Jung, *United States-Race and Hispanic Origin: 1790–1990*, prepared by the Population Division, Bureau of the U.S. Census, Washington, DC, 2002, www.census.gov/population/www/documentation/twps0056/twps0056.html.

86. James Oliver Horton, "Freedom's Yoke: Gender Conventions among Antebellum Free Blacks," *Feminist Studies* 12 (Spring 1986): 53; Phillip Lapsansky, "Afro-Americana: From Abolition to Bobalition," in *Annual Report for 2003* (Philadelphia: LCP, 2004): 36.

87. African Society, *Laws of the African Society, Instituted at Boston, Anno Domini 1796* (Boston, 1802).

88. Shane White, "'It Was a Proud Day': African Americans, Festivals, and Parades in the North, 1741–1834," *Journal of American History* 81 (June 1994): 15.

89. Mitch Kachun, *Festivals of Freedom: Memory and Meaning in African American Emancipation Celebrations, 1808–1915* (Amherst: University of Massachusetts Press, 2003), 27.

90. Maureen Daly Goggin, "Visual Rhetoric in Pens of Steel and Inks of Silk: Challenging the Great Visual/Verbal Divide," in *Defining Visual Rhetorics*, ed. Charles Hill and Marguerite Helmers (Mahwah, NJ: Lawrence Erlbaum, 2004).

91. Robert Hariman, "Political Parody and Public Culture," *Quarterly Journal of Speech* 94, no. 3 (2008): 250.

92. Eric King Watts, "'Voice' and 'Voicelessness' in Rhetorical Studies," *Quarterly Journal of Speech* 87, no. 2 (2001): 180.

93. Robin R. Means Coleman, *African American Viewers and the Black Situation Comedy: Situating Racial Humor* (New York: Garland, 2000), 53–61.

94. Douglass Bradburn, *The Citizenship Revolution: Politics and the Creation of the American Union, 1774–1804* (Charlottesville: University of Virginia Press, 2009), 1–19.

95. Barbara Young Welke, *Law and the Borders of Belonging in the Long Nineteenth Century United States* (Cambridge: Cambridge University Press, 2010), 34.

96. Jennifer R. Mercieca, *Founding Fictions* (Tuscaloosa: University of Alabama Press, 2010), 215.

97. Gary Nash, "Race and Citizenship in the Early Republic," in *Antislavery and Abolition in Philadelphia: Emancipation and the Long Struggle for Racial Justice in the City of Brotherly Love*, ed. Richard Newman and James Mueller (Baton Rouge: Louisiana State University Press, 2011), 90–117.

98. See chapter 1, note 15.

99. Leslie Harris, *In the Shadow of Slavery: African Americans in New York City, 1828–1863* (Chicago: University of Chicago Press, 2003), 97.

100. "Fancy balls," or elaborate social gatherings that invited pageantry among free African Americans, were denigrated in White newspapers, and thus, until the mid-nineteenth century, many editors of Black newspapers summarily frowned upon these gatherings as well ("From the Pennsylvania Gazette," *Freedom's Journal*, March 14, 1828).

101. Jane E. Dabel, *A Respectable Woman: The Public Roles of African American Women in 19th Century New York* (New York: New York University Press, 2008), 98.

102. Black Public Sphere Collective, *The Black Public Sphere*, 13.

NOTES TO CHAPTER 5

1. Lara Putnam, "To Study the Fragments/Whole: Microhistory and the Atlantic World," *Journal of Social History* 39, no. 3 (2006): 615.

2. Edward Williams Clay, "Life in Philadelphia," 1830, LCP.

3. *Daily National Journal* (Washington, DC), November 28, 1828.

4. Robert L. Patten, *Cruikshank's Life, Times, and Art: 1792–1835* (New Brunswick, NJ: Rutgers University Press, 1992), 288; Frederic G. Stephens, *A Memoir of George Cruikshank* (New York: Scribner and Welford, 1891).

5. Mark Hallett, *Hogarth* (London: Tate, 2006); M. George, *Hogarth to Cruikshank: Social Change in Graphic Satire* (New York: Walker, 1967).

6. Martha S. Jones, "Reframing the Color Line," in *Reframing the Color Line: Race and Visual Culture of the Atlantic World*, ed. Jones and Clayton Lewis (Ann Arbor, MI: William Clements Library, University of Michigan, Ann Arbor), 5.

7. Kay Dian Kriz, *Slavery, Sugar, and the Culture of Refinement: Picturing the British West Indies, 1700–1840* (New Haven, CT: Yale University Press, 2008), 72.

8. Ian Kenneth Steele, *English Atlantic: An Exploration of Communication and Community* (New York: Oxford University Press, 1986).

9. J. H. Elliott, *Empires of the Atlantic World: Britain and Spain in America, 1492–1830* (New Haven, CT: Yale University Press, 2006), 111.

10. Ibid.

11. Richard T. Godfrey, *Printmaking in Britain: A General History from Its Beginnings to the Present Day* (Oxford: Phaidon, 1978), 9.

12. Stuart Hall, ed., *Representation: Cultural Representations and Signifying Practices* (Thousand Oaks, CA: Sage, 2007), 1.

13. William Summers, *"Shall I hab de honour to dance de next quadrille?,"* 1833, in "Life in Philadelphia" series, , London Set, LCP.

14. Richard T. Godfrey, *Printmaking in Britain: A General History from Its Beginnings to the Present Day* (Oxford: Phaidon, 1978).

15. Amelia Faye Rauser, *Caricature Unmasked: Irony, Authenticity, and Individualism in Eighteenth-century English Prints* (Newark: University of Delaware Press, 2008), 56.

16. Pierce Egan, *Tom & Jerry: Life in London* (London: Hotten, 1869).

17. Mark Bryant and Simon Heneage, comps., *Dictionary of British Cartoonists and Caricaturists, 1730–1980* (Aldershot, England: Scholar Press, 1994). For more about "Life in London" and Cruikshank, see Marcus Wood, *Radical Satire and Print Culture, 1790–1822* (New York: Oxford University Press, 1994).

18. Cara Finnegan, "Studying Visual Modes of Public Address: Lewis Hine's Progressive-Era Child Labor Rhetoric," in *Handbook of Rhetoric and Public Address*, ed. Shawn J. Parry-Giles and J. Michael Hogan (Malden, MA: Wiley-Blackwell, 2010), 256.

19. Kathleen Wilson, *Island Race: Englishness, Empire and Gender in the Eighteenth Century* (New York: Routledge, 2003). This notion was not always honored by jailers, who refused to release enslaved people to their "god parents" (F. O. Shylon, *Black Slaves in Britain* [New York: Oxford University Press, 1974], 20).

20. Gabriel Shire Tregear, "Tregear's Black Jokes: Being a Series of Laughable Caricatures in the March of Manners amongst Blacks," 1834, LCP.

21. Bernth Lindfors, *Ira Aldridge: The Vagabond Years, 1833–1852* (Rochester: University of Rochester Press, 2011).

22. Marcus Wood, *Blind Memory*, 158.

23. Mary Louis Pratt, "Arts in the Contact Zone," in *Mass Culture and Everyday Life* (New York: Routledge, 1997), 63.

24. E. Ann Kaplan, *Looking for the Other: Feminism, Film, and the Imperial Gaze* (New York: Routledge, 1997).

25. Lester C. Olson, *Benjamin Franklin's Vision of American Community: A Study in Rhetorical Iconology* (Columbia: University of South Carolina Press, 2004).

26. Sarah Salih, *Representing Mixed Race in Jamaica and England from the Abolition Era to the Present* (New York: Routledge, 2010), 47.

27. Ibid., 49. For more on the enduring meaning of color and "brown" in Jamaica, see Deborah A. Thomas, *Modern Blackness: Nationalism, Globalization and the Politics of Culture in Jamaica* (Durham, NC: Duke University Press, 2004).

28. Gwyn Campbell, Suzanne Miers, and Joseph C. Miller, eds., *Women and Slavery: The Modern Atlantic* (Athens: Ohio University Press, 2008), 6–10.

29. William A. Green, *British Slave Emancipation: The Sugar Colonies and the Great Experiment, 1830–1865* (Oxford: Clarendon, 1976), 12.

30. Kathryn Kish Sklar and James Brewer Stewart, eds., *Women's Rights and Transatlantic Antislavery in the Era of Emancipation* (New Haven, CT: Yale University Press, 2007).

31. Peabody, *"There Are No Slaves in France,"* 7.

32. Annette Gordon-Reed, *Hemingses of Monticello: An American Family* (New York: Norton, 2009), 688.

33. Eliga H. Gould and Peter S. Onuf, *Empire and Nation: The American Revolution in the Atlantic World* (Baltimore: Johns Hopkins University Press, 2005), 381.

34. Michael Duffy, "The French Revolution and British Attitudes to the West Indian Colonies," in *A Turbulent Time: The French Revolution and the Greater Caribbean*, ed. David Barry Gaspar and David Patrick Geggus (Bloomington: Indiana University Press, 1997), 80; James, *Black Jacobins*.

35. Lawrence C Jennings, *French Anti-Slavery: The Movement for the Abolition of Slavery in France, 1802–1848* (Cambridge: Cambridge University Press, 2000).

36. Jane Landers, *Atlantic Creoles in the Age of Revolutions* (Cambridge: Harvard University Press, 2010), 63.

37. Gretchen Holbrook Gerzina, "Black Loyalists in London after the American Revolution," in *Moving On: Black Loyalists in the Afro-Atlantic World*, ed. John W. Pulis (New York: Garland, 1999), 85.

38. Shylon, *Black Slaves in Britain*, 11–13.

39. Gretchen Gerzina, *Black London: Life before Emancipation* (New Brunswick, NJ: Rutgers University Press, 1995), 26.

40. Ibid., 17.

41. John Carlos Rowe, "Nineteenth-Century United States Literary Culture and Transnationality," *PMLA* 118, no. 1 (2003): 80.

42. Van Gosse, "'As a Nation, the English Are Our Friends': The Emergence of African American Politics in the British Atlantic World, 1772–1861," *American Historical Review* 113, no. 4 (2008): 1027.

43. Anne McClintock, *Imperial Leather: Race, Gender, and Sexuality in the Colonial Contest* (New York: Routledge, 1995), 36.

44. Jacqueline Jones, *Labor of Love, Labor of Sorrow: Black Women, Work and the Family from Slavery to the Present* (New York: Basic, 2010).

45. Hazel Carby, "White Women, Listen! Black Feminism and the Boundaries of Sisterhood," in *Black British Cultural Studies: A Reader*, ed. Houston A. Baker Jr., Manthia Diawara, and Ruth H. Lindelborg (Chicago: University of Chicago Press, 1996), 65.

46. William Summers, *Life in Philadelphia: A Black Tea Party*, 1833, in "Tregear's Black Jokes," 1833, LCP.

47. Deborah Gray White, "Jezebel and Mammy: The Mythology of Female Slavery," in *Race, Ethnicity and Gender: Selected Readings*, ed. Joseph F. Healey and Eileen O'Brien (Thousand Oaks, CA: Pine Forge Press, 2004), 127.

48. Hortense Spillers, "Mama's Baby, Papa's Maybe: An American Grammar Book," *Diacritics* 17 (Summer 1987): 65–81.

49. Saidiya V. Hartman, *Lose Your Mother: A Journey along the Atlantic Slave Route* (New York: Farrar, Straus and Giroux, 2007), 80.

50. Jennifer DeVere Brody, *Impossible Purities: Blackness, Femininity, and Victorian Culture* (Durham, NC: Duke University Press, 1998).

51. Lamin O. Sanneh, *Abolitionists Abroad: American Blacks and the Making of Modern West Africa* (Cambridge: Harvard University Press, 1999).

52. Michael de Certeau, *Practices of Everyday Life* (Berkeley: University of California Press, 2002), 117.

53. Ibid., 118.

54. Falstaff, *New Comic Annual for 1831* (London: Hurst, Chance, and Co., 1830), 224.

55. Ibid, 225.

56. Ibid.

57. Ignatius Sancho, *Letters of the Late Ignatius Sancho, An African*, ed. Vincent Carretta (New York: Penguin, 1998); Sören C. Hammerschmidt, "Character, Cultural Agency and Abolition: Ignatius Sancho's Published Letters," in "Slavery and Antislavery," ed. Brycchan Carey, *Journal for Eighteenth-Century Studies* 31 (June 2008): 259–74.

58. Falstaff, *Comic Annual*, 234.

59. Robert P. Emlen, "Imagining America in 1834: Zuber's Scenic Wallpaper 'Vues d'Amerique du Nord,'" *Winterthur Portfolio* 32 (Summer/Autumn, 1997): 190.

60. Ibid., 195.

61. Odile Nouvel, Deke Dusinberre, and Musée des arts décoratifs, *French Scenic Wallpaper, 1795–1865* (Paris: Musée des arts décoratifs: Flammarion, 2000), 146.

62. Jacques Gérard Milbert, *Picturesque Itinerary of the Hudson River and the Peripheral Parts of North America*, trans. Constance D. Sherman. (Saddle River, NJ: Gregg, 1968).

NOTES TO THE EPILOGUE

1. Jasmine Nichole Cobb, "No We Can't! Post-Racialism and the Popular Occurrence of a Rhetorical Fiction," *Communication Studies* 62 (September 2011): 406–21.

2. Hortense Spillers, "Views of the East Wing: On Michelle Obama," *Communication & Critical/Cultural Studies* 6, no. 3 (2009): 309.

3. James A. Abbot and Elaine M. Rice, *Designing Camelot: The Kennedy White House Restoration* (New York: Van Nostrand Reinhold, 1998), 21; *A Tour of the White House with Mrs. John F. Kennedy*,(CBS Broadcasting, 2004).

4. Barack Obama, "769—Remarks on the Natural Disasters in the South Pacific and Indonesia and the Situation in Iran," October 1, 2009, in Gerhard Peters and John T. Woolley, The American Presidency Project, www.presidency.ucsb.edu/ws/?pid=86694.

5. Erica R. Edwards, "The Black President Hokum," *American Quarterly* 63 (March 2011): 52.

6. Barack Obama, "A More Perfect Union," March, 18, 2008, www.americanrhetoric.com/speeches/barackobamaperfectunion.htm.

7. Leigh Raiford, *Imprisoned in a Luminous Glare: Photography and the African American Freedom Struggle* (Chapel Hill: University of North Carolina Press, 2011), 148.

Index

Figures and illustrations are indicated by italic page numbers.

About the Author

Jasmine Nichole Cobb is assistant professor of communication studies at Northwestern University.